The Rebecca Notebook
and Other Memories

Daphne du Maurier

The Rebecca Notebook and Other Memories

DOUBLEDAY & COMPANY, INC., GARDEN CITY, NEW YORK

1980

"Someday I'll Find You", permission granted, Chappel Music Publishers, London.

Permission granted to quote from Miss Frith's book, LEAVES FROM A LIFE.

"Charmaine" reproduced by permission of Keith Prowse Music Publishing Co., Ltd. 138–140 Charing Cross Road, London WC2H OLD.

Library of Congress Cataloging in Publication Data
Du Maurier, Daphne, Dame, 1907–
    The Rebecca notebook and other memories.

    I. Title.
PR6007.U47R54   823'.912
            ISBN: 0-385-15885-8
Library of Congress Catalog Card Number: 80-652

Contents

MEMORIES

POEMS

THE REBECCA
NOTEBOOK AND
EPILOGUE

INTRODUCTION

It is now over forty years since my novel *Rebecca* was first published. Although I had then written four previous novels, *The Loving Spirit, I'll Never Be Young Again, The Progress of Julius* and *Jamaica Inn,* as well as two biographies, *Gerald: A Portrait* and *The du Mauriers,* the story of Rebecca became an instant favourite with readers in the United Kingdom, North America and Europe. Why, I have never understood! It is true that as I wrote it I immersed myself in the characters, especially in the narrator, but then this has happened throughout my writing career; I lose myself in the plot as it unfolds, and only when the book is finished do I lay it aside, I may add, finally and forever.

This has been more difficult with *Rebecca,* because I continue to receive letters from all over the world asking me what I based the story on, and the characters, and why did I never give the heroine a Christian name? The answer to the last question is simple: I could not think of one, and it became a challenge in technique, the easier because I was writing in the first person.

I was thirty years old when I began the story, jotting down the intended chapters in a notebook, and I am now in my seventy-third year, with memory becoming hazier all the time. I apologise for this, but it cannot be helped. All I can tell the reader is that in the fall of 1937 my soldier husband, Boy Browning, was commanding officer of the Second Battalion, Grenadier Guards, which was stationed in Alexandria, and I was with him. We had left our two small daughters, the youngest still a baby, back in England in the care of their nanny, with two grandmothers keeping a watchful eye.

Boy—Tommy to me—and I were living in a rented house, not far from the beach, Ramleh I believe it was called, and while he was occupied with military matters I was homesick for Cornwall.

I think I put a brave face on the situation and went to the various cocktail parties which we were obliged to attend, but all I really wanted to do was to write, and to write a novel set in my beloved Cornwall. This novel would not be a tale of smugglers and wreckers of the nineteenth century like *Jamaica Inn*, but would be set in the present day, say the mid-twenties, and it would be about a young wife and her slightly older husband, living in a beautiful house that had been in his family for generations. There were many such houses in Cornwall; my friend Foy Quiller-Couch, daughter of the famous "Q," with whom I first visited Jamaica Inn, had taken me to some of them. Houses with extensive grounds, with woods, near to the sea, with family portraits on the walls, like the house Milton in Northamptonshire, where I had stayed as a child during the First World War, and yet not like, because my Cornish house would be empty, neglected, its owner absent, more like—yes, very like—the Menabilly near Fowey, not so large as Milton, where I had so often trespassed. And surely the Quiller-Couches had told me that the owner had been married first to a very beautiful wife, whom he had divorced, and had married again a much younger woman?

I wondered if she had been jealous of the first wife, as I would have been jealous if my Tommy had been married before he married me. He had been engaged once, that I knew, and the engagement had been broken off—perhaps she would have been better at dinners and cocktail parties than I could ever be.

Seeds began to drop. A beautiful home . . . a first wife . . . jealousy . . . a wreck, perhaps at sea, near to the house, as there had been at Pridmouth once near Menabilly. But something terrible would have to happen, I did not know what. . . . I paced up and down the living room in Alexandria, notebook in hand, nibbling first my nails and then my pencil.

The couple would be living abroad, after some tragedy, there would be an epilogue—but on second thoughts that would have to come at the beginning—then Chapters One, and Two, and Three . . . If only we did not have to go out to dinner that night, I wanted to think. . . .

And so it started, drafts in my notebook, and the first few chapters. Then the whole thing was put aside, until our return to England in only a few months' time.

Back home, Tommy and his battalion were stationed at Aldershot, and we were lucky enough to rent Greyfriars, near Fleet, the home of the great friend in the Coldstream Guards who had taken over from Tommy in Alexandria. Reunited with the children, and happy in the charming Tudor house, I was able to settle once more to my novel *Rebecca*. This much I can still remember; sitting on the window seat of the living room, typewriter propped up on the table before me, but I am uncertain how long it took me to finish the book, possibly three or four months. I had changed some of the names, too. The husband was no longer Henry but Max—perhaps I thought Henry sounded dull. The sister and the cousin, they were different too. The narrator remained nameless, but the housekeeper, Mrs. Danvers, had become more sinister. Why, I have no idea. The original epilogue somehow merged into the first chapter, and the ending was entirely changed.

So there it was. A finished novel. Title, *Rebecca*. I wondered if my publisher, Victor Gollancz, would think it stupid, overdone. Luckily for the author, he did not. Nor did the readers when it was published.

Its success was such that a year later I adapted the story for the stage, then later the film rights were sold. War came in 1939. We had moved from Greyfriars to Hythe, to the Senior Officers' School where Tommy became commandant. I forgot all about *Rebecca*, if its readers had not. And it may have been because of its popularity that I was asked, some eight years later, to contribute an article to a book entitled *Countryside Character*. I called my article "The House of Secrets," and this can be read in the present volume, preferably as soon as the reader has skipped this Introduction.

And what became of the original notebook? That is another matter, which I will tell briefly.

The Hitchcock film of *Rebecca* became an even greater success than the book, and was made—I think I am correct in this—around 1940, in the States. Then, some years later, a suit for plagiarism was brought against Selznick International Pictures by the family of a Mrs. MacDonald—I trust I have the name right—who said the story was a copy of a novel she had written called *Blind Windows*. I had never heard of Mrs. MacDonald or her

Blind Windows. The novel was sent to me, and I glanced through it. It was nothing like my *Rebecca,* save for the fact that the man in the book had been married twice. Nevertheless the suit was brought, and I was called as a witness for the defence.

So in 1947 I went to America with Nanny and my two younger children—I had a boy of six and a half by then, and Tessa, the eldest daughter, was at boarding school—and once in New York I stayed with my American publishers, Nelson and Ellen Doubleday. They became the dearest of friends. My only memory of the plagiarism suit was that the notebook was produced in court, and after cross-questioning the judge dismissed the case. I gave the notebook to dear Ellen Doubleday as a memento, and all I can recollect, after that first visit to the States, was being seasick all the way home in the *Queen Mary.*

When, after many more visits to the Doubledays, dearest Ellen died, she left the notebook to her daughter Puckie. Puckie returned it to me. And I reread it, for the first time in thirty years, when I received it.

And so I bring my *Rebecca* saga to an end. Perhaps the reader may care to compare it, and the original epilogue, with the published novel. If not, never mind. Skip through it, then turn to my early stories!

The Rebecca Notebook

Epilogue. Written.

Chapter I. A companion, sketch of early life. Father a doctor in Eastbourne, mother dead. Left with little money. Detail of companion's existence. Hotel dining room. Henry for the first time. The courtesy of H compared to other men.

Chapter II. Progress in friendship: drive perhaps somewhere, Manderley, descriptions. More of Henry. Asks her to marry him. And Mrs. Van Hopper, "My dear, you're a very lucky girl." (Mrs. V.H. had given her notice anyway, going back to America.) "Don't flatter yourself he's in love with you, my dear. Poor fellow, he's incorrigibly lonely, like all widowers who can't forget their first wife. He practically told me as much."

Chapter III. Married, and so to Manderley. The house, the rooms, determined to do well. Mrs. Danvers, such opposition. "It is a little difficult, madam, for us. You see we were all very fond of Mrs. de Winter."

Chapter IV. Henry's sister, Barbara. Rather brusque, not unfriendly. Looks her up and down a bit. "You don't mind my saying so, but you ought to do something to your hair"—and then when she goes, "You're very different from Rebecca."

Chapter V. Atmosphere rather getting her down. And then the drive over to see the old grandmother. Deaf and rather senile. "Well, old lady, how are you?" Self anxious to please, and ill at ease. "Who are you, I don't know you, I haven't seen you before. Henry, who is this girl? I want Rebecca: where is my Rebecca? What have you done with Rebecca?" The nurse comes in, everyone stands up, awful embarrassment, "I think perhaps you had

better go, rather too much excitement for her." Henry in the car
very white and silent. "I'm so terribly sorry. I had no idea she
would do that." "Don't be absurd, it's absolutely all right."

Chapter VI. Riding efforts, no good at all, Henry overkind. The
serving-women, and the dress in the cupboard, Rebecca's. "How
tall she must have been?" "Yes, m'm, she was, what you would
call statuesque." The meet, the flashy loose-lipped cousin. Glance
of derision. "I thought I'd pay my respects to your wife."
Henry's anger. "Keep away from Manderley in future, do you
hear? You dirty swine." They stared at one another. Self frightened and bewildered. Never seen Henry angry before. Looked
upon something that she was not meant to see.

Chapter VII. The woodman, and the summerhouse. A bit senile
too. "You're kind, and you've got gentle eyes. You're not like the
other one." "The other one? Who do you mean?" He looked very
sly, he laid his finger against his nose. "She used to come here,"
he whispered, "I seen her with me own eyes. Be night she'd
come, she'd not be alone. And then I run against her face to face.
'You've never seen me before, have you?' she said. 'No,' I said.
'And you'll not know me if you see me again, will you?' says she.
'No, ma'am,' says I. 'I'm not going to give you any money,' she
says, 'but if you tell anyone you have seen me here I shall have
you put to the asylum. You don't want to go there, do you?' she
says. 'No, ma'am,' I says, I don't want no harm to come to a living soul. She's dead now, ain't she? Tall she was, and dark, she'd
give you the feeling of a snake. Have you come to put me to the
asylum too?" He was crazy, of course, poor old fellow, and yet—
how puzzling his description. It was not one's idea of Rebecca.

(Must separate these two chapters by a more intimate depressing reaction. The coat under the stairs, the handkerchief in
the pocket. Then the snapshot, Henry laughing, bending over
her—I couldn't see her face. It was my favourite corner of the
garden, where we had sat yesterday for tea, spoiling my memory. Mrs. Van Hopper had been right. "I can't see you mistress
of a place like Manderley, somehow I feel you'll regret it." I felt
now I had no right to be there. What had happened to those
weeks, and days—nothing died, nothing was wasted. That moment, when Henry and Rebecca stood there, side by side, where

had it gone? He was my husband and I knew nothing of him. Sitting in the library, staring in front of him. No sound but the clicking of my needles. Probably an irritation?

Chapter VIII. The dance. Chooses a dress of one of the pictures. Doesn't tell Henry. It's to be a surprise. Great preparations. Looks very well. Goes to the head of the staircase and stands there. The sea of faces looking up. A hum. Then Henry, white-faced, his eyes blazing with anger. "What the hell do you think you're doing?" Pause, a hand on the bannister. "It's the picture, the one in the drawing room." A deathly silence. "Go and change, at once. Put on an ordinary evening frock—anything, it doesn't matter what. We won't wait for you."

Back to the bedroom, the little maid crying, trembling fingers. Sat on the bed, twisting and turning her fingers. Knock on the door. Barbara comes in, swift and firm. "It's all right, my dear—put on anything, that charming white. I knew at once it was just a terrible mistake. You could not possibly have known."

"Known what?"

"Why, you poor silly child, that dress, the picture you copied, it was identical with the one Rebecca wore, the last fancy-dress dance at Manderley."

I sat stunned. "I ought to have known," stupidly over and over again. "I ought to have known."

"Of course Henry thought it was deliberate on your part—I said at once it was not, how could you have known? It was sheer bad luck you chose that particular picture."

"I can't go down now. I can't face them all."

"You must; if you don't they will all think you meant to do it. I'll explain everything. Just slip down in your white frock."

"No—Barbara, I can't. After dinner, I'll try."

Goes down and stands by his side in the hall. The interminable evening winds on. Henry, with set white face, does not speak to her at all. To bed, and he goes to his dressing room.

Chapter IX. The next morning. Aftermath of the ball. I could not face the guests. Sent a note down. And they all go away. Verbal message from Henry, "Gone up to London." The silence of the house. Potters through the woods, utterly lost and miserable. It should have been so different. Henry made a terrible mis-

take in marrying me, that's evident. He wanted to be alone with
his memories, and I had intruded upon him and Rebecca. Mrs.
Van Hopper had been right. I was making a mistake, she had
said, "I don't think you'll be happy." Rebecca still dwelt in Manderley, and she resented me. Overwrought and hysterical. I went
and unlocked the secret door in my desk. I took out the snapshot
of Rebecca. I was very calm. I knew what she wanted me to do.
It was as though she was sitting by my side. "We don't want you
here, we don't want you. Henry wants to be alone with me."

I sat down at the desk and wrote to Henry. The letter. Then I
went upstairs and took the bottle of Lysol from the bathroom
cupboard.

Chapter X. The delirium, and here I can use the early bits if I
like (unless already used), Eastbourne and the rest in disjointed
form. That can be worked up. The beat of the metronome—*un
deux, un deux, un deux,* and the burning of my throat. Yes, of
course, it was the tar, the liquid tar that the men were pouring
down my throat. "My darling, my darling, why in the name of
God didn't you tell me? My beloved, my sweet." His hands and
his voice, his hands pulling me back, his cheek against mine. "Of
course she stood between us, of course I could not love you with
her diabolical shadow haunting me, standing forever like a living
threat. Don't you understand, darling, that I killed Rebecca, she
was never drowned, that body that was washed up, that I
identified, was not hers at all. I shot her that night in the cottage
in the woods, I carried her vicious damnable body down to the
boat—and laid it in the cabin. It was I who set sail, I who slipped
the moorings, and when we were three miles out I opened the
sea cocks, bored holes in the planking to make my work more
swift—then, casting the life buoy over the side and the fenders
and her oilskins to act as evidence, I jumped into the dinghy and
pulled away. The boat sank in ten minutes. And Rebecca lies
there now, ten fathoms deep, in the cabin of that little boat—and
no one will ever know, my darling, no one will ever know."

Chapter XI. Recovered, on the lawn, tea, and raspberries.
Wood pigeons, the atmosphere entirely changed. Henry ten
years younger. Rather a Menabilly-ish description. Perhaps people to cricket. At any rate strike the peaceful note.

Chapter XII. Overcast summer day. Here perhaps the leaves blowing off the table. Sense of foreboding. They go indoors to escape a tropical shower. Leaves scatter fast. Feel there won't be tea on the lawn again. The last time. Later on rockets—go to the end of the lawn to see. Mist too thick.

Chapter XIII. Henry goes to London. Lonely without him. News of the wreck over breakfast. I go out to see her. She was about three miles offshore, a desolate-looking sight. Chat with an old fellow on the cliff. "They are going to send divers down, the cargo was valuable." They were rowing out in the boat even as I watched. The diver in his red-stockinged cap. Rather monotonous. Rather chilly. When I got back I found there was a telephone message from Henry, saying he would be back by the evening train.

Chapter XIV. Sitting quietly together in the library. Entrance of maid—the inspector. Twists his hat. I always liked Inspector Booth. "The divers came upon another wreck this afternoon, the wreck of a small sailing boat. Lying in fifteen fathom of water, sir. Do believe me, sir, I simply hate to come here and distress you, but from what they say the boat is unquestionably the late Mrs. de Winter's little *Gypsy*."

Chapter XV. Reactions of Henry—the pause—the tense atmosphere. He swallowed. "It was kind of you, Inspector, to come and tell me personally. I appreciate it very much." Discuss what is to happen. Leave it in peace perhaps. The inspector goes. So it was all to happen again, that shadow of Rebecca coming between us. And Henry, standing by the window, "It's warm in here, isn't it?" His voice strained and unnatural. "My darling, I'm sorry, so desperately sorry." He did not answer. I went up to him and took his hand. "Just as we were forgetting her, just as we were beginning to be so happy." Still he did not move. It was unnatural. "What's the matter?" and then he broke down, like a child, I held out my arms to him and rocked him. "It's come at last, what I've dreamt about, what I have foreseen. This is the end of our brief happiness. You see—I killed Rebecca, and her dead body is lying in that cabin now."

Chapter XVI. The confession, she consoles him, they cling to each other. "We can't do anything until the morning."

Chapter XVII. Breakfast. Untasted. The glorious day. "Is it true Mrs. de Winter's boat has been found?" Mrs. Danvers, hungry, a ghoul scenting disaster. I was cold. "They are not sure." The telephone. We looked at each other. He went into the study and I followed him. The one-sided conversation. "Yes—yes, it's me speaking, Booth. Yes. Ah." I went out onto the terrace. Too good a morning. Unfair, and shameless. He came out. He took my hands. "They've found the body in the cabin of *Gypsy*. I'm going down right away."

Chapter XVIII. Waiting for him to return, it seemed hours. At last the sound of the car. I was sick with apprehension. He was not alone. Major Gray, the chief constable, was with him. Impossible to catch Henry alone. Goes to wash his hands. "This is a most distressing thing, Mrs. de Winter, I do feel for you and your husband very acutely. It makes it all the more difficult, you see, your husband having identified that original body, over a year ago." "Then—then something was found in the cabin."

"Oh, yes," he lowered his voice, "it was her, without a doubt. Of course—the actual body was completely decomposed, you know—but the remains were sufficient for your husband to attest—" He stopped, Henry had come into the room. "Lunch is ready," he said briefly. "Shall we go in?" "I wish I could spare you the formality of an inquest," he said, "but I'm afraid it's impossible." Discuss it from every angle. He goes at last. Henry seemed calm now. "Everything will be all right. No one has any suspicion. It's simply a case of mistaken identity. That's all. I'm not afraid. How can I regret having killed Rebecca? I don't, I never have. There's never been one pang of remorse at that part of it. But it's you—marrying you under false pretences, dragging you through this." But she is with him.

Chapter XIX. The coroner's court. The witness of the diving and then Henry. Quite straightforward, though rather tricky about why the body was in the cabin. Henry skates well over thin ice. Then the member of the jury. The boat builder. A nasty little man. (Not really, I suppose.) "What I don't understand, sir, is this. I've been and looked at the little boat, I ought to know, it was my young nipper that built her. She was well built, strongly built, and where she was lying ten fathoms deep is just off the rocky ground. Now, what is the meaning of these holes drilled in the bows—that's never rocks has done that, nor natural corrosion of sea water. Them holes have been drilled with a vice and bit."

Chapter XX. The coroner suggests adjourning until the afternoon, for further evidence to be obtained. (Again Major Gray and the coroner to lunch.) Another wretched meal. Then the afternoon. The planks are produced. The boat builder's son has had time to make a full investigation. He goes in the box. "Yes, sir, these planks have been drilled right through. And there's one other thing, sir, that I don't think was noticed. The sea cocks was turned full on." "I'm afraid I do not quite follow." "Why, sir, the plug that brought water to the sink. They are closed when an owner puts to sea. This one was full on, and what with the holes drilled and this as well it wouldn't take long for a small craft to sink. Not much above fifteen to twenty minutes, sir. I built her, sir, and I was proud of my work, and so was Mrs. de Winter. She was soundly built. It's my opinion that the little craft was deliberately scuttled." Sensation. "I see no alternative but to call Mr. de Winter again." Apologises. "Can you suggest any reason for this?" "It was shock enough to learn that I identified the wrong body a year ago. Now it is thrust upon me that my late wife was drowned in the cabin of her boat, and furthermore that the cabin was bored to let in the water. Are you suggesting that this was done deliberately, by my wife, before sailing, and that she calmly sat in the cabin and watched the water pour through the floorboards?" The coroner was nonplussed. "I realise this is very distressing for you, and for Mrs. de Winter." I felt all eyes in my direction. "But the evidence seems overwhelming. Mr. de Winter, have you any reason to suspect that your late wife wished to put an end to herself?" "None at all." "I think we had better go into the facts of last year in rather more detail." (Work this up when the time comes.) Getting more and more exhausted. The atmosphere stifling. A note handed to the coroner. He looked

up, like a stuffed owl, over his spectacles. "There is someone
here who wishes to give evidence. Mr. Paul Astley, please."

Chapter XXI. It was the loose-lipped cousin. Henry looked
very tired. He is questioned. The cousin. "Quite impossible for
Mrs. de Winter to have committed suicide. She had was not the
type, and certainly would never have chosen the manner. If her
husband suggests so I say he is being deliberately misleading.
Mrs. de Winter wrote me a letter the evening she died. Here it
is. I should like the letter to be read aloud. 'H going to London
tomorrow night. Come to the cottage and discuss plans. Have a
far better alternative to Paris—Rebecca.'" "What do you wish the
jury to infer from this?" "It's quite simple, isn't it? Mrs. de Winter and I were in love with each other. She was going to leave
her husband. We had thought of flying to Paris. But in that note
she asks me to meet her in the old woodman's cottage at Manderley, to discuss plans. You see the note was written at nine-
fifteen. Would she have written that and gone straight off and
committed suicide?"

"Mr. Astley, was Mr. de Winter aware of the relations between you and his wife?"

"Of course he was, ask him, he can't deny it."

"Do you imply that he shut his eyes to the fact?"

"No, he was madly jealous. She often told me so."

"Did you understand he was ignorant of this Paris plan?"

"As far as I know he was ignorant. But it is quite within the
bounds of possibility that she told him that evening, that they
had a row, and that he, in one of his stinking rages, plugged
holes in that boat knowing that it would sink. Go on, ask him,
ask him to prove that he's innocent, can't you—ask him to prove
it!"—the terrible white look on Henry's face—that terrible white
lost look.

The evidence is overwhelming. Leads up to the question,
"Then, Mr. de Winter, you never at any time had a suspicion
that your wife might do away with herself?" (Overwhelming relief, because it looked all the time as though they were working
up to a leading question on murder.) "Will somebody take my
wife home? She is going to faint." I think it was little Dr. Mars-
den who caught my hands as I fell. End of chapter.

Chapter XXII. Back home. Sits in a sort of stupor. Henry returns. Aged, and very tired. Verdict of suicide, without sufficient evidence to show the state of mind of the deceased. "We'll have to get away." "Won't it look suspicious?" "Let's go away this evening, Henry, quietly, to some stodgy respectable hotel in London, where no one will know us, where we are just two people out of eight million." "Yes—" very wearily, "yes." "We had better go away tonight then?" "No, not tonight." "Why not?" "Because something has to be done first. It was Gray who suggested this evening. If we do it in the day there might be a morbid crowd of sightseers. I've arranged for it to be tonight at half past nine." "Yes, of course, I understand." It was as though Rebecca had died but yesterday. There was that particular atmosphere about the house connected only with the aftermath of death. A sort of standing by—marking of time. Mrs. Danvers. She had been crying. "Please, Mr. de Winter, I understand Mrs. de Winter is to be buried this evening. With your permission I should like to be present. She was always very good to me." I wondered why she looked at Henry like that, an unfathomable question in her eyes. "Yes, Mrs. Danvers, of course. I appreciate your wish. You understand, though, the ceremony is to be entirely private. There will be no one attending but myself. I must ask you to say nothing about it to the servants." "They none of them know, sir." "Very well, then." We did not talk much during dinner. When he had gone I went upstairs to pack. I felt that I was doing things for the last time. When the stable clock struck ten, its odd high-pitched note, it seemed to me that I would not hear it again. Packing rather mechanically, and then the knock on the door. "Do you know how long Mr. de Winter will be?" "I don't suppose he'll be much after half past ten. Why?" "Mr. Paul Astley is below, and wants to see him."

Chapter XXIII. She has a short interview with him first. "You know what has happened, of course? I don't know that Henry will see you. All this has been very upsetting, and we are going away." He kept examining his nails, and there was something about his half-smile that I did not like. "Going away. Yes, I think that's very wise of you. Gossip is an unpleasant thing, and it's always more pleasant to avoid it."

"I don't think we are going for that reason."

"No? Of course, it's been a great shock to me. Rebecca was my second cousin, you know, I was devoted to her." Work up the scene. And then Henry returns.

"What are you doing here?" "Well, actually I came to offer my congratulations."

"Do you mind leaving the house; or do you prefer to be chucked out?"

"Steady a moment, Henry. You've done very well out of this affair. You realise of course that I can make things extremely unpleasant for you, I might almost say dangerous?" I gripped the hands of my chair. Henry was unmoved. He lit a cigarette. The evidence is torn to shreds, the copy of the note is produced. "If this was made public, if I told my full story—damn the consequences to my reputation—it would put a very different light on the affair, wouldn't it?" "Well, what do you propose to do? There's the telephone. Ring up Gray and tell him your story."

"Wait a bit, wait a bit. No need to get rattled. I'm a poor man, Henry, I don't want to smash you up. Why don't we come to an agreement? Here, I'll put all my cards on the table. Let me have a settlement of two thousand a year and I swear to God I'll never trouble you again." "Get out." "No, wait," I said. I turned swiftly to Paul Astley. "I see what you're driving at. It happens, by some devilish stroke of ill fortune, that things could be twisted round to make it very difficult for Henry. Perhaps he does not see it as clearly as I do. I think we ought to consider this offer of yours." "Don't you interfere with this. Don't you see that it's blackmail? Give him two thousand a year for life?" "It depends how much you value your own. Mrs. de Winter doesn't fancy being pointed at as the widow of a murderer, a fellow who was hanged, do you?"

"You think you can blackmail me, Astley, but you're wrong." Very white. "I'm not afraid of anything you can do. There's the telephone. Shall I ring up Gray, ask him to come over?"

"You would not dare. This evidence is enough to hang you." Henry walked to the telephone. "Give me Cutty 17, please." I saw our safety fall from us piece by piece. Rings Gray. "Will you come along here?" Gray comes. "Good evening, Henry. What's happened?" "You know Paul Astley, Rebecca's cousin." "Yes, we have met, I think." "Very well, Astley, go ahead." (Wind out of sails.) "Look here, Gray, I'm not satisfied with the verdict." "Isn't that for De Winter to say?"

"No, I don't think it is. I have a right to speak, not only as Rebecca's cousin but, if she had lived, as her prospective husband."

"Is this true, Henry?" Henry laughed shortly.

"So he says, Arthur, if you want to believe it you can."

"Supposing you tell me exactly what's wrong."

"Listen here, Gray, this note was written to me half an hour before Rebecca was supposed to have set out on that suicidal sail. Here it is, I want you to say whether you think a woman who wrote that note had made up her mind to kill herself?"

"No—on the face of it, no. What does the note refer to? What were these plans?"

"We were going to Paris. It was her idea, she loathed Manderley, loathed every stick and stone in the place. Henry was going to London, it was an escapade after her own heart."

" 'I've got something to tell you.' What do you suppose that means?"

"I don't know. One never knew with Rebecca. It might mean anything. But there was the meeting—nine-thirty—in the cottage, it's as plain to me as though she were standing here now."

"What are you suggesting, get done with these insinuations and speak out."

"Rebecca never plugged the holes in that boat, Gray, Rebecca never committed suicide, she was murdered, and if you want to know who the murderer is, why there he is—standing there with his God damned superior smile, he couldn't even wait till the year was out before marrying again, the first chit of a girl he set his eyes on—there's your murderer for you, Mr. Henry de Winter of Manderley." He began to laugh, high-pitched and foolish, the laugh of a drunkard, and all the while pointing his finger at Henry, who stood very still in his corner by the window.

Chapter XXIV. They go into it more carefully. "You say you were Mrs. de Winter's lover. Can you prove it? Have you other letters? I want to remind you of this, because in a court of law you might find yourself making a big mistake." (Henry interposes about the blackmail.) "No, I didn't. Rebecca was not the sort of woman to write love letters."

"Does anybody know?"

"Yes—there's one person knows. But whether she'd speak the truth or not I don't know. But she might speak, if she thought it would help Rebecca." Already I had an inkling of what was to come.

"Well, who is it?"

"Mrs. Danvers."

"Then I think the simplest thing to do would be to ask Mrs. Danvers to come here."

Mrs. Danvers comes. Tall and gaunt. She had evidently been weeping.

"Mrs. Danvers, were you aware of the relationship between the late Mrs. de Winter and Mr. Astley?"

"They were second cousins, so I've always understood."

"No—I was not referring to blood relationship. Were you aware that there existed a closer relationship than that?"

"I don't understand you." Astley laughed coarsely.

"Come off it, Mrs. Danvers. You knew damn well that Mrs. de Winter and I (etc., etc.). I've already told Major Gray, but he won't believe me. Come now, admit what you know, she was in love with me, wasn't she?"

Mrs. Danvers considered him a moment. I can't describe her smile, it had all the meaning of disdain and of scorn.

"She was not."

"Listen here, Mrs. Danvers—"

"She was not in love with you, no, nor with her husband. She was above you all, she despised all men."

"Look here—didn't she creep down the woodland path to me at nights, weren't you waiting up for her sometimes, didn't she spend nights with me in London?"

"Well"—with sudden passion—"what if she did, hadn't she a right to amuse herself the way she liked? Love-making was a game with her, she told me often, she did it because it made her laugh, it made her laugh, I tell you," etc., etc., torrent of passion.

It was horrible, unexpected, and it was not helping Henry.

"Can you suggest any reason why she should have taken her life?"

"No—I've lain awake at nights, Major Gray, reproaching my-self. If I'd been at Manderley that night."

"You were not here?"

"No—I'd gone into Stanebury. I usually went on Friday after-noons, and I missed my bus. I didn't get back till after nine. She had gone then." I felt pity for Mrs. Danvers now. If only that loyalty was ours.

"Mrs. Danvers, you knew Mrs. de Winter very well, we can gather that from what you've already told us." Astley would have spoken but he motioned him to be quiet. "Can you think of any reason, however remote, why Mrs. de Winter should have taken her own life?" She shook her head slowly. "No," she said, "no, Major Gray. Ever since the verdict I've been thinking about it, turning it over and over in my mind."

"There you see," Astley said swiftly, "it's impossible, I've told you that."

"Be quiet, Astley," he thundered, "give Mrs. Danvers time to think. If we'd known how she'd spent her day in London it might help."

"She had a hair appointment from twelve till one-thirty. She lunched alone at her club, and came down by a train about half past three."

"It ought to be easy to verify that. What was she doing from two until three?"

"Wait—I've got her engagement diary. You know you let me have all those little mementoes, when she went. They're locked in my room. Everything she did she'd write down, and tick off with an X."

Goes to fetch it. "Yes—here it is—'Hair 12.00. Lunch at Club. 2 o'clock. Baker.'"

"Who's Baker?"

"Baker, Baker. Never heard of the fellow."

"Baker. I don't know the name. But look here, she's put a great X after that, as though as a special gesture. I believe if we knew who Baker was we'd be near to solving Mrs. de Winter's suicide. Mrs. Danvers, she wasn't in the hands of moneylenders?" "No." "Blackmailers?" A glance at Astley. Too careful for that. "She had no enemy, no one she was in fear of?"

"Mrs. de Winter afraid? She was afraid of no one and nobody,

there was only one thing that she was afraid of—and that was
pain."

We all of us stared. Paul Astley looked astonished.

"What on earth do you mean? What about the falls she had
out hunting? What about the dogs she looked after?"

"Not that sort of pain, Mr. Paul. She was, like all strong people, afraid of being ill, and most of all of having operations.
'When I die, Danny,' she said to me, 'I hope it will be quick, like
the snuffing of a candle. If I knew I was to suffer—I think I'd go
clear off my head.'"

That seems no good.

"That's why I was glad it was a quick death. They say drown-
ing is painless, don't they?" Eagerly. I felt sorry for Mrs.
Danvers. At any rate, I thought, Henry and I both knew that
Rebecca had died painlessly.

"When did she say that?"

"She always felt that way, all the time I knew her. But she did
say it to me not long before she died."

"What in hell's the use of all this, we're getting away from the
point all the time. Baker, if we only knew." Mrs. Danvers had
been going through the diary. Suddenly she gave an exclamation. "There's something here, right at the back, between a number of loose pages. Baker—and the number 1057. That's the telephone number. No exchange, though."

"Try all the London exchanges with that number. It will take
you a week. What's the time?" (Make it earlier.) I could see that
Henry, like the rest of us, considered the tracing of Baker a wild
goose chase. However, it served to delay. It might quieten Gray
for the time.

"This will cost you a bit. [Explain about telephone books.]
Give us this book again. Is that a dash after the number?
Couldn't it, with a little ingenuity, be twisted into M?" He tries
one number, etc. Couple named Carter lived there for seven
years. "Try Museum, sir," from Mrs. Danvers. He does so. Night
porter. Anyone named Baker. "No, sir, I've only been here six
months. There may have been. I believe there was a gentleman
of that name once." "Could you inform me, is it a private house
or offices? Ah—" He turned, an odd, rather triumphant look in his

eyes. "The man said he believed there was a man named Baker there once and it's not offices."

"What are they?" from Astley.

"The address is 113 Harley Street, and are a number of doctors' consulting rooms." Then I knew at once. Of course Rebecca spent the hour from two to three with the doctor who had told her that, etc.

Chapter XXV. Journey to London to Harley St. Baker of course retired six months ago through ill-health. Living in Hampstead. Trek to Hamp—(noose drawing tighter round his neck). Baker out when they get there. They sit round the room, description of, etc. Baker comes in. Different somehow. Gray takes the initiative, and asks the question. On the thirteenth of last year, between two and three, a Mrs. de Winter.

Shakes his head, no idea of the name.

Perhaps she did not come under her own name. Here, he looks up his diary. "I see a Mrs. Winter booked an appointment for that day. Hold on, I'll go through my files. Yes—here we are. H'm. Yes—of course you know, unprofessional conduct."

"This is Mr. de Winter. In strict confidence, she committed suicide, we strongly believe, and it is possible, just possible, you may furnish us with the motive." I waited for his denial, for his inevitable, "Mrs. Winter, if I remember rightly, did not strike me as being the sort of woman who would be afraid to have a child." But instead he glanced through his files again. "She had been to have some X rays taken, and she came to know the results. She told me, 'I want to know the truth, no gentle bedside manner for me.' She had a deep-rooted malignant growth, and since she had asked for the truth I let her have it. The pain was slight as yet, but in six months' time, perhaps in less than that, she would have to be under morphia. An operation might have done some good, personally I believe not."

"Dr. Baker," Henry leaning forward, "you are quite certain of this? There is no possibility of mistake?"

"None at all. Outwardly Mrs. Winter was a perfectly healthy woman. There was a certain malformation of the u, she could never have had a child, for instance, but that had nothing to do with the disease."

We sat silent. It was Arthur Gray who first rose to his feet. "I think Dr. Baker has told us all we wanted to know. If you could let us have a copy of that analysis."

"Oh, certainly."

We went outside.

"I think you two had better go off on your own," he said. "I'll deal with Astley. This"—he tapped the document—"and Mrs. Danvers' statement give us our motive. There's no twisting about of that. And blackmail is a very ugly charge. You can leave it all to me."

He hailed a taxi. "God bless you both," he said abruptly. And then he was gone. We got into the car.

"He knows, of course," said Henry.

"Yes," I said.

And we went along the North Circular Road, etc., etc.

Chapter XXVI.   Going towards Manderley. We still have to go away—they take the decision, they go over it all. After all that has happened. Perhaps Rebecca will have the last word yet. The road narrows before the avenue. A car with blazing headlights passed. Henry swerved to avoid it, and it came at us, rearing out of the ground, its huge arms outstretched to embrace us, crashing and splintering above our heads.

Epilogue?

1. Atmosphere.
2. Simplicity of style.
3. Keep to the main theme.
4. Characters few and well defined.
5. Build it up little by little.

The Rebecca Epilogue

If you travel south you will come upon us in the end, staying in one of those innumerable little hotels that cling like limpets to the Mediterranean shore. You will be passing through to somewhere more attractive, but we are fixtures there, and have been for many months. As you walk into the dining room you will not notice us at first, for we have a table in the corner by the window; but when you have eaten your inevitable hors d'oeuvre, and are considering the plate of roast veal and haricot beans that the obliging but clumsy little waiter has put before you, you will hear my voice for a moment, raised above the clatter of plates, demanding a bottle of Evian water in ineffectual French. You groan inwardly, and hope that we will not edge into conversation with you when the time comes to take coffee in the lounge. The nuisance is spared to you, however, for when *déjeuner* is over we make for the shady side of the verandah without glancing once in your direction.

You see then that he is crippled, he walks slowly and awkwardly with the aid of sticks, and it is some little time before I have settled him for the afternoon. There is the long chair to adjust, the pillows to arrange, and the rug over his knees; and when this is done to his satisfaction, and he has rewarded me with a smile, I sit down beside him and open my bag of knitting.

You watch us covertly for a while from behind the concealing pages of the continental *Daily Mail*, and speculate idly upon our identity. His face is vaguely familiar to you. There is something arresting about his profile and the line of his jaw, but it is impossible to put a name to him. Of course there are replicas of us all over Europe. Both of us bear upon our persons the unmistakable signs of the wandering English who live abroad.

He very immaculate, with fresh linen, smelling of eau de co-

logne and bath salts, a copy of *The Times* on his lap, his panama
hat set at just the right angle, and I with faded hair and colour-
ing, dark glasses concealing eyes that have lost their brightness,
and upon my rather dumpy body one of an unending series of
cotton frocks, too long for me and sagging at the hem. Later in
the day you run up against me in the English library, the bag of
knitting still under one arm and three books under the other, and
as I pass you I leave a little whiff of lavender water in my wake.
I dab it on with the stopper behind each ear every morning, and
it lasts me for the day.

During your brief visit you notice that we live very much by
routine. The chairs are put out on the verandah after breakfast
and we stay there, with intervals for meals, until sundown.
Sometimes I wander off for walks alone, carrying a cardigan I
have knitted myself and a local walking stick with a spike at the
bottom, but I am always back in time for tea. He has had a nap
whilst I was gone, and wakes just in time for my return, pre-
ceded by the little waiter with tea. We shift with the sun, and
when the first chill of evening falls upon the verandah I put a
marker in the book I have been reading to him, and start the
small task of getting him indoors. You gather that changing for
dinner at half past seven is rather a business for us, but nevertheless we appear in the nick of time, he faultless as usual and
reminding you once again of some familiar face, and I in black
lace with a fur round my shoulders. We keep very much to ourselves, and beyond a courteous good morning and good night to
the few other inhabitants of the hotel, and a more genuine smile
to the staff, you never see us talk to anyone.

The day comes for you to leave for your more exciting rendez-
vous. This spot is deadly dull, of course, but the rest has done
you good, and as you stand on the verandah for the last time,
waiting for your luggage to come down, you see us sitting in our
usual corner of the verandah, sipping our midmorning coffee.
Something prompts you to walk across and say good-bye. You
come upon us unawares, and for the first time you notice that
there is an indefinable air of sadness about us, a sort of aftermath of tragedy, and you feel a little uncomfortable, as though
you had clumsily stumbled against a barrier. You are saved from
embarrassment by our smiles, and there is nothing tragic in the

way we wish you bon voyage, and chat for a moment quite pleasantly about your destination. We both look rather hungrily at your luggage, and the thought comes to you, very surprisingly, that perhaps we wish we were going too.

"Are you making a long stay here?" you ask; and I pause a moment before replying, throwing him a glance, "Our plans are rather indefinite," leaving it at that. The stout hall porter has assembled your luggage and is waiting for his tip. There is nothing to delay you now.

"Well, so long," you say, "we shall probably meet at home someday."

The Englishman shakes your hand and wishes you good luck. "No," he says, half to you, half to himself, "no, we shall never go home again."

And then you smile, and wave, and disappear round the corner of the verandah. You think about us vaguely when you get into the train. Why do they do it, you wonder; leading apparently aimless lives? For what purpose? Are they really in quest of the sun, or is their existence a way of escape, from something or someone?

We shall never live in England again, that much is certain. The past would be too close to us. Those things we are trying to forget and put behind us would stir again, and that sense of fear, of furtive unrest struggling at length to master unreasoning panic—now mercifully stilled, thank God—might in some manner unforeseen become a living companion, as it did before. We are not unhappy, that I would impress upon you. Henry at least knows something of the peace of God, which, poor darling, he never possessed before. He is wonderfully patient and never complains, not even when he is in pain, which happens, I think, rather more often than he would have me know. I can tell by the way he will look puzzled suddenly, and lost, all expression dying away from his dear face as though swept by an unseen hand, and in its place a mask will form, a sculptured thing, formal and cold, beautiful still but lifeless. He will fall to smoking cigarette after cigarette, not bothering to extinguish them, and the glowing stubs will lie around him on the ground like petals. He will talk quickly and eagerly about nothing at all, an unusual thing

for such a silent person, snatching at any subject, however trivial, as a panacea to pain.

I remember my father expounding once upon the theory that
men and women emerge stronger and finer after suffering, and
that to advance in this or any world we must endure ordeal by
fire. He should have known, of course—he was a doctor. And I,
at the time a chubby schoolgirl in tearing health from a scramble
on the south downs, considered it a dreary doctrine. Since then I
have known fear, and loneliness, and very great distress. I have
watched my beloved husband come through a great crisis, and
I—I was not a silent spectator. I know now that it is not easy to
live. Sooner or later, in the life of everyone comes a moment of
trial. We all of us have our own particular devil who rides us
and torments us, and we must give battle in the end. Henry and
I have conquered ours, or so we believe. The devil does not ride
us any more. But we are shorn of our little earthly glory, he a
cripple and his home lost to him, and I, well, I suppose I am like
all childless women, craving for echoes I shall never hear, and
lacking a certain quality of tenderness. Like a ranting actress in
an indifferent play, I might say that this is the price we have to
pay for our freedom. But I have had enough of melodrama in
this life, and would bereave my Henry of his five senses if it
would ensure him his present peace and security until eternity.

As I said before, we are not unhappy. We have money to live
without discomfort. Granted that the little hotel you found us in
was cheap, the food indifferent, and that day after day dawns
very much the same, yet we would not have it otherwise. We
both appreciate simplicity, and if we are sometimes bored—well,
boredom is a pleasing antidote to fear. The only time Henry
shows impatience is when the postman lags, for it means we
must wait perhaps another day before hearing the result of some
match played a week ago. We have tried wireless, but the noise
is such an irritant, and we prefer to store up our excitement
against the arrival of our mail. Oh, the Test Matches that have
saved us from ennui, the boxing bouts, even the billiard scores.
Finals of schoolboy sports, dog racing, strange little competitions
in the remoter counties, all these are grist to our hungry mill.
Sometimes old copies of the *Field* come our way, and I am
transported from this indifferent shore to the reality of an Eng-

lish spring. I read of chalk streams and the mayfly, of harbours where the tide is at the flood, of sorrel growing in meadows, and rooks circling above church towers as they used to do at Manderley. The smell of wet earth comes to us from those thumbed and tattered pages, the sour tang of moorland peat, and handful upon handful of green and soggy moss, spattered white in places with the herons' droppings.

Once there was an article on wood pigeons, and as I read it aloud to Henry it was as though I was once again in the deep woods at Manderley, the pigeons fluttering above my head. I heard their soft complacent call, so comfortable and cool on a hot summer's afternoon, and there would be no disturbing of their peace until Jasper came loping through the bracken to find me, his damp muzzle questing the ground, his spaniel ears adroop, his jowl saggy, and his great eyes a perpetual reproach. Then like old ladies caught at their ablutions, the bathroom door ajar, the pigeons would flutter from their hiding place, shocked into silly agitation, and making a monstrous to-do with their wings streak away from us above the treetops, and so out of sight and sound. While I, yawning idly, would recollect that the sun by now had left the rose garden, there were languid heads upon lean stalks calling for water, but most important of all there were fresh raspberries for tea. . . .

It was the grey look on Henry's face that made me stop abruptly and turn the pages until I found an article on cricket, very practical and dull. Middlesex batting on a hard wicket at the Oval, piling up interminable dreary runs—how I blessed their stolid flannelled figures—and in a few minutes his face had settled back into repose, the colour had returned, and he was deriding the Surrey bowling in healthy irritation. We were saved a retreat into the past and I had learnt my lesson. That grey look meant hunger and regret, and bitterness too for this exile we had brought upon ourselves, so in future I must keep away from colour and scent and sound, rain and the lapping of water. Read English news, yes, and English sport, politics and pomposity, but keep the things that hurt to myself alone. They can be my secret indulgence.

Some people have a vice for reading Bradshaws, and plan innumerable journeys across country for the fun of linking up im-

possible connections. I, on the contrary, am a mine of informa-
tion on the English countryside. I know the name of every owner
of every British moor, and their tenants too. I know how many
partridge are killed on such-and-such an estate, how many
pheasants, how many head of deer. I know where trout are rising, and where salmon are leaping; even the names of those who
are walking hound puppies are familiar to me. I attend all meets,
I follow every run. The state of the crops, the price of fat cattle,
the mysterious ailments of pigs, I relish them all. A poor pastime,
perhaps, and not a very intellectual one, but I breathe the air of
England as I read, and can face this glittering sky with greater
courage.

That afternoon you saw me set forth upon my walk, stick in
hand, was passed by me in the west country on a misty afternoon. I did not notice the scrubby vineyards and the crumbling
stones because I was picking foxgloves and campion from a wet
streaking hedge. Yes, I know my cotton frock sagged at the back,
and my cardigan had stretched, and I came back worn and
dusty-looking. I noticed your pitying, indulgent smile. For all
that I had enjoyed my afternoon, and it was worth being away
from Henry to find his smile of welcome when I returned.

Although you were hiding behind the *Daily Mail* I know you
were watching the little ritual of our tea. The order never varies.
Two slices of bread and butter each, one Indian tea, one China
(I take mine with lemon), and two brioches with apricot jam. No
cake. Henry has a theory that it gives him indigestion. What a
hidebound, pernickety couple we must seem to an outsider like
yourself, clinging to our routine and living like slaves to the
clock. Having a sit-down tea at half past four because we always
did in England. You should have seen us at Manderley—there it
was even more of a ritual. In winter we had it in the library, the
table put within comfortable distance of the roaring log fire. On
the stroke of the half hour old Robert would fling open the door,
followed by that nervous young footman he was in the process of
training, who will never become proficient until he can control
his hands from shaking, and the performance of laying the table
would be carried out under the forbidding eye of Robert, who
now and again communicated with his minion by way of dumb
show.

Such a feast would be laid before us always, and yet we ate so little, Henry faithful always to his slice of bread and butter and his apricot jam. I must admit I went a little further. Those dripping crumpets, I can taste them now, alternating with piping-hot floury scones and tiny crisp wedges of toast. Sandwiches of a delectable but unknown nature, mysteriously flavoured, and that very special gingerbread. Angel cake that melted in the mouth, and its rather stodgier companion, bursting with peel and raisins. There must have been enough food there to keep a starving family for a week. I never knew what happened to it all. The waste used to worry me sometimes, but I never dared ask Mrs. Danvers what she did about it. She would have looked at me in scorn and smiled that freezing superior smile of hers. I can hear her say, "There were never any complaints when Mrs. de Winter was alive," before she swept away, leaving me standing on one foot. Poor Mrs. Danvers, I wonder what she is doing now. She always despised me. I think it was the expression on her face that gave me my first feeling of unrest. Instinctively I thought, "She is comparing me to Rebecca," and sharp as a sword the shadow came between us.

Well, it is over now, finished and done with. I ride no more tormented, and Henry is free. Even my faithful Jasper has gone to the happy hunting ground, and this summer Manderley opens as a country club. The prospectus was sent to me the other day. I did not show it to Henry, but put it away in the bottom of my trunk. They have demolished the old gun room and the flower room in the east wing, and my little morning room, and have built what they call a "sun loggia," Italian style, with vita glass, so that the guests can sprawl about in negligée and acquire the fashionable tan.

Four concrete squash courts stand where the stables used to be, and they have sunk a swimming pool in the wilderness. The rose garden is a rose garden still, but they have discovered its possibilities for tea, and with gay little tables and bright umbrellas intend luring their clients there on summer afternoons. I have no doubt that Joe Allan and his Boys will look very well in the minstrels' gallery, so appropriately placed for their convenience above the great hall, where I gather the Saturday dances are to be held. Apparently the golf course will not be ready until the winter, for the park does not lend itself easily to conversion, and there are so many trees to come down. The place will be packed for the opening weekend, every room is booked already, and a famous film star is to start the proceedings by diving into the swimming pool in evening dress. The dress no doubt to be auctioned afterwards. Whether the venture is a success or not, one thing at least is certain. The guests will sleep soundly in their beds. Our ghosts will never trouble them. I shall keep the prospectus, though, and use it now and again as a lash when I fail in humour. It might stimulate in me an affection for cactus bushes and olive groves, stony vineyards and dusty bougain-villea.

And you, perhaps you will visit Manderley one weekend, jaded and out of sorts from your London season. The west country is not so far in these days of easy flying, and they are sure to clear a landing ground for planes somewhere in the park. If you are stouthearted and not overburdened with imagination you can walk anywhere in Manderley with impunity, but if London life has put a strain upon your nerves there are one or two places I should avoid. The deep woods, for instance, after dark, and the little woodman's cottage. Here there may linger still a certain atmosphere of stress. That corner in the drive too, where the stump of a tree encroaches upon the gravel, it is not a spot in which to pause. Your fancy might play odd tricks upon you, especially when the sun has set. When the leaves rustle they sound very much like the stealthy movement of a woman in evening dress, and when they shiver suddenly, and fall and scatter before you on the ground, they could be the patter-patter of a woman's hurrying footstep, and that mark in the gravel the imprint of a high-heeled satin shoe.

No, if I were you I should toy with my cocktail in the new American bar, that billiard room always lacked atmosphere; and remain downstairs where you can hear the crooner braying, do not wander alone along the passages upstairs. There is a moment, just after twilight, if the moon is full, when the light streams through that long narrow window in the old west wing; and you could swear that in the corner there, against the door, where the shadows are darkest, there is a figure crouching, a woman surely. But perhaps the west wing is ablaze with electric light now, and dressing rooms and shower baths abound, and all the shadows have been swept away.

As you stand in the doorway of the hall, waiting for Joe Allan to strike up with one of his hot numbers, and light a cigar feeling at peace with yourself and the world, you will never connect Manderley with that fellow in the chaise longue and the panama hat, and his dull little wife in her faded cotton frock; yet it was not so long ago that Henry stood where you are standing now, whistling and calling to the dogs, and the step that you have sprinkled so freely with the ash from your cigar was thick with the crumbs I had scattered for the linnets. . . .

I suppose we are both very changed. Henry looks much older, of course, and his hair has gone very grey; but there is a certain stillness about him, an air of tranquillity that was not there before, and I—rather too late in the day—have lost my diffidence, my timidity, my shyness with strangers. Perhaps Henry's dependence upon me for every little thing has made me confident and bold at last. At any rate I am different from that self who drove to Manderley for the first time, hopeful and eager, handicapped by a rather desperate gaucherie, and filled with an intense desire to please. Those preceding years of companionship with Mrs. Van Hopper had scarcely engendered in me great qualities of confidence, and it was my lack of poise that made such a bad impression on people like Mrs. Danvers. What must I have seemed like after Rebecca ; . . ?

As we sit today at our table in the window, quietly working our way through from hors d'oeuvre to dessert, I think of that other hotel dining room, larger and far more splendid than this, that dreadful Côte d'Azur at Monte Carlo, and how, instead of having Henry opposite me, his steady, well-shaped hands peeling a mandarin in methodical fashion, I had Mrs. Van Hopper, her fat bejewelled fingers questing a plate heaped with ravioli, her small pigs' eyes darting suspiciously from her plate to mine for fear I should have made a better bargain.

Only a few years ago—far fewer than you would suppose—she dominated my small world; the salary she paid me was one hundred and fifty pounds a year, and Manderley was unknown to me. There was I, with straight bobbed hair and youthful unpowdered face, trailing in her wake like a subdued mouse. Now, with Henry by my side, in spite of all we have lost, in spite of his maimed body and scarred hands, those days, the terror, the distress, are over, and I feel a glow of contentment come upon me. His maimed body and my disfigurement are things of no account, we have learned to accept them, we live, we breathe, we have vitality, the spark of divinity has not passed us by. This factor alone should be enough for us; we have been spared to one another, and because of this we shall endure.

Déjeuner is over. The little waiter wipes the last crumbs from our table, and when I have helped Henry to his feet we make our usual pilgrimage to the verandah. The sun has lost its morning brilliance and is streaking to the west, leaving an afterglow which is easier to bear. Henry draws the rug over his knees, throws away his cigarette, then closes his eyes. I fix my dark glasses, reach for my bag of knitting. And before us, long as the skein of wool I wind, stretches the vista of our afternoon.

The House of Secrets

It was an afternoon in late autumn, the first time I tried to find the house. October, November, the month escapes me. But in the west country autumn can make herself a witch, and place a spell upon the walker. The trees were golden brown, the hydrangeas had massive heads still blue and untouched by flecks of wistful grey, and I would set forth at three of an afternoon with foolish notions of August still in my head. "I will strike inland," I thought, "and come back by way of the cliffs, and the sun will yet be high, or at worst touching the horizon beyond the western hills."

Of course, I was still a newcomer to the district, a summer visitor, whose people had but lately bought the old "Swiss Cottage," as the locals called it, a name which, to us, had horrid associations with an underground railway in the Finchley Road at home.

We were not yet rooted. We were new folk from London. We walked as tourists walked, seeing what should be seen. So my sister and I, poring over an old guidebook, first came upon the name of Menabilly. What description the guidebook gave I cannot now remember, except that the house had been first built in the reign of Queen Elizabeth, that the grounds and woods had been in the last century famous for their beauty, and that the property had never changed hands from the time it came into being, but had passed down, in the male line, to the present owner. Three miles from the harbour, easy enough to find; but what about keepers and gardeners, chauffeurs and barking dogs? My sister was not such an inveterate trespasser as I. We asked advice. "You'll find no dogs at Menabilly, not any keepers either," we were told, "the house is all shut up. The owner lives in

Devon. But you'll have trouble in getting there. The drive is nearly three miles long, and overgrown."

I for one was not to be deterred. The autumn colours had me bewitched before the start. So we set forth, Angela more reluctant, with a panting pekinese held by a leash. We came to the lodge at four turnings, as we had been told, and opened the creaking iron gates with the flash courage and appearance of bluff common to the trespasser. The lodge was deserted. No one peered at us from the windows. We slunk away down the drive, and were soon hidden by the trees. Is it really nigh on twenty years since I first walked that hidden drive and saw the beech trees, like the arches of a great cathedral, form a canopy above my head? I remember we did not talk, or if we did we talked in whispers. That was the first effect the woods had upon both of us.

The drive twisted and turned in a way that I described many years afterwards, when sitting at a desk in Alexandria and looking out upon a hard glazed sky and dusty palm trees; but on that first autumnal afternoon, when the drive was new to us, it had the magic quality of a place hitherto untrodden, unexplored. I was Scott in the Antarctic. I was Cortez in Mexico. Or possibly I was none of these things, but a trespasser in time. The woods were sleeping now, but who, I wondered, had ridden through them once? What hoofbeats had sounded and then died away? What carriage wheels had rolled and vanished? Doublet and hose. Boot and jerkin. Patch and powder. Stock and patent leather. Crinoline and bonnet.

The trees grew taller and the shrubs more menacing. Yet still the drive led on, and never a house at the end of it. Suddenly Angela said, "It's after four . . . and the sun's gone." The pekinese watched her, pink tongue lolling. And then he stared into the bushes, pricking his ears at nothing. The first owl hooted. . . .

"I don't like it," said Angela firmly. "Let's go home."

"But the house," I said with longing, "we haven't seen the house."

She hesitated, and I dragged her on. But in an instant the day was gone from us. The drive was a muddied path, leading nowhere, and the shrubs, green no longer but a shrouding black, turned to fantastic shapes and sizes. There was not one owl now, but twenty. And through the dark trees, with a pale grin upon his face, came the first glimmer of the livid hunter's moon.

I knew then that I was beaten. For that night only.

"All right," I said grudgingly, "we'll find the house another time."

And, following the moon's light, we struck through the trees and came out upon the hillside. In the distance below us stretched the sea. Behind us the woods and the valley through which we had come. But nowhere was there a sign of any house. Nowhere at all.

"Perhaps," I thought to myself, "it is a house of secrets, and has no wish to be disturbed." But I knew I should not rest until I had found it.

If I remember rightly the weather broke after that day, and the autumn rains were upon us. Driving rain, day after day. And we, not yet become acclimatized to Cornish wind and weather, packed up and returned to London for the winter. But I did not forget the woods of Menabilly, or the house that waited. . . .

We came back again to Cornwall in the spring, and I was seized with a fever for fishing. I would be out in a boat most days, with a line in the water, and it did not matter much what came on the end of it, whether it would be seaweed or a dead crab, as long as I could sit on the thwart of a boat and hold a line and watch the sea. The boatman sculled off the little bay called Pridmouth, and as I looked at the land beyond, and saw the massive trees climbing from the valley to the hill, the shape of it all seemed familiar.

"What's up there, in the trees?" I said.

"That's Menabilly," came the answer, "but you can't see the house from the shore. It's away up yonder. I've never been there myself." I felt a bite on my line at that moment and said no more. But the lure of Menabilly was upon me once again.

Next morning I did a thing I had never done before, nor ever did again, except once in the desert, where to see sunrise is the peak of all experience. In short, I rose at 5:00 A.M. I pulled across the harbour in my pram, walked through the sleeping town, and climbed out upon the cliffs just as the sun himself climbed out on Pont Hill behind me. The sea was glass. The air

was soft and misty warm. And the only other creature out of bed
was a fisherman, hauling crab pots at the harbour mouth. It gave
me a fine feeling of conceit, to be up before the world. My feet
in sand shoes seemed like wings. I came down to Pridmouth
Bay, passing the solitary cottage by the lake, and, opening a
small gate hard by, I saw a narrow path leading to the woods.
Now, at last, I had the day before me, and no owls, no moon, no
shadows could turn me back.

I followed the path to the summit of the hill and then, emerging from the woods, turned left, and found myself upon a high
grass walk, with all the bay stretched out below me and the
Gribben head beyond.

I paused, stung by the beauty of that first pink glow of sunrise
on the water, but the path led on, and I would not be deterred.
Then I saw them for the first time—the scarlet rhododendrons.
Massive and high they reared above my head, shielding the entrance to a long smooth lawn. I was hard upon it now, the place
I sought. Some instinct made me crouch upon my belly and
crawl softly to the wet grass at the foot of the shrubs. The morning mist was lifting, and the sun was coming up above the trees
even as the moon had done last autumn. This time there was no
owl, but blackbird, thrush and robin greeting the summer day.

I edged my way onto the lawn, and there she stood. My house
of secrets. My elusive Menabilly . . .

The windows were shuttered fast, white and barred. Ivy covered the grey walls and threw tendrils round the windows. The
house, like the world, was sleeping too. But later, when the sun
was high, there would come no wreath of smoke from the chimneys. The shutters would not be thrown back, or the doors unfas-
tened. No voices would sound within those darkened rooms.
Menabilly would sleep on, like the sleeping beauty of the fairy
tale, until someone should come to wake her.

I watched her awhile in silence, and then became embold-
ened, and walked across the lawn and stood beneath the windows. The scarlet rhododendrons encircled her lawns, to south,
to east, to west. Behind her, to the north, were the tall trees and
the deep woods. She was a two-storied house, and with the ivy
off her would have a classical austerity that her present shaggy
covering denied her.

One of her nineteenth-century owners had taken away her
small-paned windows and given her plate glass instead, and he
had also built at her northern end an ugly wing that conformed
ill with the rest of her. But with all her faults, most obvious to
the eye, she had a grace and charm that made me hers upon the
instant. She was, or so it seemed to me, bathed in a strange mystery. She held a secret—not one, not two, but many—that she
withheld from many people but would give to one who loved
her well.

As I sat on the edge of the lawn and stared at her I felt as
many romantic, foolish people have felt about the Sphinx. Here
was a block of stone, even as the desert Sphinx, made by man for
his own purpose—yet she had a personality that was hers alone,
without the touch of human hand. One family only had lived
within her walls. One family who had given her life. They had
been born there, they had loved, they had quarrelled, they had
suffered, they had died. And out of these emotions she had
woven a personality for herself, she had become what their
thoughts and their desires had made her.

And now the story was ended. She lay there in her last sleep.
Nothing remained for her but to decay and die. . . .

I cannot recollect, now, how long I lay and stared at her. It
was past noon, perhaps, when I came back to the living world. I
was empty and lightheaded, with no breakfast inside me. But the
house possessed me from that day, even as a mistress holds her
lover.

Ours was a strange relationship for fifteen years. I would put
her from my mind for months at a time, and then, on coming
again to Cornwall, I would wait a day or two, then visit her in
secret.

Once again I would sit on the lawn and stare up at her windows. Sometimes I would find that the caretaker at the lodge,
who came now and again to air the house, had left a blind
pulled back, showing a chink of space, so that by pressing my
face to the window I could catch a glimpse of a room. There was
one room—a dining room, I judged, because of the long sideboard against the wall—that held my fancy most. Dark panels. A
great fireplace. And on the walls the family portraits stared into
the silence and the dust. Another room, once a library, judging

by the books upon the shelves, had become a lumber place, and in the centre of it stood a great dappled rocking horse with scarlet nostrils. What little blue-sashed, romping children once bestrode his back? Where was the laughter gone? Where were the voices that had called along the passages?

One autumn evening I found a window unclasped in the ugly north wing at the back. It must have been intuition that made me bring my torch with me that day. I threw open the creaking window and climbed in. Dust. Dust everywhere. The silence of death. I flashed my torch onto the cobwebbed walls and walked the house. At last. I had imagined it so often. Here were the rooms, leading from one to another, that I had pictured only from outside. Here was the staircase, and the faded crimson wall. There the long drawing room, with its shiny chintz sofas and chairs, and here the dining room, a forgotten corkscrew still lying on the sideboard.

Suddenly the shadows became too many for me, and I turned and went back the way I had come. Softly I closed the window behind me. And as I did so, from a broken pane on the floor above my head came a great white owl, who flapped his way into the woods and vanished. . . .

Some shred of convention still clinging to my nature turned me to respectability. I would not woo my love in secret. I wrote to the owner of the house and asked his permission to walk about his grounds. The request was granted. Now I could tread upon the lawns with a slip of paper in my pocket to show my good intentions, and no longer craw belly to the ground like a slinking thief.

Little by little, too, I gleaned snatches of family history. There was the lady in blue who looked, so it was said, from a side window, yet few had seen her face. There was the cavalier found beneath the buttress wall more than a hundred years ago. There were the sixteenth-century builders, merchants and traders; there were the Stuart royalists, who suffered for their king; the Tory landowners with their white wigs and their brood of children; the Victorian garden lovers with their rare plants and their shrubs.

I saw them all, in my mind's eye, down to the present owner, who could not love his home; and when I thought of him it was not of an elderly man, a respectable justice of the peace, but of a small boy orphaned at two years old, coming for his holidays in an Eton collar and tight black suit, watching his old grandfather with nervous, doubtful eyes. The house of secrets. The house of stories.

The war came, and my husband and I were now at Hythe, in Kent, and many miles from Cornwall. I remember a letter coming from my sister.

"By the way, there is to be a sale at Menabilly. Everything to be sold up, and the house just left to fall to bits. Do you want anything?"

Did I want anything? I wanted her, my house. I wanted every stick of furniture, from the Jacobean oak to the Victorian bamboo. But what was the use? The war had come. There was no future for man, woman or child. And anyway, Menabilly was entailed. The house itself could not be sold. No, she was just a dream, and would die, as dreams die always.

In '43 changes of plans sent me back to Cornwall, with my three children. I had not visited Menabilly since the war began. No bombs had come her way, yet she looked like a blitzed building. The shutters were not shuttered now. The panes were broken. She had been left to die.

It was easy to climb through the front windows. The house was stripped and bare. Dirty paper on the floor. Great fungus growths from the ceiling. Moisture everywhere, death and decay. I could scarcely see the soul of her for the despair. The mould was in her bones.

Odd, yet fearful, what a few years of total neglect can do to a house, as to a man, a woman. . . . Have you seen a man who has once been handsome and strong go unshaven and unkempt? Have you seen a woman lovely in her youth raddled beneath the eyes, her hair tousled and grey?

Sadder than either, more bitter and more poignant, is a lonely house.

I returned to my furnished cottage, in angry obstinate mood. Something was dying, without hope of being saved. And I would not stand it. Yet there was nothing I could do. Nothing? There was one faint, ridiculous chance in a million. . . . I telephoned my lawyer and asked him to write to the owner of Menabilly and ask him to let the house to me for a term of years. "He won't consent for a moment," I said. "It's just a shot at random."

But the shot went home. . . . A week later my lawyer came to see me.

"By the way," he said, "I believe you will be able to rent Menabilly. But you must treat it as a whim, you know. The place is in a fearful state. I doubt if you could do more than camp out there occasionally."

I stared at him in amazement. "You mean—he would consent?" I said.

"Why, yes, I gather so," answered my lawyer.

Then it began. Not the Battle of Britain, not the attack upon the soft underbelly of Europe that my husband was helping to conduct from Africa, but my own private war to live in Menabilly by the time winter came again. . . .

"You're mad . . . you're crazy . . . you can't do it . . . there's no lighting . . . there's no water . . . there's no heating . . . you'll get no servants . . . it's impossible!"

I stood in the dining room, surrounded by a little team of experts. There was the architect, the builder, the plumber, the electrician, and my lawyer, with a ruler in his hand which he waved like a magic baton.

"I don't think it can be done. . . ." And my answer always, "Please, please, see if it can be done."

The creeper cut from the windows. The windows mended. The men upon the roof mortaring the slates. The carpenter in the house, setting up the doors. The plumber in the well, measuring the water. The electrician on the ladder, wiring the walls. And the doors and windows open that had not been open for so long. The sun warming the cold dusty rooms. Fires of brushwood in the grates. And then the scrubbing of the floors that had felt neither brush nor mop for many years. Relays of charwomen, with buckets and swabs. The house alive with men and women. Where did they come from? How did it happen? The whole thing was an impossibility in wartime. Yet it did happen. And the gods were on my side. Summer turned to autumn, autumn to December. And in December came the vans of furniture; and the goods and chattels I had stored at the beginning of the war and thought never to see again were placed, like fairy things, about the rooms at Menabilly.

Like fairy things, I said, and looking back, after living here two years, it is just that. A fairy tale. Even now I have to pinch myself to know that it is true. I belong to the house. The house belongs to me.

From the end of the lawn where I first saw her, that May morning, I stand and look upon her face. The ivy is stripped. Smoke curls from the chimneys. The windows are flung wide. The doors are open. My children come running from the house onto the lawn. The hydrangeas bloom for me. Clumps of them stand on my piano.

Slowly, in a dream, I walk towards the house. "It's wrong," I think, "to love a block of stone like this, as one loves a person. It cannot last. It cannot endure. Perhaps it is the very insecurity of the love that makes the passion strong. Because she is not mine by right. The house is still entailed, and one day will belong to another. . . ."

I brush the thought aside. For this day, and for this night, she is mine.

And at midnight, when the children sleep, and all is hushed and still, I sit down at the piano and look at the panelled walls, and slowly, softly, with no one there to see, the house whispers her secrets, and the secrets turn to stories, and in strange and eerie fashion we are one, the house and I.

EARLY STORIES

INTRODUCTION

The last chapter in my book of memoirs—*Growing Pains* in the United Kingdom, *Myself When Young* in the States—is entitled "Apprenticeship": the subtitle of the book itself, *The Shaping of a Writer*. In brief, the chapter "Apprenticeship" explains how I began to write short stories before embarking on my first novel, and some of these stories are now included here. One or two were published in *The Bystander*, thanks to the interest and kindness of my maternal uncle, William Comyns Beaumont, who was editor at the time, and two or three of the others also found space in other magazines. The rest, to the best of my recollection, were not published until many years later, when I had become known as a professional writer, and then the whole collection was printed in paperback under the same title as the one which they bear now, *Early Stories*.

The reason for their inclusion in this present volume is that very few readers will have known about the paperback, and the stories do show something of my development as a writer. They are set in various locations, in France, in London, in Cornwall, and one in Switzerland. It so happens that during my late teens and early twenties I spent much of my time between London, France and Cornwall, and so let my imagination have full play. I would sit in a café in Paris, or listen to the conversation of my dear French friend Fernande Yvon, when she was chatting to her fellow countryfolk, and something observed, something said, would sink into the hidden places of my mind, and later a story would form itself. The same held good for London, and for my home in Hampstead, conversations overheard in my father Gerald's dressing room, or at lunch at our house, Cannon Hall, on Sundays; nothing definite, nothing solid or factual, but an impression, an association of persons, places and ideas, so that weeks, possibly months later, the germ of a short story suddenly became quite clear in my mind, and I knew that I must write it down and rid my system of it. Whether it would ever be published did not bother me. The writing of it was all. "So?" asks the reader, disenchanted. "Nobody in any of the stories is real? They are all made up?"

Made up . . . My father Gerald makes up his face to become another man upon the stage. I myself sit in front of a seedy hotel in the Boulevard du Montparnasse and imagine what happens within it, or wander into a small church in Brittany with nobody inside. I see a bouquet of flowers and wonder who will buy it. I watch a small yacht putting to sea in Fowey Harbour, with members of the Yacht Club watching it too. I am travelling in the London underground, a woman passes me. I am in the foyer of a theatre. I am in a dressing room. I watch a queue of people hoping for my father's autograph. A distinguished clergyman comes to a Hampstead garden party . . . And so on and so on. The people and the places and the events are real to the writer, and that is all that matters. Read for yourself and see!

Panic

The hotel was in one of those narrow obscure streets that lead from the Boulevard du Montparnasse.

It was a grey drab house that shrank away from the pavement and flattened itself between two buildings, as if ashamed, as if conscious of its own squalor. The very sign appeared unwilling to attract attention as it swung high above the door, in faded gold letters, "Hotel"; and then lower down, humble and mean, the word "Confort."

There seemed no purpose in its being there, no reason for its existence. There was not even a café in the street, with gay checked tablecloths spread over little tables, and a large menu, illegible but generous, to welcome passers-by. Nothing but the street and the hotel, and next door a shabby fruit shop with dusty windows; hard greengages that no one would ever buy, and sad wizened oranges. The flies settled on them wearily, too tired to move.

In the hotel no one stirred. The *patronne* sat huddled at her desk in the dark little office, her fat white face resting on her hands, her mouth open. She breathed heavily, she was nearly asleep.

Who could possibly remain awake in such weather?

Every year it was the same. The fierce, dead heat that descends on Paris like a white blanket in July, stifling the body, stifling the brain. A fly crept onto her arm and ran up her shoulder. She was aware of it in her sleep, she shook it away and woke yawning, grumbling to herself, pushing her dyed red hair from her forehead with hot sticky fingers. She fumbled about on the floor, looking for her shoes, and dragged them on, still yawning, not realising what she was doing.

"The heat has made my feet swell," she thought stupidly.

She rose from her chair and went to the door. Still not a breath of air. The sky was white, the pavement burned her shoes. She stood looking up and down the street. She could hear the clanging of trams and the screaming horns of the taxis, as they rattled and shook; part of the ceaseless traffic in the Boulevard du Montparnasse.

A taxi broke away from the block and came down the street, slowly, uncertainly, the driver looking from right to left. He drew up with a jerk before the hotel.

"Would you like to try here, m'sieu?" he asked. "It's not much of a place, but I tell you Paris is packed—packed—you'll be lucky to find anything tonight."

The sweat poured down his face. He was tired, uninterested; wouldn't these English people ever be satisfied?

The girl stumbled from the taxi and looked up at the hotel, and then at the fat, greasy *patronne,* who stood at the door, a false smile of welcome on her face.

"*Vous désirez, madame?*" she began, her eyes closing together, her tongue running over her lips.

The girl drew away instinctively, and then laughed, in case her companion should notice.

"I don't know—what do you think, it's sordid, rather depressing."

The man made a movement of impatience.

"Of course it's sordid, these places always are. What did you expect? But we must decide somewhere."

He made no effort to conceal his irritation. Why must she persist in being tiresome? Women always wanted things to be romantic, attractive; they liked to drape the truth in pretty colours. She had been difficult all day, silent, not in the right mood. Supposing this adventure was going to be a failure?

He turned to the *patronne.* "*Vous avez une chambre pour ce soir?*" he said in his slow, careful French.

"*Entrez, monsieur. On va vous trouver quelquechose. Gaston—Gaston,*" she called.

A boy in a dirty shirt appeared, wiping his hands on a towel. He took the two suitcases from the taxi. The woman went into the dark office, and came back clutching a handful of keys.

"*Une chambre avec salle de bain . . . ?*" began the girl.

"*Ah! Non, c'est impossible. On n'a pas d'eau courante ici,*" snapped the woman.

She led the way up the dingy staircase.

"What does it matter?" whispered the man fretfully. "We can't be particular. . . ."

There was a strange smell in the passage, the air was full of it, it seemed to come from the woman herself. Stale scent and staler powder. The smell of people who sleep in the afternoon, who do not take off their clothes. Cigarette ash, not thrown away, and overripe fruit eaten in bedrooms.

The woman knocked at a door. From within came an exclamation, quickly stifled, and the sound of heavy naked feet crossing the floor. The door opened about a foot and a man's head appeared, tousled, damp.

He smiled, showing a row of gold teeth. "*Je regrette, madame, mais je ne suis pas présentable.*"

The woman laughed. She seemed pleased, she raised an eyebrow. "*Excusez-moi, je vous croyais parti,*" she murmured, and closed the door softly. She led the way to a room at the end of the passage. "*C'est ce que nous pouvons trouver de mieux pour ce soir.*"

It was small and incredibly hot. She threw open the window, which looked upon a narrow courtyard. There were two cats in the yard, and a girl washing something under a tap. A large bed, recently made, with a heap of unnecessary bedclothes, stood in the corner of the room. In another corner a washstand—a fat jug with a crack down the middle. There was an ugly pattern on the wallpaper, and a red carpet on the floor. The man glanced uneasily at the girl—

"Sordid, but necessary," he said, forcing a laugh. "Let's go out and get something to eat."

They had dinner at a restaurant on the Boulevard du Montparnasse. She was not hungry, she poked at her food, and then pushed away the plate with a sigh.

"But look here, you must eat," he began. "You scarcely touched anything on the train. What's the matter? You're surely not scared, you, of all people?"

"Don't be silly—of course not. I'm not hungry, that's all." She turned away and pretended to watch the people passing in front of the restaurant. He glanced at her anxiously. She looked different this evening, quite different from what she had been in London. Perhaps it was because they were alone at last. Nearly always before there had been people, and she had seemed cool, definite, provocative, with a depth of knowledge behind her eyes, a world of experience. This was what had attracted him. Tonight she looked younger, much younger, almost a child. She wouldn't drink anything either. He read the wine list very carefully. It was impossible to do this sort of thing unless one was a little drunk.

It was all being utterly different from what he had planned. Why couldn't she make an effort? Why bother to come away if this was how she was going to behave? He resented the fact that she was not being attractive to him. Her face was like any other face. He began to suspect he did not want her so very much after all. Oh, but this idiotic feeling would pass, they were both a trifle shaky, he supposed. Funny little things, women; one never knew really what they felt or why.

Funny, but necessary from time to time. It was a long while since he had been so attracted to anyone, he didn't want it to stop now, before anything had happened.

"That's the worst of being temperamental," he thought, "one's emotions are so utterly out of control."

In his mind he drew a picture of himself, odd, eccentric, a bit of a genius, driven by passion, hypnotised by this girl.

The picture intrigued. "*Garçon!*" he called, shaking the wine list. "*Garçon!*"

He was beginning to enjoy his dinner.

It was dark when they returned to the hotel. The *patronne* must have retired for the night, the little office was empty. The boy in the dirty shirt appeared from nowhere, yawning, rubbing his eyes. He watched them anxiously as they went upstairs.

"There's something evil about this hotel," whispered the girl. "I wish now we hadn't come here." She laughed, trying to pass it off as a joke. From one of the rooms they could hear the low murmur of a woman's voice, and a man's cough. Then silence. A blind rattled somewhere. Although the window was open the heat in their bedroom was unbearable. A ray of moonlight shone on the cracked water jug and a strip of the ugly wallpaper.

He sat down on a chair and began to take off his shoes. "This is a terrible place," he admitted, "but for God's sake let's try and keep our sense of humour." He wished he had drunk a little more; he still felt coldly and insanely sober.

She did not reply. She poured some water into the tooth glass and drank thirstily. Her hands trembled. She did not know why she had come, or what was going to happen, but it was too late to think about this now. She felt tired and sick, and deep down inside her something was cold with fear. Why had she come? Curiosity, adventure, a senseless spirit of bravado. He might have been a complete stranger to her.

"Supposing we're found out?" she said.

"Don't be absurd, no one will ever know, at least, not about me. Didn't you arrange everything on your side?"

Surely she hadn't forgotten, or done anything foolish?

"Of course—it's all right."

She felt as if this was happening to somebody else. This was not her. She was at home, putting the car away in the garage.

"What would happen if they found out?" he wondered uneasily. Perhaps he would be expected to marry her. It was too late now, though, trying to think this out. Why was she putting difficulties in the way? She sat down on the bed, a pale, frightened-looking child. What an impossible situation.

He crossed over to the basin and started to clean his teeth. He wanted to hit her. Damn women. Why could they never be in the right mood at the right time? He was not going to give way, though, it wouldn't be fair to himself. Coming all this way, fagging over to Paris. He supposed he must make some effort to hide his annoyance. He threw down the towel and sat beside her on the bed.

"Cold feet?" he said carelessly. "What do you generally do when you do this sort of thing? What have you done before?"

She backed away from him, smiling nervously.

"That's just it. I've never done anything like this before."

He waited, not understanding. "What on earth do you mean?" He felt the colour rise from his throat, spreading over his face. He shook her arm angrily, his face scarlet. "If you think you're going to fool me . . ."

He woke suddenly, startled, dragged from the depths of a sleep that was like death.

What was the matter? Was she dreaming aloud, a nightmare? "What is it?" he whispered. "What is it?"

She was breathing strangely, quickly, as if suffocating, and all the while a funny little noise in her throat. He fumbled with a match, and peered into her face. It was white, ghastly, drained of all colour. Her hair was wringing wet. Her eyes stared up at him, without recognition, two pieces of glass, no light in them. There was no sound in the room but her terrible choking breathing, inevitable, persistent.

"Be quiet," he said desperately. "Be quiet, somebody will hear." He left the bed and poured some water into the tooth glass. "Drink this, darling, drink this."

The glass rattled against her teeth, the water spilt on her chin. Still she made no sign.

"What shall I do?" he thought helplessly. "What in Christ's name shall I do?" He crept to the door and listened. The passage was still dark, but a ray of daylight was creeping through an open window.

He stood in the middle of the room. He saw her garter-belt pushed underneath her chemise on the chair. Stupidly the thought ran through his mind. "Pink, why a pink garter-belt?"

He passed his hand over his forehead. His fingers were wet with sweat. He could hear himself swallow.

Suddenly the breathing stopped. Not a sound came from the bed. He stood motionless, unable to move, unable to think, listening to silence.

A grey light began to filter through the open window. The furniture took shape, he could distinguish the pattern of the wallpaper. He wondered who had chosen it, and if it had been on those walls a long, long time. His brain refused to work properly.

"It's no good standing here," he thought. "It's no good standing in the middle of the room."

She was dead, of course. He knew that. She was dead. Funny —he felt no sort of emotion. Fear had taken it all away. He leant over the bed and gazed at her. She looked pinched and small, her mouth was open. No breath came from her now, no sound. Yes, she was dead. He went over to the basin and washed his face and hands. He wondered senselessly what had killed her. Heart, perhaps, she had never looked strong. She should have told him, it was not his fault. No, of course it was not his fault. Had he killed her? He did not know enough about women. He had not realised.

"I don't know what one does quite when a person dies," he thought, drying his hands on the towel.

He was frightened because he felt no emotion. Perhaps it was repressed, stifled; perhaps something had happened to his brain. He must not allow himself to become hysterical. Supposing he laughed, supposing he laughed in the silence of this dark sinister room and woke the other people in the hotel. Supposing they crawled in at the door, queer, shadowy figures, peering over the fat shoulder of the *patronne*. The man with the gold teeth, smiling, bowing—"*Je regrette, mais je ne suis pas présentable.*" He could imagine his grey unshaven face, the grin fading away as he saw the still figure on the bed.

This was awful. He was going to laugh—he was terrified he was going to laugh.

The silly line of an old song, heard years ago, came into his brain: "Cheer up, Jenny, you'll soon be dead—A short life but a gay one." Supposing he threw open the door and sang down the passage . . . "A short life but a gay one."

An hysterical giggle rose in his throat and broke the silence of the room. The sound brought him to his senses. He must dress quickly and get away. He must not be found here with her. The police—and questions, endless questions. The truth being dragged from him, and her family arriving—an appalling inquest —scenes and questions, more questions. There would never be an end to it, never. Panic came upon him, like an unseen hand seizing him by the throat. Why had this terrible thing happened to him? Why should he have been chosen to play this part? If he could get away now, though, no one would ever know. He pulled on his clothes, his fingers slippery with sweat. There was no reason why his identity should be discovered, he had given no name. The cards still lay on the mantelpiece, waiting to be filled in. He pushed his things into his suitcase and closed the lid. Out of the tail of his eye he saw the dark outline of her body on the bed. He pretended to himself he had not seen. The idea came to him that this scene would stay forever before his eyes. The small, hot bedroom, the dead girl on the bed, and the ugly paper on the wall behind her head. He turned away, afraid.

He crept down the stairs, his suitcase in his hand, his hat pulled over his eyes. Somewhere a clock struck the half hour. He heard a door creak. He flattened himself against the wall, drawing in his breath.

A woman came into the top passage and stood listening. She was holding something in her hands. Then she stole softly along the passage and went into a different room.

The man on the stairs waited, it seemed to him that his feet had turned to stone. Once more the vision of the bedroom flashed before his eyes, the silence, the dark figure on the bed.

He left the hotel and started to run. He ran down the street, and into another street, and across the boulevard, and so on into a meaningless procession of streets. Grey houses, all alike, and dreary deserted cafés. This was not the Paris he knew, it was a nightmare in his brain, it was an inferno. And all the while the patter of his feet beat time with his heart to the senseless repeating tune. "Cheer up, Jenny, you'll soon be dead—A short life but a gay one."

He could run no longer. He walked steadily, his bag in one hand, his coat over his arm. Paris awoke to another day, white, blistering, like the days that had gone before. People came into the streets. Sleepy boys rolled aside the shutters of the shops and wearily dusted the tables in the cafés.

Someone leant out of a window and shook a mattress. A woman, her hair falling about her face, brushed the steps of a house with her broom. A yellow dog stretched itself, and sniffed at a lamppost. Traffic began to rattle over the cobblestones.

The man could go no farther. He sat down, at a table outside a café, and rested his head in his hands. He could remember nothing but that he was tired, so tired that he desired only to lay himself upon the ground and sleep, his head in the gutter.

The drowsy *garçon* stood before him. He heard himself ordering coffee. Trams passed by, and a few early taxis.

"A short life but a gay one. A short life but a gay one." Would the tune never leave him? Senseless, utterly senseless. Yes, he must find some train and get away, right away. Somewhere down on the Mediterranean. He would be able to write a play there, perhaps—do a little work.

He called the *garçon* for his bill. He must go now and find out about trains, he would take the first one that left for the south. He fumbled in his pockets, staring at the slip of paper. Then a tight band slipped away from his head, leaving his brain clear, cold.

Something, like the clutch of a clammy hand, closed upon his heart. His back weakened. A little trickle of sweat ran down his forehead and crept upon his cheek.

He remembered that he had left his pocketbook and everything that it contained—letters, money, addresses—in the bedroom of the hotel by the Boulevard du Montparnasse.

La Sainte-Vierge

It was hot and sultry, that oppressive kind of heat where there is no air, no life. The trees were motionless and dull, their drooping leaves colourless with summer dust. The ditches smelt of dead ferns and long-dried mud, and the grasses of the fields were blistered and brown. The village seemed asleep. No one stirred among the few scattered cottages on the hillside; strange, uneven cottages, huddled together for fear of loneliness, with white walls and no windows, and small gardens massed with orange flowers.

A greater silence still filled the fields, where the pale corn lay heaped in awkward stacks, left by some neglectful labourer. Not even a breeze stirred the heather on the hills, lonely treeless hills, whose only dwellers were a host of bees and a few lizards. Below them the wide sea stretched like a sheet of ice into eternity, a chart of silver crinkled by the sun.

Away from the hills, towards the scattered houses, was a narrow, muddy lane leading to nowhere. At first it seemed one of those shy, twisting lanes, tempting to explore, that finish in a distant village or an unknown beach, but this one dissolved into a straggling path that soon lost itself among tall weeds. In a sheltered corner of the lane Marie was washing her linen in a pool.

The water looked like a basin of spilt milk, white with soft soap, and the clothes lay limp upon the slippery stones. Marie scrubbed hard, scornful of the heat, her black hair screwed behind her head in a tight knot; now and again she brushed away with an impatient hand the streaks of perspiration that trickled from her forehead.

Her face was thin and childish, rather plain and pathetic, and though she was twenty-three she looked little more than seventeen. There were tired lines under her eyes, and her hands were rough and uncared for. She was a typical Breton peasant, hard-working and reserved, whose only beauty was her youth, which would quickly pass. When the Breton women sorrow they show no grief upon their faces, they would rather die than let their tears be seen; thus Marie bore no outward trace of the pain that was in her heart.

She was thinking of Jean, her husband. She lived for him; there was nothing else in her life. She was a woman who would love but once, and give everything. There was no part of her body and soul that did not belong to him; she had no thought and no wish beyond his happiness. He was her lover and her child. Yet she never told him this, she did not even understand it herself. She was ignorant and unintelligent; it was only her heart that knew.

"He is going away from me," she was thinking, "he is going in his boat on that terrible sea. Only a year ago now since my brother was drowned in the sudden gale that came after the hot weather. I am afraid, so terribly afraid. Jean is ashamed of me; he thinks I am not fit to be the wife of a fisherman. I cannot help it. The coast is dangerous, more dangerous than anywhere else in Brittany. And these storms—the mists—the odd currents. Jean is rash and he loves danger, he does not mind. If he could be safe and return to me unharmed, I would work my fingers to the bone."

Every few months Marie would go through this agony, when Jean and the other fishermen went to sea and stayed for ten days without sight of land. The weather was uncertain and storms were frequent; the frail boats stood very little chance against a heavy sea. "I must not let him see I am afraid," she said to herself. "He cannot understand it, and I irritate him."

She paused in her work and sank back upon her heels. Her throat was dry, and she had an aching, sick feeling below her heart. It would be terrible to be alone without him, worse than it had ever been before. Something was going to happen. If only she had not the feeling that something was going to happen. The sun shone down upon her uncovered head, and she was aware of her great weariness.

There was no one near her, and through the trees the village looked dusty and lifeless. The linen lay in an untidy heap by her side. What did it matter whether it was clean or dirty?

She closed her eyes, and was filled with a sense of unbelievable loneliness. "Jean," she whispered, "Jean."

From across the fields came the sound of the chapel bell striking the hour. Marie sat up and listened, and over her face came a strange smile, a smile in which hope and shame were mingled. She had suddenly remembered the Sainte-Vierge. In her mind she saw the figure in the chapel, Notre Dame des Bonnes Nouvelles, with the infant Jesus in her arms.

"I will go this evening," she thought. "When it is dark I will go to the Sainte-Vierge and tell her my trouble. I shall ask her to watch over Jean when he is at sea." She rose to her feet and began to lay her washing in the basket.

Her memory of the chapel had stopped the sick feeling in her heart, and as she walked through the fields and the village she was conscious only of her weariness. When she had left her basket in the cottage Marie went down the hill to the harbour, where she hoped to find Jean.

She walked towards a group of men who were standing on the edge of the quay, by a heap of old nets and discarded sails. Jean was among them, laughing and talking. Marie felt so proud as she looked at him. He was a good head taller than any of the others, with great broad shoulders and a mass of dark hair.

She ran forward, waving her hand. Jean's eyes narrowed as he saw her, and he muttered a curse under his breath. "Shut your mouths," he said to the other men, "here comes the child." They laughed awkwardly, and some of them began to move away.

"What are you doing down here?" asked Jean.

"It is settled, then, that you sail," said Marie breathlessly. "What time do you leave?"

"At midnight, so as to catch the tide," he replied. "But listen here, I must have supper early tonight, there are a lot of things I have to do. Jacques here wants me to help him with his boat."

He winked at the young fisherman next to him, who carefully avoided Marie's eye.

"Yes," said the lad, "that's right," and strolled away towards the beach. Marie did not notice anything, but the sick feeling had begun again in her heart.

"Come away," she said to Jean, "I have something to tell you." He followed her rather unwillingly up the hill.

They paused halfway, and turned back to look at the sea. The heat of the afternoon had passed, and in about four hours' time the sun would sink below the horizon. The sea shone like splintered silver, while westward beyond the beacon streams of burnt clouds were massing in a purple haze. Down in the bay some children were bathing, and the sound of their voices and splashes floated up to the hill. The gulls wheeled and screamed around the harbour, searching for food.

Marie turned away and climbed towards the village. She had a vivid mental picture of the sea and was aware that it was the last time she would look at it with Jean. Subconsciously, in the depths of her being, she consecrated the spot. Jean spat out the fag end of his cigarette; he was not thinking of anything.

Theirs was the last cottage beyond the village shop—a funny little white place with a prim garden. Marie went straight to the living room, and began to lay the supper things on the table. She went about her work mechanically; she had no idea what she was doing. There was only one thought in her mind—in a few hours he would be gone.

Jean's shadow loomed in the doorway. "You were wanting to tell me something?" he asked. Marie did not answer for a moment. Her love for him was so great that she felt it would choke her if she spoke. She wanted to kneel at his feet, to bury her head against him, to implore him to stay with her. If only he would understand to what depths of degradation she would sink for his sake. Everything she had ever felt for him came back to her at this moment. Yet she said nothing, and no sign appeared on her stolid little face.

"What is it?" he asked again.

"It is nothing," she answered slowly, "nothing. The curé was here today, and hoped you would see him before you go."

She turned to pick up a plate, conscious of the lie, conscious of her failure. He would never know now.

"I will see," said Jean, "but I don't think there will be any time. This boat of Jacques's—and the nets." He left the rest unfinished, and went out into the garden.

The next few hours passed rapidly. After supper Marie

washed up the dishes and put away her clean linen. Then she had her mending to do, mostly things for Jean.

She worked until it became too dark to see, for she was very thrifty and would not use a lamp. At ten o'clock Jean came in to say good-bye. "May I come with you and help Jacques with his boat?" she asked.

"No, no, you will be in the way," he replied quickly. "We cannot work and talk as well."

"But I will not say a word."

"No, I won't have you come. You are tired, too; it is this heat. If I know that you are here in bed I shall be happy, and think about you."

He put his arms round her and kissed her gently. Marie closed her eyes. It was the end of everything. "You will be careful, you will come back to me?" She clung to him like a child.

"Are you mad, you silly girl?" he said, and he laughed as he shut the door and left her. For a few minutes Marie stood motionless in the middle of the room. Then she went to the window and looked out, but he was already out of sight. It was a beautiful evening, very clear and bright, for there was a full moon.

Marie sat down by the window, her hands in her lap. She felt as if she were living in a dream. "I think I must be ill," she said to herself. "I've never felt like this before."

There were no tears on her cheeks, only deep shadows in her eyes. Slowly she rose to her feet, and after putting a shawl round her head and over her shoulders she opened the door and stepped outside. There was no one about, and everything was quite still. Marie slipped through the garden and crossed the lane. In a few minutes she was running across the field that led to the chapel.

The chapel of Notre Dame des Bonnes Nouvelles was very old and was no longer used for services. The door remained open day and night, so that the peasants could go in and pray when they wanted, for they always felt a little in awe of the new church at the end of the village.

Marie pushed open the creaking door, then paused to listen. The chapel was quite deserted. Through the low window by the altar the moon shone now and again, lighting the nave. There had probably been no one inside for days. A few leaves lay on the rough stone floor, where they had blown in from the open door. The whitewashed walls were grimy, and great cobwebs hung from the rafters in the roof.

Hanging by nails on the wall, on either side of the altar, were gifts presented by the peasants who had prayed there: roughly carved models of ships, pathetic little toy boats, brightly coloured balls, and strings of glass and wooden beads. They had lain there many years, perhaps, and were covered in dust. There were even a few wedding wreaths, now old and faded, given by the brides of long ago. All over the walls were inscriptions written in pencil, prayers and thanksgivings to Notre Dame des Bonnes Nouvelles, *"Mère, priez pour nous,"* *"Notre Dame des Bonnes Nouvelles, sauvez mon fils qui est sur la mer."*

Marie went slowly to the rails and knelt down. The altar was bare of flowers, and alone in the centre stood the figure of the Sainte-Vierge. Her golden crown was crooked on her head, and covered in cobwebs. Her right arm had been lost, and in the other she held the little figure of the infant Jesus, who had no fingers on his hands. Her robe had once been blue, but the colour had come off long ago, and it was now a dirty brown. Her face was round and expressionless, the face of a cheap doll. She had large blue eyes that looked vacantly before her, while her scarlet cheeks clashed with her cracked painted lips. Her mouth was set in a silly smile, and the plaster was coming off at the corners. Round her neck she wore string upon string of glass beads, the offerings of the fishermen, and someone had even hung a wreath over her baby's head. It dangled sideways and hid his face.

Marie knelt by the rails and gazed at the Sainte-Vierge. The figure was the most beautiful and sacred thing in her life. She did not notice the dust and the broken plaster, the toppling crown and the silly painted smile—to Marie she was the fulfiller of all prayers, the divine mother of the fishermen. As she knelt she prayed, not in words but in the thoughts that wandered at will through her mind, and her prayers were all for Jean, for his safety and his return.

"Oh! Mother," she said, "if it is wrong for me to love him so much, then punish me as you will, but bring him safely back to me. He is so young and brave, yet helpless as a child, he would not understand death. I care not if my heart breaks, nor if he should cease to love me and should ill-treat me, it is only his happiness I ask, and that he shall never know pain or hardship."

A fly settled on the nose of the Sainte-Vierge, and brushed a scrap of coloured plaster off her cheek.

"I have put all my trust in you," said Marie, "and I know that you will watch over him when he is at sea. Though waves rise up and threaten his boat, if you protect him I shall have no fear. I will bring fresh flowers every morning and lay them at the feet of the little Jesus. When I am working in the day I will sing songs and be gay, and these will be prayers to you for his safety. Oh! Mother, if you could only show me by a sign that all will be well!"

A drip of water from the roof fell down upon the Sainte-Vierge and left a dirty streak across her left eye.

It was very dark now. Away across the fields a woman was calling to a child. A faint breeze stirred in the trees, and far in the distance the waves broke dully on the shingle beach.

Marie gazed upon the figure until she drooped from weariness, and everything was blurred and strange before her eyes. The walls of the chapel lay in shadow; even the altar sank into nothingness. All that remained was the image of the Sainte-Vierge, her face lit up by a chance ray of moonlight. And as Marie watched the figure it seemed to her that the cracked, painted smile became a thing of beauty, and that the doll's eyes looked down upon her with tenderness and love. The tawdry crown shone in the darkness, and Marie was filled with awe and wonder.

She did not know that it shone only by the light of the moon. She lifted up her arms and said: "Mother of pity, show me by a sign that you have heard my prayers." Then she closed her eyes and waited. It seemed an eternity that she knelt there, her head bowed in her hands.

Slowly she was aware of a feeling of peace and great comfort, as if the place were sanctified by the presence of something holy. She felt that if she opened her eyes she would look upon a vision. Yet she was afraid to obey her impulse, lest the thing she would see should blind her with its beauty. The longing grew stronger and stronger within her, until she was forced to give way. Unconscious of her surroundings, unconscious of what she was doing, Marie opened her eyes. The low window beside the altar was filled with the pale light of the moon, and just outside she saw the vision.

She saw Jean kneeling upon the grass, gazing at something, and there was a smile on his face, and slowly from the ground rose a figure which Marie could not see distinctly, for it was in shadow, but it was the figure of a woman. She watched her place two hands on Jean's shoulders, as if she were blessing him, and he buried his head in the folds of her gown. Only for a moment they remained like this, and then a cloud passed over the face of the moon, and the chapel was filled with darkness.

Marie closed her eyes and sank to the ground in worship. She had seen the blessed vision of the Sainte-Vierge. She had prayed for a sign, and it had been given her, Notre Dame des Bonnes Nouvelles had appeared unto her, and with her own hands had blessed Jean, and assured him of her love and protection. There was no longer fear in Marie's heart; she felt she would never be afraid again. She had put all her faith in the Sainte-Vierge, and her prayers had been answered.

She rose unsteadily from the ground and found her way to the door. Once more she turned, and looked for the last time at the figure on the altar. It was in shadow now, and the crown was no longer gold. Marie smiled and bowed her head; she knew that no one else would ever see what she had seen. In the chapel the Sainte-Vierge still smiled her painted smile, and the vacant blue eyes gazed into nothing. The faded wreath slipped a little over the ear of the infant Jesus.

Marie stepped out into the evening. She was very tired and could scarcely see where she was going, but her heart was at peace and she was filled with a great happiness.

In the corner of the narrow field, sheltered by the chapel window, Jean whispered his desire to the sister of Jacques the fisherman.

A Difference in Temperament

He leant against the mantelpiece, nervously jingling the change in his pockets. He supposed there would be another scene. It was so unreasonable the way she minded him going out without her. She never seemed to realise that he just had to get away sometimes—for no particular reason, but because it gave him a sense of freedom. He loved to slam the front door behind him and walk along the street to a bus, swinging a stick. There was something about the feeling of being alone that he could not explain to anyone, not even to her. The delicious sense of utter irresponsibility, of complete selfishness. Not to have to look at his watch and remember, "I promised to be back at four," but at four to be doing something quite different that she would not know. The feeblest thing. Even driving in a taxi she had never seen; to have the sensation of leaning back and smoking a cigarette without turning his head and being aware of her beside him. He would come back in the evening and tell her about it; they would sit in front of the fire and laugh; but at least it would have been his afternoon—not theirs, but his alone.

This was what she resented, though; she wanted to share everything. She could never imagine doing things apart from him. She had an uncanny way of reading his thoughts, too. If he was thinking of something that had no connection with her, she would know it at once. Only she exaggerated it in her mind. She would immediately think he was bored with her, that he did not like her any more. It wasn't that, of course; it wasn't that at all. Naturally, he loved her more than anyone in the world; in fact, there literally did not exist anyone but her. Why did she not realise this and be thankful? Why must she chain him to her, his mind, his body, his soul, without allowing the smallest part in him to stray, even for a little distance? She should understand that he would never go far, he would never go out of her sight—metaphorically; but surely just to the top of that hill, to see what was on the other side. No, even this she must share with him.

"Don't you see," she would explain, "that when I see anything or do anything there is no joy in keeping it to myself? I want to give everything to you. If I am alone and I see a picture that I love, or if I read some passage from a book, I think to myself, 'There is no meaning in this unless he knows it too.' You are such a part of me that to stand alone leaves me dumb, without speech, without eyes. A tree with hatched branches, like someone with no hands. Life is valueless unless I can share everything with you—beauty, ugliness, pain. There must be no shadows between us, no quiet corners in our hearts."

Funny!—yes, he saw what she meant, but he could not feel like this. They were on different planes. In the universe they were two stars, she far higher, burning with a steady light, but he flickering unsteadily, always a little ahead—and in the end falling to earth, a momentary streak in the sky.

He turned to her abruptly. "I guess I'd better go and have lunch in town today after all. I promised the chap I'd see him again before he leaves, and I don't want to offend him. I'll be back early, of course." He smiled a shade too sincerely.

She looked up from the letter she was writing. "I thought you had arranged everything the last time you were together?"

"Yes—more or less. But I feel I ought to see him again, just once. It's a good opportunity today, don't you think? I mean, we weren't going to do anything; you're busy." He spoke easily, naturally, as if there was no question of her minding.

She was not deceived, though, not for a moment. Why was he never frank with her? Why not admit that he was no longer content to be with her, but must go out and seek any sort of distraction? It was his reticence that hurt her, his refusal to speak the truth. Like a wounded animal, she spread out her claws to protect herself.

"You enjoy his company so much, when you have only known him for three weeks?" Her voice was hard and metallic.

He knew this voice. "Darling, don't be ridiculous. You know I don't care a damn whether I see this fellow or not."

"Why do you go, then?"

There was no answer to this. He yawned self-consciously and avoided her eyes. She waited without saying a word. He pretended to lose his temper.

"I've told you I don't want to offend him. It's a bit thick; there's always this same old argument whenever I go out. Good God, it's only for a few hours! If you had your way you'd leave me without a friend in the world. You seem to be jealous if I speak to a dog."

Jealous! She laughed contemptuously. He had misunderstood her again. As if she could possibly be jealous of the people he knew. It would be different if there was someone worth while. But this careless, selfish way he left her for anyone, for some creature he might not even see again! She despised the weak manner in which he shifted responsibility from himself.

"Go then," she said, shrugging her shoulders, "since it pains you to hurt a comparative stranger. I'm glad you've let me know. I shall remember in future. Perhaps you've forgotten that last Monday you promised this sort of thing would never happen again. I realise now that I can't depend on you at all. I've been making rather a fool of myself over you, haven't I? Well, aren't you going?"

Her eyes were cold. She had wrapped herself in a sheet of armour.

He turned his back and looked out of the window. "Charming little scene for nothing at all," he laughed lightly. "It's pleasant, isn't it, living like this? Makes such an attractive atmosphere in the house. Scarcely a day passes without some sort of discussion, does it?" He rocked backwards and forwards on his heels, whistling a tune. He knew that every word tore at her like a knife. He was pleased. He wanted to hurt her. He didn't care.

She sat quite still, pretending to do accounts on a piece of paper. Calmly, dispassionately, she wondered why she loved him. His cruel, selfish nature, the way he took everything from her and gave nothing in return. If he would only realise that the smallest touch of recognition from him, the faintest sign that he would give up something unimportant for her sake, would send a flood of warmth to her heart. He did nothing. She felt herself drawing farther away from him, a lonely figure in an imaginary train. A grey shadow in a world of shadows. There was no one even to wave good-bye.

He watched her out of the tail of his eye. Why must she always parade her suffering before him? Not openly, not something that he could get hold of and flaunt in her face, but quietly, with the resignation of a martyr. A tear ran down her cheek and fell onto the blotting paper. Oh, hell!—he wasn't going to stand for it. It was damn selfish of her, spoiling his day.

"Look here," he started, as if nothing had happened, "it's too late to put the whole thing off now. If you'd said something earlier, naturally I'd have done so. I won't be long, I promise. I'll be back soon after lunch."

Surely this was a compromise. He was going out of his way to be nice to her. He waited to see how she would take it.

"Don't forget your coat, there's a bitter east wind," she told him, and went on writing.

He hesitated a moment, wondering what to do. Did that mean everything was all right? No, he knew her too well. She would suffer the tortures of the damned until he returned. She would imagine every sort of accident. She would bottle up this scene in her mind, making more out of it than there had been. Why didn't he chuck away this footling lunch and stop with her? He didn't want to go now at all. He never had, really, all the time.

Another tear fell onto the blotting paper.

"Shall I not go after all?" he suggested weakly, pretending not to notice the tear.

She made a movement of impatience. Did he think she was to be won as easily as this? He was trying to save himself. He was anxious to make up to her, to kiss and be friends like a child, and then forget all about it until the same thing happened again. Did he really want to stay with her? She gave him one more chance.

"Do just as you think best. Don't attempt to stay unless you feel like it." Her voice was cool, impersonal.

Damn it all, she might show some sort of emotion. He had offered to stop, and this was how she took it. No, he didn't see why he should be always giving in to her. What a bore everything was. Why couldn't they live in peace? It was all her fault.

"Perhaps I'd better go, it looks rather rude," he said carelessly, and strolled from the room, banging the door on purpose. He wouldn't bother to put on his coat, it would serve her right if he caught pneumonia. He had a vision of himself, stretched on a bed, coughing and gasping for breath. She bending over him with an agony of fear in her eyes. She would fight for his life, but she would lose. It would be too late. He could see her planting violets on his grave, a solitary figure in a grey cloak. What a ghastly tragedy. A lump came into his throat. He became quite emotional thinking of his own death. He would have to write a poem about this.

From behind the curtains she watched him walk to the end of the street. She was sure he had forgotten her already. She felt she did not care what he did any more. It was all over. She rang the bell and began to scold the maid for no reason.

He hated the lunch, the man was a bore—he couldn't even listen to what he was saying. He felt ill, too. His wish was probably coming true, and he was catching pneumonia. What a Godforsaken fool he was to have come. There was no point in it at all. He had probably mucked up his life just for this. And all the while the fellow was rambling on about a whole lot of damned silly people he never wanted to see again. He'd cut everyone out of his life in future, nobody mattered but her. They'd leave this beastly country and go and live abroad. Perhaps when he went home he would find she had left him for good. There would be a note pinned on the desk. What would he do? He couldn't live without her. He'd commit suicide, he'd chuck himself into the river. Surely she loved him too much to do this. He could imagine the house blank and silent, the wardrobes empty of her dresses, the desk bare. Gone, leaving no address behind her. No, she wouldn't do it, it was impossible. It was cruel, it would kill him. What on earth was this idiot jabbering about?

"I told her frankly I wasn't going to stand for it. I haven't the money for one thing, and besides, I've got to consider my reputation. Don't you think I was right?"

"Oh! perfectly—absolutely." He hadn't listened to a word. As if he cared about this fellow's hellish reputation.

"You know, I must push off, I've got an appointment with my publisher," he lied.

Somehow he managed to get away. What did it matter if he was rude? The man had ruined his life anyway. He leapt into a taxi. "Drive like the devil!" he shouted. Stop, though, he suddenly had a longing to buy her something. The most priceless jewel—the most marvellous furs—anything. He would like to shower gifts at her feet. Perhaps there wasn't time for all this. It would have to be flowers after all. It was months since he had bought her flowers. How foul of him. He chose an azalea, an enormous one with pink waving buds. "This will last a month or more if it's watered frequently," said the woman.

"Will it really?" He became quite excited, he walked out of the shop clutching the pot in his arms. She would be pleased with this. A month! Pretty good value considering. The buds were small now, but they would open a little every day, they would get bigger, the plant would grow into a small bush. "The symbol of my love," he thought sentimentally.

Supposing she had gone, though, supposing she had killed herself? He would go mad, he would scatter the petals of the azalea over her body with a wild, despairing cry. Rather an effective scene for the last act, he must remember this. No, by God, he would never write another line again, he would dedicate the whole of his life to her, to her alone. Oh! how he was suffering. If she only knew what he was going through. His heart was bursting, it had never happened to anyone in the world before. What had he done that he should suffer so? He was certain there would be an ambulance outside the door, they would be carrying her limp form on a stretcher. He imagined himself leaping from the taxi and covering her pale dead hand with kisses. "My beloved—my beloved." No, the street was empty. The house seemed unchanged. He paid the taxi and opened the front door—silently, like a thief. He crept upstairs, and listened outside her room. He heard her move. Thank God! Nothing had happened then. He wanted to shout for joy. He burst open the door, a fatuous smile on his face.

Poor darling, had she been writing letters all day? Her face was white and strained. Why on earth was she looking so unhappy? Wasn't she pleased to see him back?

"Look," he stammered foolishly, "I've bought you an azalea."

She did not smile, she scarcely noticed the flower. "Thank you," she said in a dull voice. How inevitable of him. How unfeeling and unintelligent. Would he never understand her? Did he think he could just go off and enjoy himself after having broken her heart, and then bring back this plant as a peace offering? She could picture him saying to himself, "Oh! I've only got to buy her a flower, and then kiss her, she'll forget all about this morning."

If only it was as easy as that. His attitude wounded her, distressed her beyond measure. He had no heart, no delicacy of thought. "Don't you like it?" he asked her, like a spoilt child.

Why had he bought the beastly thing? His agony at lunch, his terrible impatience in the taxi, meant nothing to her. Everything was a failure. The azalea looked foolish and conceited in its big pot. It had seemed quite different in the shop. Now it mocked him, the colour was vulgar, much too pink. It was a hideous type of flower altogether. It didn't even smell. He wanted to crash it to the ground.

"Are you going to make a habit of this in future—a reminder for each time you hurt me?" she asked him.

She loathed herself, she hated her words, she longed to say something entirely different. The atmosphere was terrible. Why couldn't they be themselves again? He had only to make the first move. But her speech stung him, she insisted on ignoring every word he said.

"My God," he shouted, "there'll never be another time. I'm finished with the whole damned business, finished. Do you understand?"

He left the room, and went out of the house. The door slammed behind him.

"But that's not what I meant," he thought, "that's not what I meant at all."

Adieu Sagesse

Richard Ferguson was a dull man. Everybody said so. He was the sort of man whom people turned into a shop to avoid, if they saw him walking along the street: "Let's go into Smith's for a minute or we shall run into old Ferguson." They knew that, if he should meet them, he would only raise his hat and pass on. He would not attempt to fall into conversation with them. No, it was just that he was dull, deadly dull. It was a mystery to the people of Maltby how he had ever come to be manager of the Western Bank. How he had married—well, everyone had long since ceased to discuss it. They had forgotten what he had been like as a young man. He had surely never been attractive.

His wife was such a charming woman too, really charming. Always ready to entertain and join in any of the local amusements. A keen sense of humour, of course—a real Maltby sense of humour. And the three daughters—the life and soul of any party. It was a wonder that the four of them could bear to live with old Ferguson.

Oh! he was dull. People said that he was henpecked. Well, it served him right. Maltby liked a man who had some spirit. Not Ferguson, though, he hadn't an ounce. No manners either, for that matter. If he were asked to dinner, he'd sit in a chair or stand by the window and never listen to a word that was spoken. He wore a funny sort of smile all the time. Superior, perhaps. Yes, that was it, superior. Maltby resented it. What did he mean by it, sulking in a corner, smiling to himself?

Poor Mrs. Ferguson. Amazing how she put up with such a stick of a man. See Mrs. Ferguson at a party! Her big cheerful laugh ringing out above the others. Hear her in church on Sunday, her voice drowning the choirboys, "Praise ye the Lord." Watch Mrs. Ferguson at the Maltby regatta in August. She was

superb in grey satin. And she wandered to and fro on the club
terrace, complete with a sunshade the same tone as her dress.
She dug young Shipton in the ribs. "Isn't it time, Jack, you
thought of settling down?" A good joke, this! She was thinking of
Helen, who was still unmarried. Never mind. Perhaps later in
the summer he would take her sailing. She turned with a smile to
someone else. Her daughters were bound to marry sooner or
later. Such striking, amusing girls. Wonderful woman, Mrs. Ferguson. Once more her laugh rang out, strong and true.

The girls were drinking tea inside the clubhouse. They whispered and nodded over their cups. "Mrs. Marshall has the same
dress as last year. Would you believe it? Dyed, of course." Their
eyes glittered among the guests. "I swear to you, the look she
gave was positively—well—you know. Do they? Oh, my dear,
don't tell me."

They laughed scornfully, they shook their shoulders like so
many birds ruffling and shaking their feathers. Young Shipton
passed with a friend. At once the girls moved differently. They
became enemies. They held venomous thoughts towards each
other. He threw them a word and moved away. Young Shipton
was conscious of his power.

The sun shone, the sea sparkled, the brass band played a
shade too slowly. Maltby was *en fête*.

"What a success it has been. What a delicious day," the voices
said to one another. And then in a minute, whispering, muttering, "What on earth has she got on her head—a tea cosy?" . . .
"There must be something in it. He's never left her side all the
afternoon."

Happy, brilliant Maltby.

Old Ferguson continued to turn his back on the club guests
and to watch the crowd below. He puffed thoughtfully at his
cigarette.

What were the thoughts of the dullest man in Maltby?

Directly beneath him was a rowing boat filled to the brim with
folk. It was Sam Collins the crabber, with his family. The "family" were dressed in their best clothes. They hopped about in the
boat and dangled their hands in the water. Sam's wife sat in the
stern with her sister and a friend, and a friend's sister . . . "an' I
said it was turrible, really, the way she was goin' on, an' her hair

all over her face and rouged up something awful, ee woud'en believe it!"

Sam sat on the centre thwart, the oars in his hands. His best
suit worried him considerably and he longed to take off his coat.
He hated the noise and the fuss of many boats. On his face was a
wistful expression. He gazed sadly towards the harbour mouth,
where the jumping water told its own tale. He heaved a sigh and
shook his head. "I bet there's mackrail out there."

Nobody heard him. Yes, somebody. He heard a chuckle above
him. He raised his eyes and saw the bank manager leaning
against the club railings. Sam flushed and then smiled a little
sheepishly. They both smiled; they both looked towards the harbour mouth; they both sighed; and old Ferguson winked, positively winked, at Sam the crabber.

"He's a dull fellow," thought young Shipton, watching his
back, "deadly dull."

Old Ferguson sat at his desk in the private room belonging to
the manager of the Western Bank. His papers lay untouched before him; his fingers drummed on his knee. It was no use, he
could not settle down to work. It was not that he was ill—not a
bit of it. He'd never felt better in his life.

No, there was nothing the matter with his health. But he felt
queer, damned queer. There was something at the back of his
mind he wanted explained. It had been growing on him for
weeks—months. Just the feeling that nothing in life really mattered.

He began to wonder why he sat here day after day, year after
year. No worries, no sorrows. Even the war had left him untouched. Here he was, sixty, nearly sixty-one, with one of the
best positions in Maltby, with a loving faithful wife, with three
devoted daughters. What about his house, The Chestnuts?
Hadn't he got the finest view in Maltby—one of the finest gardens? On the very top of the hill, above the town, overlooking
the harbour.

There was his own particular summerhouse, at the end of the
garden. He used to sit there sometimes with his telescope and
watch the ships as they left the harbour. Half a minute . . . wait
. . . he'd nearly got it . . . . it swung before him out of the mist,

the first moment when the queer feeling had come upon him. He had been sitting one evening long ago, last summer, in his favourite haunt. He must have dropped asleep, because in his sleep he had heard a challenge. A challenge, a call, a summons from the depths of his being, clutching at his heart, seizing his mind.

He had awakened with a start, expectant and alert. There . . . it sounded again . . . a summons! He had risen to his feet and gazed about him. And then he had realised what it had been. Merely the siren of a ship. A ship leaving port. Leaving Maltby. That was all. It happened every day. But why had it entered into his sleep? Why had it sounded to him like a call from the dead?

He remembered standing in the summerhouse, his telescope under his arm, watching the ship steam into the open sea. Three times she blew her siren—three prolonged blasts. Signal of farewell. Farewell to Maltby. Soon she had become a smudge on the horizon, then only a far faint ribbon of smoke. Farewell to Maltby.

Then the feeling had come to Ferguson. He was dead. They were all dead. Maltby was a dead city . . . worse than any visionary Pompeii. Worse than a place of ashes. The only living thing was the ship that had steamed away. She hadn't been caught. She had gone before they tried to hold her back. A dim haze on the horizon now. Never mind whither she was bound. Her siren had been a call to him, a summons to the dead from the living. Farewell to Maltby . . . Hullo! here was the rain. Splashing against his office window.

Old Ferguson turned to the papers on his desk before him. The sound brought him to his senses. What was he doing, dreaming like this in the middle of the day? The rain streamed down in the street outside, raining as it can only rain in Maltby.

Old Ferguson reached for his pen and began to write. The clock ticked solemnly on the wall before him. "With reference to your letter . . ." But before his eyes was the smudge of a ship on the horizon, and in his ears whispered the throb of the siren that called farewell.

Ferguson rose from the tea table and wandered towards the window. It was real Maltby weather. The rain of the morning had given way to an atmosphere of general mugginess. The sun forced a halfhearted smile and there were wide patches of blue on the flat sky. Ferguson left the room muttering something about matches. In the hall he paused to listen. No one attempted to follow him. He struggled into his old tweed jacket, seized his cap from the rack and, taking his favourite stick from the stand, left the house.

Maltby lay beneath him wrapped in a faint mist. Smoke curled from the chimneys and he could hear the cries of the children as they grubbed on the bit of beach below the town quay. Old Ferguson pretended to himself that he was just going for a stroll to breathe some fresh air into his lungs. If that had been the case he would have walked along the Esplanade and probably reached the golf course.

Why, then, did he turn in precisely the opposite direction?

Make no mistake about it. Old Ferguson knew where he was going. He made straight for the mud reach at the further end of the harbour. Here was seclusion and peace. No voices to trouble him. The tide was out, and the sea gulls dived in the mud, searching for fish ends.

On a low piece of ground, where the overhanging bough of a tree partially concealed it, lay a boat. At least, she looked like a boat. Maltby would have called her a tub. In her day she had been a seven-ton cutter and proud of the fact. She had never been a beauty even in her youth. She had too much beam for length and a high, ugly transom stern. Never mind about that. She was a boat, a real boat. Not merely a few planks of wood nailed together to form a pretty shape, to be painted white with a sky-blue waterline and then sailed on fine afternoons round the harbour mouth.

Old Ferguson ran his hands along her sides. He took his pen-knife from his pocket and poked at the wood. A slow smile spread over his face. It was rare for him to smile.

"She's sound," he said softly. "Sound as a bell." He looked at the faded gold lettering on her stern. *Adieu Sagesse.*

He remembered buying her ten years ago when her owner had died of flu. Queer sort of chap. A Frenchman who had suddenly appeared out of the blue. He had sailed into Maltby one evening on this boat, and a fortnight later he had been found,

practically dead, in the cabin. Odd fellow! Must have been as
mad as a hatter. And he, Ferguson, had bought the boat for a
song.

Nobody had ever known where the Frenchman came from,
and the boat was not registered. It had only meant half an hour's
dealing with the harbour authorities. Why had old Ferguson
bought her? Nobody knew. He did not even know himself. He
had never had the nerve to use her, and there she had lain on
the mud for—ten years.

"Such a stoopid thing to go and do," Mrs. Ferguson had com-
plained, "buying up an old tub like that. You'll be the laughingstock of the club. So unpleasant for the girls. What d'you propose to do with her now you've bought her?"

To this her husband made no reply. He scratched his head. He
couldn't think of an answer. He had merely obeyed an impulse,
if you like, but there it was. Something had whispered to him,
like the throb of the siren—"Buy her, you never know."

Ten years lying on the mud. *Adieu Sagesse!* Old Ferguson
cocked his head on one side and sniffed the air. He looked just
like an overgrown mongrel dog.

Somebody was coming along the beach, sinking into the mud
with heavy feet. He appeared round the corner of the tree. It
was Sam the crabber. Like conspirators, they smiled at one another.

"Good evening, Sam."

"Evenin', sir . . ."

Old Ferguson lit a cigarette, Sam coughed and spat behind his
hand.

"I've been taking a look at the boat, Sam. She seems as sound
as when she first lay here. I've been testing her hull with my
knife. No soft spots."

Sam stroked his beard and winked.

"There b'ain't nothin' wrong with her, sir. An' never has bin.
Her only wants a coat o' paint, to be ready fur sea."

They smoked awhile in silence.

"I'd sail her to America, I wud, an' niver ship a bucket o'
warter th' whole way over," boasted Sam. "Take a look at the
beam of 'er," he went on. "Look at thim timbers. Ye don't foind
'em buildin' boats today like 'un."

Silence again. Then old Ferguson spoke.

"I've got the key, Sam. Let's get aboard and have a look round." He glanced over his shoulder like a guilty schoolboy.

They climbed the rickety legs, damp with seaweed, and stood on the bare deck. Ferguson stamped with his feet. "Firm as a rock," he said.

His companion was digging his knife into the mast. "She's a good spar," he muttered. "'Twould only be a matter o' scrapin' an' a coat o' varnish."

Together they lifted the dirty piece of tarpaulin that covered the hatchway. They stepped into the cockpit and Ferguson drew a key from his pocket.

The door creaked and groaned, and finally opened. Eagerly they gazed down the companionway and into the cabin. There were two long berths on either side and a swinging table in the centre. Ferguson peered into the lockers and fitted cupboards, while Sam lifted the dusty skylight. Now and again they threw remarks at one another, neither expecting a reply.

"She's scarcely damp at all, after lyin' here all these years."

"Aye—she's roomy too. I'd sail in her afore I'd set foot in one o' them big loiners."

Forrard of the cabin were the tiny galley and pantry in one, and the lavatory. Then the fo'c'sle and the big cabin locker.

They moved around, muttering to themselves, touching everything with inquisitive fingers. They sat down on one of the berths. Sam found a chest under the table, full of old charts. He pored over them, licking his dirty thumb.

"How long would it take to get her into shape?" said Ferguson softly, gazing up the companionway so as to avoid Sam's eyes.

Sam coughed discreetly.

"She don't want nothin' doin' to her, so far as I ken see. Mast scraping and decks. Coat o' paint all over. All her gear's good. I've seen it meself, up in Steven's loft. 'Twouldn't take no toime to rig 'er out. Could do't meself easy." He made great play of blowing his nose.

Old Ferguson whistled self-consciously. Then he rose and went on deck. They closed the skylight and locked the door, covering the hatch once more with the ragged tarpaulin. On the beach they stood and gazed at the boat. The sun had set below the hill. The tide was creeping in, sucking its way along the mud. Golden patterns formed in the water, and the air seemed filled with splendour.

A seagull lifted its wings and settled on the masthead. The two men sighed and smiled, conscious of each other's thoughts.

"I believe she'd stand any amount of bad weather," said one.

The song of the sky and sea in unison, the creaking of the mast, the rattle of the shrouds. White foam, white clouds. The world to roam in. Alone. Alone.

"Aye, she'd sail too. Like a bird she'd be," said the other.

Stinging spray and the tang of salt. Brown sails spread to the sky. A tiller that kicked like a bucking horse. A ship that laughed and shook herself from the seas like a live thing. No land . . . and a wild, wild wind.

Something distant sounded through the dusk. Sam turned his head and listened. Ferguson closed his eyes. It was the summons he knew so well. The throb of a ship's siren as she left the harbour—outward bound.

Then Sam moved awkwardly to the stern of the boat and spelt out the name in the faded gold lettering. "Niver could make head nor tail o' this, sir. Nonsense, I reckon."

"*Sagesse* is the French for wisdom, Sam. And *adieu* means farewell."

"It's turrible queer languidge these furrin chaps do speak. Farewell to wisdom, that's what he reckoned to say. Must-a bin touched. Howsumever . . ." Sam considered the matter for a moment. "Kind o' grows on ye," he admitted, "but he must-a bin touched for sartin."

Old Ferguson smiled in the darkness. He felt young and at peace. He wanted to run to the top of the hill and wave his hand.

Adieu Sagesse. Once more the siren called from the sea. The cry of something that escapes. Grey seas, grey skies. "Good night, Sam."

"Good night, sir."

"What's come over old Ferguson?" said the club secretary one day. "I ran into him this afternoon on the golf links and the man was actually whistling to himself. He waved his stick at me and smiled all over his face. I've never been so surprised in my life. Must be goin' potty."

"If you ask me," came the voice of the Very Rev. Mr. Travers, now retired, "it's something very different, very different indeed. I hate to say this sort of thing against an old friend, and nobody respects Ferguson more than I do. But if you ask me and you really wish to have my candid opinion, it's this. The poor fellow drinks." He shook his head sorrowfully and sipped his whisky and soda with a thoughtful air.

"Where on earth does he get the stuff?" muttered Colonel Strong, ex-Indian Army. "I've never seen him take anything but ginger ale here. He's never offered me a drink in his life."

"Probably sneaks into the bar at the Queen," suggested the secretary, "and has a good old souse. Or else keeps the stuff up at his house. Jolly disgustin', if you like, a man in his position. I think people ought to be told about it."

"I'm sincerely relieved he is not on the committee," stated the Very Rev. Mr. Travers. "It would put us all in a most embarrassing position. I feel it my duty to enquire into the whole business. Delicately, of course. I shall call upon Mrs. Ferguson one day this week." Incidentally he remembered the excellence of Mrs. Ferguson's homemade seedcakes. Also he would be able to judge for himself the brand of Ferguson's whisky.

"Personally, I've always thought him a bit peculiar," said the secretary, following another train of thought. "Remember how he bought up that old tub ten years ago? Never even used her, as far as I know. Rather peculiar, to say the least of it. I was walking along that way about a week ago and somebody had been down there. The masts were scraped and half of one side was painted. The skylight was opened, too. I climbed up the bank to have a look. However, it's no business of mine."

The Rev. Mr. Travers coughed and blew his nose.

"I hope—er—that the boat is not being used for any—er—wrong purpose? I don't like the sound of all this at all. Has anybody noticed a light there after dark? For all we know . . ." He looked around him significantly.

Who could say there were not orgies of a bacchanalian nature taking place even in Maltby?

"I did see him talking to that very pretty daughter of Sam the crabber," said the secretary eagerly, "only the other day. It's just come back to me. It was in rather a dark corner, by the church. Funny sort of a place to be, now I come to think of it. Secluded and all that, don't you know?"

"Decidedly!" exclaimed the clergyman.

"Did you—er—happen to overhear what he was saying to her?"

"Yes—as a matter of fact I did," admitted the secretary carelessly. "He was askin' her if she depended on old Sam for her livelihood. Rather suggestive, what?"

Colonel Strong rose from his chair, scarlet with indignation.

"Good God! That means one thing—and one thing only. The damned old satyr, he ought to be horsewhipped."

"Well, I've lived in Maltby thirty years and I've never heard of such a thing," said the Rev. Mr. Travers. He was quite overcome. He rang for the steward and ordered another whisky to calm his nerves. "To think that what we have always believed to be a respectable, God-fearing member of society should turn out such a ruffian. Drinking himself to death, and apparently debauching the youth of Maltby. And using that old hulk of his for immoral purposes. This is really very distressing."

"What are we going to do about it?" enquired the secretary, his inquisitive nose in the air.

"Don't see what we can do, short of tackling him to his face," said the colonel gloomily.

"I suppose you wouldn't let me get hold of the girl and draw the story out of her? I don't mind gettin' in touch with her." The secretary was perhaps too eager to make himself of use.

"Certainly not," Travers replied with great dignity. "At any rate, not at present. The unfortunate girl would probably start a scandal. We must have no scandal in Maltby."

"No—no—of course not," agreed the others hastily. "Because, if there is something I abhor and detest," declared Colonel Strong, Indian Army, now retired, "it's anything in the nature of gossip or scandal."

If the members of the Maltby Yacht Club had taken the trouble to find out, they would have discovered that the manager of the Western Bank had been in the habit, during the last week, of locking himself in his office every evening and examining a number of titles, documents and deeds. His behaviour was, to say the least of it, suspicious. If he was not gambling in secret with the precious bonds entrusted to him by the worthy inhabitants of Maltby, then he must be preparing to decamp with their worldly goods.

Could it be that old Ferguson, the dullest man in Maltby, was a crook, a swindler, in short, a criminal of the deepest dye? It looked extremely like it. And yet, if the said members had possessed the powers of invisibility, and had stolen into the manager's room and glanced over his shoulders as he read his documents, they would have been baffled and intrigued. It seemed that he was examining the exact state of his own private finances, with a view to making a settlement on his wife and three daughters. Yet, in spite of his sixty years, old Ferguson looked strong and healthy. He had surely many more years to live.

Could it be that he was a victim of some deadly illness, and expected death at any moment? The suspense would have proved too much for the members of the club. For the manager was arranging not only his own affairs but also those of a certain Sam Collins, crabber. Yes, he was actually declaring a certain sum to be paid quarterly to Martha Collins, wife of Sam Collins, and those dependent on him.

Ah! Maltby, what sinister secrets are these? Gentlemen of the Yacht Club, what is going on under your very eyes!

On Wednesday evening, old Ferguson leant back in his chair with a sigh of satisfaction. His papers lay before him on his desk, neatly docketed and labelled. His work was finished. All was now in order. Nothing more remained to be done. He gazed round at the familiar walls. The heavy roll-top desk, the books of reference, the plain brown walls, the map in the corner. Strange that after so many years he should feel no affection for them—no regret.

He rose and stretched himself. He straightened his tie and looked in the little mirror by the mantelpiece.

"You're sixty," he told himself. "Nearly sixty-one, and a damned ridiculous old fool."

And then he laughed aloud. Twenty minutes later Ferguson was standing by his boat on the mud flats near the harbour mouth. What a change three weeks had made in her appearance. The mast was scraped and varnished, the hull painted, the decks scrubbed. The rigging had been set up and the mainsail bent. A dingy brown sail if you like, patchy in places, but strong. Below, everything was in order. There were cushions in the cabin, a clock, an oil stove. Even the cupboards were filled. The little pantry was stocked with crockery. Ferguson peered into every corner. No—nothing had been forgotten.

"Sam," he called softly, "Sam, where are you hiding?"

An edge of beard appeared round the fo'c'sle door.

"Here I be, sor," said a hoarse voice. "Jest seein' all were shipshape an' Bristol fashion."

His wife would have sighed at Sam's appearance. His jersey was spotted with tar, his sea boots coated with grime and filth. A disreputable old sou'wester was stuck on the back of his head. From his mouth hung the fag end of a cigarette.

"Where's your Sunday suit, Sam?" said Ferguson, winking an eye.

"Good Lard, sir! You'm surely not goin' to ask me that?" Sam's face was a study of despair. "Why, sir, I've got rid of 'un over to Maltby, quiet like. I was'n goin' to refoose good money. As it es, I reckon that chap got et turrible cheap."

"Never mind, Sam, the days of tight collars are over. No more beastly suits for either of us."

They climbed on deck.

"What time's high water?"

"'Bout 'arf an hour, sir, and we'll get it two foot higher tomorrow, d'un ee forget it."

"D'you think she'll lift, man?"

"Aye, like a bird. Her won't be no trouble."

"Right, Sam, I don't think there's anything more, then. I'll be here without fail. No regrets, eh?"

Sam spat into the water.

"What about the weather?"

"Wind's backing. We'll have it strong from the sou'west, I shouldn't wonder. She'll stand it. It'd take more'n a summer breeze to put her down."

"I believe it would, Sam."

Ferguson scrambled into the little dinghy. The letters on the boat's stern were no longer faded. They stared out in bold relief, challenging the world. *Adieu Sagesse!* The two men smiled at one another, saying not a word.

"Until tomorrow, Sam."

"Aye, aye, sir."

Ferguson climbed the steep hill that led to his house, The Chestnuts. The sun was setting behind the distant hills. Dark orange, sombre, while the grey clouds gathered. A steady wash ran past the harbour mouth.

Rain and wind, what did it matter? Beneath him lay Maltby, secure and snug. He hated her general air of self-righteousness. The prim aspect of the houses, the narrow gardens with their stiff flowers, their shingle paths. The elderly spinsters who peered from the closed windows; the retired officers who stumped up and down the Esplanade. The people who formed the congregation in church, the members of the club, the inquisitive shopkeepers, the officious harbour authorities—all those who had robbed Maltby of her living soul, and stamped her with the death's-head seal—"A seaside town." How he hated them.

Only the gulls were true, and the quiet, grave waters of the harbour. The spirit that still lurked beneath the cobbled stones of the market square; the smoke that curled from the few huddled cottages; the call of the rooks at evening; the tall silent trees on the hillside; the calm beauty of the sea after the sun had set; the soft white mists that came with the rain in summer—only these remained.

Wherever he went, he would carry in his soul a love for these things—but Maltby was dead. No regret, no fear. Something lay before him that was splendid, intoxicating, immense. The call rose strong within him, supreme. The call of life itself. And he, sixty-one, stood on the threshold of his dream.

He threw back his head and laughed. He was old, old, but nothing mattered. Nobody cared. The world was his.

His last evening. It was typical of his life. He remembered that Travers was coming to dinner. He thought of the group seated round the table in the dining room. Helen's new dress. The parlourmaid's heavy breathing as she handed the vegetables. The most comfortable house in Maltby. "Well, you can have it. You can have the lot," he cried aloud.

Adieu Sagesse! As he entered the house he heard the sound of his wife's loud laugh coming from the drawing room. One of the girls had started the noisy gramophone. On the hall table lay the black hat of the Very Rev. Mr. Travers. Old Ferguson glanced at it with a glint in his eye and made for the drawing room. He was going to enjoy himself for the first and last time in Maltby.

"Now, Richard, what in the world have you been doin'? The gong will sound in a minute. You knew perfectly well Mr. Travers was comin' to dinner." Mrs. Ferguson frowned at her husband impatiently.

"I know. That's why I came in so late. I waited till the last possible moment," replied old Ferguson cheerfully.

Mrs. Ferguson opened her mouth in astonishment, while the girls turned round from the gramophone and gazed at their father. As for the Very Rev. Mr. Travers, he drew out a large handkerchief from his pocket and proceeded to blow his nose. How extremely awkward and distressing, the wretched fellow was drunk already.

"How are you, Ferguson?" he enquired, ignoring his host's unfortunate remark. "I don't seem to have seen you about lately—except of course in church on Sunday."

"I don't know if it's the approach of autumn," declared old Ferguson with an innocent smile, "but certainly these last Sundays I've slept sounder in church than I've ever slept in my life. And you too, my dear," he added, turning to his wife, "I noticed that it was only Mrs. Druce's voice singing, 'Peace, perfect peace,' that roused you at all after the sermon last Sunday."

Mrs. Ferguson turned a deep purple; the girls coughed, and the Rev. Mr. Travers bent down and pretended to stroke the spaniel's ears.

At that moment the gong sounded and the agitated hostess led the way into the dining room.

As he entered the room the clergyman glanced surreptitiously at the sideboard. Alas! It was as he had feared. The whisky decanter was half empty. Of course, his host was on the verge of delirium tremens; probably kept the drink locked up in his room.

The party seated themselves at the table. Everyone appeared to be nervous and ill at ease, except old Ferguson, who had never been in a better humour in his life.

The soup was handed in silence. No one seemed willing to start speaking. The minutes passed. The noise of people eating became intense.

Towards the end of the meal the clergyman remembered his promise to the members of the club, to find out the meaning of Ferguson's sinister behaviour.

"It's curious how the young people of Maltby have changed," he began, as he carefully peeled his pear. "They seem to think of little but their appearance. I was walking along High Street this afternoon and really, to see some of the girls from the shops, you'd imagine they were dressed for the theatre. No sleeves, silk stockings, their faces powdered and painted. Sometimes I doubt their respectability."

"Oh, come, Mr. Travers, you're exaggeratin'," Mrs. Ferguson exclaimed. "They merely believe in fresh air. Short sleeves hurt nobody. Though I must say I hate to see girls of that class apin' their betters. We shall have them trying to join the Golf and Tennis Club, unless we keep them in their places."

"Would it matter if they did?" asked her husband.

"Matter? My dear Richard, what a thing to say. I, for one, should never want to play a game again if I had to mix with them."

"I don't approve of all these modern ways," said Mr. Travers. Wasn't he going to be offered any port? Really, his host's manners were atrocious. "Life was far more romantic when I was a boy. I doubt even if these games improve your appearance, as people try to make out. A womanly woman has sweeter qualities than all these sturdy modern creatures. By the way, that little May Collins, old Sam's youngest daughter, is a pretty type of girl." He stole a stealthy look at his host.

"I know her well," replied Ferguson. "She's a very charming girl. I've found her an excellent job at Penleath. I'm even thinking of settling some money on her."

The clergyman turned scarlet with embarrassment. His eyes glistened behind his spectacles. Really, his host was going a little too fast.

"Richard is jokin', of course, Mr. Travers," said Mrs. Ferguson in icy tones. "Would you care for some grapes? They come from our own vines."

"No, thank you, dear lady."

The girls gazed stonily before them. What on earth had happened to Father?

"Yes, as I was saying," continued their guest awkwardly, "it's scarcely a romantic period."

"I agree, Mr. Travers," broke in Helen in a sullen voice. "Men, for instance, are quite hopeless nowadays. Years ago, I believe, if a man was attracted to a girl, he sent her flowers and things. Now he doesn't even bother to remember a promise to play a round of golf, or anything else." She laughed scornfully. "I despise men!" she added.

"In my opinion, girls don't make the most of their chances. Things were very different in the old days," retorted her mother.

"There's a jolly sight too much competition, I consider," muttered one of the girls.

Helen glared at her sister.

"Hum! It's all very sad," sighed the Rev. Mr. Travers, wiping his mouth with his napkin. "The present age is far from ideal. Don't you agree with me, Ferguson?"

"No, Travers, not at all. I think it's a great age."

The family looked at him in astonishment. Most extraordinary for Father to venture such an opinion.

"May we ask why, Richard?" asked his wife, raising her eyebrows.

Old Ferguson waited a moment before replying. Then he turned to the clergyman with a bland smile.

"There's a general lack of morality I find extremely pleasant," he said.

There was a minute's horrified silence.

The Very Rev. Mr. Travers was entirely speechless. He could only stare and blink his eyes. Then Mrs. Ferguson rose majestically from the table, followed by the three girls.

"Wait a moment," cried her husband. "I've got something to say to you all. You think I'm mad and off my head. Well, perhaps you're right. But I'm proud of it and, if I'm mad, then I'm going to commit the most sublime piece of folly that ever came into a madman's head.

"I'm starting out on a great adventure. I've had to wait sixty years for it, but it's not too late. What comes of it I neither know nor care. There's something in the quality of the unknown that holds more beauty than the peace of God. One thing I know full well, and that is, if I pass away, Maltby will not pass away. You will live here, year after year, happy in your supreme self-righteousness. The congregation will continue to sleep in church on Sundays and to discuss their duty towards their neighbour during the week. You girls will marry, if your mother works hard enough, and you in your turn will produce sons and daughters to the everlasting glory of Maltby.

"They will sail their little boats on fine afternoons in the summer and hack round the golf course in the winter. I sincerely hope the annual balls will always be successful. I trust the Borough Council will gain their wish to erect what they term 'a smart promenade to attract visitors'! I shall be bitterly disappointed if my wife gives up the bridge parties that have made her so famous and which, incidentally, have added not inconsiderably to her private income.

"I shall feel I have failed as a father should my daughters forsake their very excellent habit of following young men who have no use for them. May gossip, backbiting and slander continue to be the mainstay of the club, and may members make up in argument the points they lose in sailing. As for the retired, worthy representative of the Church of England, I pray that his profound spiritual inclination, his devotion to the God of Whisky, may remain as fervid and as unremitting as it is at present."

He turned in the doorway and reached for his old tweed jacket and cap that were hanging on the stand in the hall. He paused a moment to light his pipe. Then he smiled, winked his pale blue eye and bowed to the group in the dining room.

"Good night to you all."

The front door banged and he was gone in the darkness.

Seven o'clock and a grey morning. The wind was blowing strong from the southwest, with a hint of rain behind it. No anger in it yet, for the gale signal was not hoisted on the top of Castle Hill.

The trees shivered and swayed, the rough harbour water sucked and splashed against the steps of the houses. The little boats rocked at their moorings. Grey clouds flew low on the wind-streaked sky, and high in the east gleamed a wild wet sun.

A small black boat with patched brown sails was beating her way out of the harbour. Her lee gunwale was awash, but she faced her way through the heavy seas like a seagull bred to the wind.

Holding to the mast was a figure in a torn yellow oilskin much too big for him, a sou'wester on his head and a smile on his face that reached from ear to ear. Seated at the tiller was somebody in a faded blue shirt and an old tweed jacket. His grey hair was wet with spray, but he laughed as he shook it off.

"Aren't you going to say good-bye to Maltby, Sam?"

The figure in the yellow oilskin spat into the water. It was his last supreme gesture.

The mast creaked, the wind screamed and whistled in the rigging, and the boat rose and fell through the waves with a heavy ponderous sigh.

Behind lay Maltby, wrapped in her morning mist.

The man at the tiller never once looked round. Before him stretched the open sea, mournful, terrible, mysterious. The call rose within him and became part of him forever. Grey skies—grey seas.

Adieu Sagesse.

Piccadilly

She sat on the edge of a chair swinging her legs. Her frock of black satin was too tight for her, and too short; as she tilted on her chair the dress rose above her knees, and I could see the beginning of a ladder in her stocking, hastily mended, the thread jumbled in a knot. Her hair was unnaturally light and over-waved; the vivid red of her lipstick, smudged and thick, toned badly against the pallor of her face dusted with a mauve powder. Her patent shoes were thin for walking, and cheap. The toes were too stumpy and the heels too high. She had thrown off her black coat, the collar and the cuffs of which boasted an imitation fur, and her hat, a minute piece of velvet worn at the back of her head, now lay at her feet. Around her throat was a necklace of scarlet beads that clashed with her mouth. Her face was thin, the skin drawn tightly across her cheekbones, and her eyes —silly doll's eyes, like blue china—stared sullenly in front of her.

Every now and then she puffed at a cigarette, pursing up her lips as a child would do, vainly attempting smoke rings, playing at bravado. She had sprinkled herself freely with scent, but even so it could not altogether hide the smell peculiar to one whose skin is rarely washed, whose clothes are seldom cleaned, whose body is undernourished. She looked at me under her lashes, and then shrugged her shoulders, throwing aside her cigarette, forcing a smile that went ill with her appearance, that belonged to someone who must have been dead a long while. Then she began to talk at last, her voice hard and metallic, realising that I was not a man but a dummy thing without feeling, a notebook in my hand.

"Newspaper boy, that's it, is it?" she said. "You've got to earn your living the same as I have. It's a dirty job, isn't it? When some fellow has left his wife for a new girl your boss sends you

round to nose out where it was done and who with. Or else a kid
is run over by a tram, and you call on the mother to hear how
much blood he spilt. I guess you're popular all right in homes
where things have gone wrong. I guess it gives you a sort of
pleasure, doesn't it, to poke your fingers into people's lives?
You'd think there was trouble enough without a boy like you
trampling with heavy feet on something that ought to be kept
dark and secret.

"What's it all for, can you tell me? So that Mr. Smith can get a
thrill to himself thinking, 'I might have been that chap—unfaith-
ful,' so that Mrs. Smith can wonder, 'Might have happened to my
kid'? No—I'm not clever, I'm not wise. But I kind of get time for
thinking things now and again. Well, what do you want me to
tell you? I've no secrets, not these days. I don't know anyone
that's been murdered, nor run over, nor left sudden, nor waiting
for a baby. I haven't any friends to speak of. I rub along better
on my own. You know—I find the talk of other people silly.
Seems as though, whatever they say, it wouldn't make a pennyworth of change if they'd left it all unsaid. The weather now—ah!
that's different if you like. Weather means a lot to me. You understand that, don't you? I hate the rain—I can't afford to have it
rain. And I hate the fog—I hate the winter—they're bad times for
me. But for Lady Stuck-up in her fur coat and her car, it doesn't
hurt her. She's all right. And Miss Prim selling stockings behind
a counter, she's all right. Half the world don't worry when it
rains.

"But me, looking out of this window and seeing the sky like a
dripping bucket, and saying to myself, 'Will it stop before night?'
and 'Will my shoes let in the wet again?' Yes, and the chap who
sells sunshades—we worry. Come on, tell me it takes all sorts to
make a world. They told me that in school. I don't know why
you want to ask me questions. Is it that you're doing a piece in
your paper called 'Confessions of the Great'? I've seen that sort
of stuff before. 'How I Became an Actress,' by Florrie Flapdoo-
dle, or 'My First Step Towards the Church,' by the Archbishop
of Bunk. You want to pry into the lives of humble people like
myself. '"As a kid I loved handling corpses," said the under-
taker.' Is that it? So you want me to give it you, hot and strong,
straight from the shoulder.

"Listen, you funny little fellow with your notebook and your inky fingers. I'll tell you a story. Maybe it's true, maybe it isn't. You can make what you like out of it and print it in big letters in the *Sunday Muck*: 'What Led to My Entering the Profession,' by Maisie."

You see, in a kind of way, everything happened because of superstition. I've always been mad for superstition. Walking under ladders, crossing my salt, bowing to the moon, hunting up passages in the Bible. Even now it's the same. Every morning I open my Bible to see if it's going to be my lucky day. Laughing at me? I tell you I'm serious. A girl I knew found "God shall send a pestilence unto ye," and in a fortnight she had it. She didn't laugh. All she knew was that it didn't come from God. . . . We're like that, every one of us. Believing in legends, believing in symbols, believing in signs—the only things we don't believe in are fairies.

Listen—if I wasn't superstitious I'd be a housemaid now in Park Lane. It's a fact. I'd be wearing a cap and an apron. I'd be emptying the slops of some overfed old countess. I'd be meeting my boy Thursday night under a lamppost and going to a picture house for one and three pennyworth of cuddle. And look at me— I'm free, I don't owe anything to no one, I belong to myself. Haven't I got a room of my own? Once I was a kid that didn't know a thing. I went into service straight from the Soldiers' Orphan Home. I was happy because I was ignorant. I used to scrub myself every day with soap and wear flannel next to the skin. I didn't know any better. I thought if I rose from under housemaid to upper maybe I'd save enough at fifty to live quiet in the country.

I wanted to marry, too. I thought if you kissed a boy he took you straight away to church. Then I met Jim. Jim didn't take me to church nor did he kiss me much, but he taught me a whole lot of things housemaids don't need to know. I felt for Jim what girls in books feel for the fellow on the cover. You know, with big eyes and curly hair. Jim's hair was straight and he had a cast in one eye, but I didn't worry. I don't know if there's a name for it—what Jim and I had. In the pictures they call it Love. In the newspapers they call it an Offence. I didn't call it nothing, but it seemed all right to me. I had a pain in my heart when he wasn't there. I'd wait around in the rain; I wouldn't work proper. I thought maybe he'd leave me if I didn't look nice. So I gave up washing and bought some scent and powder, and he said I was fine. He used to say to me, "Look here, Maisie, service isn't any good to you. You're too smart." "Why," I'd tell him, "I can't do anything else." "Of course you can," he'd say, "there's heaps of things you could do. Service is drab. It doesn't lead you no-where." When I told him maybe one day I'd get to upper house-maid he laughed.

"Are you going to waste your days planning what'll come to you when you're fifty?" he said. "I thought you'd got more sense."

I told him he was mean, but I thought about it all the same. I thought maybe he'd look down on me if I stayed in service. "If I leave my place you'll have to find me a job," I said. He looked queer then, he didn't say much, but next time we went together he petted me so I felt I'd do anything he wanted as long as I didn't have to lose him. "I treat you all right, don't I?" he said. "How do you think I earn money to take you out and give you good times?"

"I don't know. You work, don't you?"

"Yes, I work, Maisie, but not the way you mean."

"Well, tell me," I said.

Then he laughed, slyly, winking at me. "Look at this," he said, and he took a necklace out of his pocket and jingled it up and down before my eyes.

"Where'd you find that?" I asked him.

"Took it off an old lady," he said.

Then I understood. Jim was a thief. I was scared. I cried, I said I wouldn't have any more to do with him. I was honest, I said. "All right," he laughed, and went off, not coming near me for three weeks.

That taught me. I saw I couldn't do without him. I wrote him he could steal the crown jewels if he liked, as long as he took me back. I thought p'raps I could reform him, and one day I'd save enough money to keep him and buy a little house in the country. I gave in my notice to the lady in Kensington. I saw an adver-tisement in a paper for an under housemaid in a place in Park Lane.

I showed it to Jim. "That's me," I said.

He laughed. "You can't do that," he said. "You come and get rich my way."

I put the advertisement in my bag.

"I'm going to answer it today," I told him.

"We'll see," he said.

He said he'd come with me. We went to the underground and booked to Down Street. I was fussed and worried, I wondered if I was doing the right thing—answering that advertisement.

"Look here," said Jim, "let's make a bargain. Either you go to Park Lane or you come and live with me, work with me. You can't do both; quick now, decide." He said this as we got into the train. I shut my eyes tight. I thought, "If only there could be a sign to tell me what to do." Then I opened my eyes, I glanced at the platform as the train carried us away. Suddenly I saw the words flash up at me in lights on a board, "Passing Down Street."

Then I said aloud to Jim, "All right. I'll come to you."

Yes, you can call it superstition. Each thing has happened to me in that way. In the underground, too. Funny, isn't it? Never up in the air, never up in the world. Always below, beneath the ground. I was with Jim for about six months. He trained me so I could steal women's handbags without their noticing. It was quite easy. I was expert after a time.

We worked the underground. I got to know every station, every lift—all the network of passages. Sometimes it was exciting, and dangerous, making me want to laugh, but more often it was hell. Sometimes I'd tremble so I'd come over faint. "Pull yourself together," Jim would whisper, "do you want to give us away?"

Sometimes he'd make me go alone. Then I'd be scared. It seemed as though everyone must be looking, and that I was there, all alone, no one near, nowhere to hide if things went wrong.

"You're not bold enough," Jim told me. "How d'you think we're ever going to get rich if you act timid the way you do? Handbags don't bring us in much unless you get a lucky haul. You've got to learn an' be more snappy. Most women nowadays wear bracelets. Why can't you have a try at them?" He'd always be worrying at me. "Can't you lift a bracelet?" he'd say. He'd complain all the time. He was lazy now, he made me do the work.

One evening when I'd only lifted one bag the whole day he turned nasty. "I'm coming out with you tonight," he said, "and we're going to get a bracelet."

I began to cry. "I can't," I said. "I don't feel sure of my fingers."

"You'll do as I tell you or I'm finished with you," he said.

We started to work the Central London line shortly after eleven. We counted on getting the after-theatre crowd. It was at Oxford Circus he saw the old lady in the fur coat walk to the booking office. She booked to Lancaster Gate. Jim nudged me, pointed to her hands.

She wore a large ring on her little finger. It looked valuable, too. We also booked to Lancaster Gate. I was trembling all over, and my hands were slippery with sweat. "I can't do it," I whispered. "I can't do it." He held my arm so tight I nearly screamed. We didn't sit next to her in the carriage. We were in another part of the train.

When we got out at Lancaster Gate she was walking up the platform. There were few people about, I saw it was going to be difficult. There wouldn't be the excuse of jostling in a crowd.

She was in evening dress. It was long at the back. She couldn't manage it proper. I thought that perhaps if she tripped in some way . . . I brushed against her—she dropped her bag. We both groped for it on the floor. The bag opened and her powder box and purse and odds and ends fell out in a mess. I talked loudly, fussing her, pretending to help, bumping her against the wall—but I had the ring. Then I left her, and ran on to catch the lift, Jim just behind me. "Something is going to happen," I thought, "something is going to happen . . ." I felt I could see prison in front of me, and I couldn't escape. If the old lady missed her ring in the lift I was done for. I wondered if I had better turn back and get through to the other platform. I knew if I went up in that lift I was finished. And as though to prove it—as though there really was something true in superstition—I saw the notice: "Stand Clear of the Gates."

I turned to Jim. "I'm going back," I said. He was rough, he shook my arm. "Get in quick—you little fool," he said. But he was scared too. I could see the whites of his eyes. He pushed me inside the lift. I saw the old lady running along the passage waving her hand. "I've been robbed," she shouted, "I've been robbed. Stop that girl."

People turned to look at me. I tried to get to the other side of the lift, but it was barred. Then they began to crowd round me and to question me.

You don't want me to tell you about gaol, do you? You can squeeze that out of somebody else. There's plenty of ex-convicts who like to get into the newspapers. I've got nothing to say. . . . Oh yes—they treated me kind. That's right, isn't it? And a lady visited me once a week and asked me if I'd been a bad girl, and wouldn't I be happier with Jesus? I told her "No," I didn't care how dirty he'd been to me, I'd go with Jim and no one else. That was true, too. Maybe he'd turned me down, but I was his girl. I only wanted to get clear of gaol to be with him again. He told me it was the same for him. He came and saw me once. You stand in a kind of place with bars around, and they let you talk to your friends. "Why, Maisie," he said, "you know I didn't mean to get you in here, don't you?"

"That's all right—I haven't split," I said.

"You aren't sore at me, Maisie, are you?" he said. "It just happened that way, and it couldn't be helped. I tried to save my skin. You won't let on to them here we were working together, will you?" he said.

I told him he needn't worry.

"You're a sweet kid," he told me, "I'm fond of you. It's lonely without you."

He didn't talk no more after that, and he went away. He never came back again neither. But somehow I pictured him waiting for me outside. I guessed he'd be helpless without me fiddling with his things and just being near him. A man likes to have a girl around if it's only to treat her rough and swear at her, don't you think? It gives him a queer kind of comfort. And loving a girl makes a man forget to wonder why it was he was born.

I guess that's what it was like for Jim, anyway. So back in gaol I'd make plans of what we'd do when I was out again. I thought we'd have to lie low for a bit because of my coming from gaol. They keep a pretty sharp eye on you, so I was told by one of the girls. It's no use working your old game again until they've slacked off from watching you. I didn't want to land Jim into trouble either.

There was a kid in there with me who said she was going to go straight when she was out. She believed in the stuff that the visiting lady handed her. I was wise, though. "You'll never be free of this," I said, "it clings like mud, don't you know that?"

"Oh, Maisie," she said, crying, too—young she was—"I wish you'd come with me, and we'd go out to the colonies together."

"What? And be treated worse than a servant, and scrubbing floors, and people above you?" I said. "I've had enough scrubbing inside here to last me a lifetime. When I get outside I'm going to live like a princess. I've got a boy waiting for me," I said.

She was free before me. "I'm going to Canada," she said. "I'm starting fresh."

Funny thing—they put her with a clergyman's wife up in Bristol, and found out a month later she had started her old tricks again, so they gave her three years. It just shows you, doesn't it?

I got out in the spring. They talked to me before I left about duty, and citizenship, and humanity, and God. They gave me some money, too. I went out and bought a chemise trimmed with lace. I wanted Jim to find me smart. There never was a day like the day I came out. Blue sky and the sun, and people smiling for no reason. I felt like dancing, and screaming with laughter, and being looked at by fellows, and running away in a corner to cry at the same time.

I kept saying to myself, "Soon I'll be seeing him, soon—soon." I had myself kind of worked up. D'you see? He'd be somewhere around. I knew that. I'd only got to go and find him; he wouldn't be far.

So I looked up at the sky and talked like a baby. "Here—you be off—you aren't any use to me," and I went down into the underground where I belonged.

I looked for him all day, and I was getting tired, and sore, too. I felt myself thinking, superstitious like—"Maybe there'll be a sign soon to show me what's going to happen." Yes, it was six o'clock, what they call the rush hour in the underground. I guessed if Jim was still working he'd be busy at that time. I took a ticket at Bond Street. I had to stand nearly five minutes in a queue. I was hot, my clothes sticking to me, my hat at the back of my head. I wanted to lie down and die. . . . And the crowd pushing into me, breathing down my neck, straining to get past me, to go their way. I got my feet on the moving stairway—I leaned against the rail. We were taken downwards, away from the light above, down into the underground.

And then I saw Jim. He was across the rail, on the other side, on the same staircase—but *coming up*. We drew nearer, we were level—and I called out to him, over the barrier that separated us: "Jim—here I am—Jim." He didn't look. He didn't speak. He heard me, but he didn't do anything. He seemed smarter, different, and there was a girl with him—hanging on his arm. I turned, I tried to push back, but there were people coming down behind me all the time and it wasn't any use. I called out to him once more—"Jim—Jim."

There wasn't anything I could do. I let the moving stair take me where it wanted—down—down. And he, the last I saw of him was a figure right at the very top, blotted against a girl—going out into the air.

She stretched across to a table and picked up a bottle of nail varnish.

"So that was my sign," she said; "he going up the staircase and me going down. That's what you wanted to know, wasn't it? It'll make a pretty picture for your newspaper. Tell me, do they pay you well for this sort of thing?"

Still she tilted on the edge of her chair, swinging her legs.

"Aren't you satisfied yet? D'you like every single scrappy detail? You ask me why I didn't go back to being a servant? Because, little newspaper boy, servants can't have the things I want. Why didn't I go on being a thief? Because I was scared, and I had to have a job that was easy to do. Why did I choose, beyond anything else in the world, to be what I am? Is that what you want, to put it in headlines?" She laughed, she shrugged her shoulders, she was no longer the Maisie who had told her story but the Maisie of the moment—ugly, older, hard, false, and without feeling.

She said: "Because when I got to the bottom of that moving

stairway I walked to a train, and I got out at a station, and I got in another train, and I got out at another station—and as I stood on the platform I prayed hard to God that He should give me a sign. And He did."

She finished her nails. She dabbed her face with powder, her lips with rouge. She pulled on her coat and her hat, she stood ready with her bag under her arm. She opened her mouth and laughed.

"What was the sign?" she said. "Why, it came straight from God, written big above my head, in letters of fire at the end of the platform—'Follow the Red Light for Piccadilly.'"

The Supreme Artist

He came away from the stage after the final curtain and went along to his dressing room, humming a tune to himself, thinking of nothing. The girl followed close behind, patting the lock of hair that had fallen over her face.

"You smudged your eye-black when you cried this afternoon," she told him, "it came off in streaks down the side of my neck—look how filthy it is. I suppose you must cry?"

"I don't know, I've never thought about it before," he said. "I'll try something else tonight. We might alter the whole of the last act. What about wearing a beard? I'm sure one could give an entirely different performance in a beard." He turned to the looking glass in his room and squinted sideways at his profile.

"I should hate you in a beard," she said, feeling his chin. "It would make you all heavy and middle-aged. Darling, promise me never to wear one?"

He picked up a hand mirror and viewed himself from another angle. "I'm not so sure," he said doubtfully, and then called over his shoulder to his dresser, "Monkton, what about a beard for the last act?"

The man coughed politely behind his hand. "Well, sir, it's hardly for me to say, but I scarcely think it would be suitable. Not for this type of part, sir."

"P'raps you're right. Why is it I'm never allowed to do as I like—Oi, where are you going?"

She turned to him from the doorway. "Upstairs to change. Have you got the car outside?"

"Yes—want throwing out anywhere?"

"Take me back to the flat like an angel, unless you've got millions of people to see. I can easily find a bus . . ."

"Don't be a mug, of course I'll drive you anywhere. Buck up

and get your things on. Monkton, there's nobody waiting, is there?" He began taking off his coat.

"One minute, sir, excuse me, but I believe there's a lady wishes to see you. Here is her card, but she said you wouldn't know the card, sir. I said I knew you generally liked to get away quickly matinee days, and she seemed disappointed. Said she'd wait in case you could spare her a few minutes."

"Give me the card." He frowned over it, twisting it in his fingers. "Mrs. John Pearce—conveys nothing to me. What's she like, Monkton?"

"Well, sir—it's rather difficult to describe. A middle-aged lady, I should say, white hair, tall—dressed almost in country clothes. A very pleasant speaking voice."

"Oh, Lord! Pour me out a drink and show her in."

He lit a cigarette, and tried to remember the second bar of the tune that was haunting him.

> Why are you so mean to me?
> Why are you . . . ?

He had forgotten all about the woman, until the door closed suddenly and she was standing there before him. She laughed at him, holding out her hands. "You haven't changed at all, have you?"

He saw someone with a mass of thick white hair under an ugly hat, someone with a bronzed, rather weather-beaten face. Her eyes were blue, and she was nice when she smiled. Her clothes were all wrong, though, her ankles thick. She obviously did not care about these things. He started back in surprise, pretending to be overwhelmed with joy and astonishment.

Of course he had no idea who she was. "My dear," he began, "but this is too marvellous. Why on earth didn't you tell me you were in front?"

It seemed as though she could not move away from the doorway, but must stand there watching him, feeling his eyes with hers, uncertain of the truth of his words.

"I didn't think you'd recognise me," she began. "I was certain you wouldn't have the remotest idea who I was. What is it—

nearly thirty years? Think of all that's happened since, so much and so much . . ."

"But you're talking nonsense," he interrupted, "of course I knew you the moment you came into the room."

He racked his memory for some light out of the past. Who on earth could she be? Mrs. John Pearce . . .

She loosened the scarf round her throat and sat down on the edge of the sofa. "This is the first time I've ever been brave enough to come round," she said. "I've wanted to so often, but something always prevented me, a sort of silly pride. A feeling you wouldn't know me, wouldn't remember. I come and see all your plays, you know. I'm still sentimental enough to cut out your notices and paste them in a book!"

She laughed at him, shaking her head. He made a little noise in his throat to save the necessity of words. "You see, I live right down in the country now," she went on. "It's quite an expedition to come up to London. When I do, about twice a year, I make a point of seeing you act. I don't know what it is, but the years don't make any difference to you. To me, a tired middle-aged woman in the stalls, you are always the boy I knew, funny, excited, with his hair rumpled. That's being a sentimentalist, isn't it? Can I have a cigarette?"

She reached out for the box on the table. He wondered why she gave him no clue to her personality, and why she did not even bother to mention the names of people or of places. Apparently they must have known each other absurdly well. Bronzed face, white hair, Mrs. John Pearce.

"Let's see"—he threw his question into the air—"let's see, how long is it really since I saw you last?"

She watched his expression with grave eyes. "I said thirty years just now, but maybe it's a little less," she answered. "Time is such a ridiculous thing. Do you know, I've only got to relax, and throw my mind back, and I can hear the sound of your cab starting, and you driving away in it, hot and furious, with me lying on my bed imagining that nobody ever got over a broken heart."

Oh! so they had been as intimate as that? Angry words—tears— and now he couldn't remember her at all. . . .

"I must have behaved like a swine," he said angrily. "I can't understand how we ever came to quarrel."

She threw back her head and laughed. "You don't mean to say you've thought it was because of a quarrel?" she asked him. "But we never had rows, you and I. You must remember that."

"No. No, of course not." He joined in her laugh, wondering whether she had noticed his slip. "I know we were the most wonderful friends in every way," he continued.

She sat silent for a minute, considering the matter, her head on one side. "That's where you're wrong," she told him. "It's because we never struck a proper basis of friendship that the whole thing finished. I think we were too young to have any judgement —too young and too selfish. No sense of values. We were like greedy children who make themselves sick with overeating."

He agreed solemnly, watching her over the rim of his glass. So this had been a passionate affair. Thirty years ago—he cast his mind back in vain. He had an uneasy feeling that he had behaved badly to this white-haired woman who sat before him. In a moment he was acquitted, though.

"I shall never regret it," she said suddenly, "never one second. Being in love—terribly in love—is the best thing in the world, don't you think? The only moment I have sometimes regretted was sending you away as I did. We might have gone on being happy."

Then it had not been his fault after all. Presumably he had gone from her brokenhearted. It was all rather touching. Why had he such an appalling memory? He was ready to cry over his youthful tragedy.

"I nearly blew my brains out at the time," he said bitterly. "I suppose you never cared for one moment how it would affect me. I felt as if there was nothing to live for—nothing in life to hold on to."

"I guessed it would be hard at first," she smiled, "but look— you soon got over it."

He was certain he had taken months in getting over it. For all he knew this woman had blasted his whole outlook thirty years ago. They had obviously been passionately in love and she had given him the chuck, breaking his heart. He forgot her ugly hat and her tired, weather-beaten face. He began to imagine somebody young, somebody slim. He pictured to himself all sorts of mad, impossible things.

"Those long days together," he began dreamily, "that frock you wore—and your hair brushed away from your face."

She frowned, puzzled by his words. "But we scarcely saw each other in the daytime."

"Nights, I meant," he said hurriedly. "Long, long nights. Sometimes there was a moon making patterns on the floor. You used to put your hands over your eyes to hide yourself from the light."

"Did I really?"

"Yes—you know you did. And often we'd come back hungry—neither of us with any money in our pockets. Perhaps only enough to halve a ham sandwich. And you'd be cold—I'd have to give you my coat—but you'd wrinkle up your nose in contempt, saying 'Who wants to get warm that way?' Then, because I loved you so much, I'd want to strangle you, and . . ."

He stopped short, dazzled by his own imagination, and a little hurt at the astonished expression on her face.

"I've forgotten all that," she told him. "I'm sure you always had plenty of money. And we never halved ham sandwiches, we nearly always dined with Mother."

He glared at her, shocked and confused. His ideas were so much more romantic. She was spoiling everything. Why must she drag in her relations?

"I always hated your mother," he said coldly, "we never got on. I didn't like to tell you at the time."

She stared at him blankly. "But whyever didn't you say so? You know it would have made all the difference in the world."

He brushed her statement aside. He would not talk about her mother. He saw himself young, miserable, very much in love. This was the only thing that mattered.

"I tried drinking at first," he went on gloomily, "but it wasn't any good. I never could get your face out of my thoughts, never for a single instant, night and day. It was complete and utter hell—"

"What about your ambition, surely that gave you some sort of interest? And then when success came to you?"

"Ambition? Success?" He laughed scornfully, throwing his cigarette into the fireplace. "What were they compared with my love for you? Don't you understand that after you sent me away I was broken, done in? You took from me the only chance of happiness I ever had. I was young, I had ideals, I believed in you more than anything in the world. Then, for some reason that I shall never know, you chucked me. You didn't care what became of me, and you have the face to sit there and tell me that the fact of my being successful should have put you out of my mind. Don't you know that success has not brought one grain of happiness to me, that always in the depth of my heart I've known that you were the only thing that mattered?"

He blew his nose noisily, and poured himself out another drink. His eyes were red and his hands trembled with emotion.

She rose from the sofa and laid her hand on his shoulder. "I'd no idea you felt it in that way," she said gently. "Please, please don't reproach me like this. I believed I was doing it for your good. I thought I would be a drag on you."

He refused to be comforted. He shook his head miserably.

"You were the sweetest influence in my life—the one reason for existence," he said. He glanced down at the wedding ring on her hand and was aware of his unreasoning jealousy. "Who is this fellow you've married, anyway?" he asked roughly. "This John Pearce—damn his eyes. So you couldn't even be faithful to one . . ."

"I met him eighteen months after you went away," she answered. "John and I have been married twenty-seven years now. Four grown-up children—just think of that! We lead a very peaceful life down in Devonshire. Don't you remember how I always loved the country? That dream has come true, anyway. I have a snapshot of my youngest boy here in my bag. He's rather a darling, don't you think? He's doing so well in Burma."

He scarcely looked at the snapshot. He wasn't interested in her children, or in her house in Devonshire.

"Does your husband know about us?"

She put the photo away in her bag.

"Oh yes! I tell him everything."

"Then he doesn't mind?"

"Why should he? He's scarcely likely to bother over something that happened thirty years ago! He's always very interested in you. We read your notices together. He's going to be terribly excited when I tell him I've been round to see you."

He did not want it to be like this. He wanted a hulking brute of a husband who treated her badly, who never understood her. He wanted her to be lonely and unloved, leaning out of a window, watching for a star. He could not allow her to be married for twenty-seven years and have four grown-up children. She seemed to take it all for granted, too. She made no allowance for his feelings.

"So much for fidelity," he said grimly, "so much for vows and promises, and all the things that go to make up belief. We used to hold each other and whisper words like 'never' and 'forever.' Just a silly little string of lies, that's what they were. You've killed my last illusions today; you've made me feel as though nothing's worth while."

She shrugged her shoulders and began to draw the gloves on her large brown hands. "You talk as though you had never made love to other women," she laughed comfortably.

"Other women?" He waved the idea away. He would not even discuss it. In his mind he saw a meaningless procession, to all of whom he had sworn the same things. The thought irritated him. He found it unattractive. He would have liked men and women to be as birds on a tree—the male bird dumb and inconsolable on a high branch, with its mate dead at the foot of the tree. The picture saddened him. He felt unhappy for no reason. She was standing now, the ugly hat crammed over her face, the scarf pulled anyhow on her shoulder.

He caught at her hand. "I don't want you to go," he said.

She smiled and made her way to the door. "I must catch my train at Paddington, John and the children expect me. It's made me so happy coming to see you. I shall sit in the train tonight and go through it all over again. It's been a great excitement in my quiet, uneventful life, you know. God bless you, and take care of yourself. You don't know how young you've made me feel."

He looked at her white hair and the bronzed, weather-beaten face. "You're taking something away with you that belongs to me," he said. "It's something that has no name, but it means a great deal to me. I wish I knew what it was."

But this time she laughed and would not believe what he was saying. "Now you're just acting," she told him.

"No," he said, "no, that's what you don't understand."

She went from him down the passage and out of the stage door. He heard her footsteps pass along the alley outside his window. He looked at himself in the mirror above the fireplace. He felt tired and listless.

"Monkton?" he called. "Monkton?"

When he had cleaned away his grease paint and washed, his face seemed thin and pale. There were little lines beneath his eyes. His hair was streaked with grey.

Somebody knocked at the door. It was the girl ready dressed, carrying her beret in her hand.

"Who on earth was that old lady with the white hair and the large bosom?" she asked him.

"I don't know," he said, "as a matter of fact I haven't the vaguest idea even now."

"Did she keep you ages, poor darling? What a bore for you."

He made no answer. She followed him to the car waiting in the street. When they came to a block in Piccadilly she looked at him, wondering what he was thinking about.

He was singing absently to himself, his thoughts miles away—

"Why are you so mean to me?
Why are you . . . ?"

He broke off in the middle of a bar. "Tell me," he said suddenly, "that woman—did she seem old to you, really old?"

Angels and Archangels

The Rev. James Hollaway, vicar of St. Swithin's, Upper Chesham Street, was seriously displeased.

For six weeks he had been obliged to leave his parish in the hands of his curate, and now he had returned to find the man had profited by his absence to preach sedition among the masses. In this incredibly short space of time the whole tone of the services had altered, the entire atmosphere of the church had changed. The inhabitants of Mayfair, the titled, the celebrated and the wealthy, who formed the congregation of St. Swithin's, had assisted at mass as usual during the beloved vicar's absence, and had found in his place a raw young man of no attraction, of no breeding, whose very accent was not above reproach.

And this was not all. Instead of officiating humbly, with an attempt at self-effacement, as one who knows he can never step into the shoes of the absent, who is there merely on sufferance, someone to be passed with averted eyes and a patient sigh, this curate had the supreme audacity to imagine himself a person of importance, authorised to attack and to condemn. He stood in the pulpit, small and plain-featured, an unworthy representative of that vicar whose voice had thrilled thousands, and whose eyes had drawn the most reserved of women to the portals of confession.

Then, before the members of the congregation had time to lose themselves in the deeper interests of their own thoughts, the unknown curate had looked down upon them with a gleam of contempt, while coldly and calmly he proceeded to tell them what he thought of them.

The venom of the snake has been described as painful, a torture that is impossible to endure, but the words of the little curate were more poisonous than the serpent's tooth, they seared

deep into the souls of his listeners. The half hour during which
he preached was the most embarrassing and uncomfortable that
has ever been passed under the roof of St. Swithin's. If ever sen-
tences screamed for censorship, it was felt that the sermon of the
Rev. Patrick Dombey should have been erased entirely with a
blue pencil. When he had finished there was not a cheek among
the congregation that was not coloured a bright puce, there was
not a throat that had not been cleared at least ten times. No man
could look his neighbour in the face. There was not a boot that
had not tapped nervously upon the floor, or a glove that had not
been torn in two places by the hot twisted hands of its wearer.

The vicar was to be away six weeks, and this was only the first
instalment. The band of the devout and faithful left St. Swithin's
that Sunday morning like a flock of agitated geese. Needless to
say, they did not return the following week, and one and all they
wrote letters of protest to their beloved vicar.

The Rev. James Hollaway received his mail on the verandah
of the lovely house in Devon where he was recovering from his
attack of influenza.

At first he did not consider the matter as desperate. He even
read some of the letters aloud to his hostess, the fair and faithful
Duchess of Attleborough.

"You see, my dear Norah," he began, with a beautiful little
gesture of resignation, "I cannot even be away for one week—
they clamour for me. What is one to do?"

She bent over his chair and fanned him gently with her handkerchief.

"You are so unselfish, Jim," she told him, "I believe you would
be ready to go back at once, and kill yourself, rather than feel
you are leaving things in the hands of an incompetent curate.
But I forbid you—I insist on keeping you here as my prisoner.
You are still so weak, you need looking after."

He shook his head with the movement she adored. "You are
spoiling me," he said gently.

"You are a child in matters of health," she went on. "It would
be suicide to return. Who is this Patrick Dombey, anyway?"

He shrugged his shoulders contemptuously. "Some Cambridge
fellow recommended to me very highly. Been working in Whitechapel, I believe. I suppose he has ridiculous socialistic ideas. I

was obliged to make use of him, I had no one. You remember Smith, my previous curate? He is in a sanatorium, with his wife. Tubercular, poor fellow, not much hope for him, I'm afraid."

He smiled peacefully as she handed him his morning peach.

"Then you will promise to stay here till you're really well, and leave St. Swithin's to look after itself?" she pleaded.

He caught at her hand and pressed it.

"'O woman, in our hours of ease . . .'" he quoted softly.

The weeks passed, and disquieting rumours continued to reach the vicar in Devon. It appeared that the curate, far from being dismayed at the revolt of the faithful flock, had even encouraged their absence, and had filled the church with followers of his own, men and women from the lowest ranks of life. These people came from the worst quarters of the East End, and, ill fed, ill clad and dirty, sprawled across the pews so lately occupied by the lovely ladies of society.

The glory of St. Swithin's was no more. The famous church in Mayfair, whose incense-laden atmosphere had caused strong hunting peers to weep with emotion, and whose soulful organ and sweet-voiced choirboys against a background of glittering candles had brought the gayest revue actress to her knees, was now given up to a sordid crowd of slum dwellers from Whitechapel who did not even know the meaning of genuflexion.

The vicar, despite his conscience and his clear call to duty, might yet have dismissed the matter temporarily from his mind, confident that on his return all would be well and that, anyway, the rumours were exaggerated, had it not been for a certain column in a prominent newspaper.

"During the absence of the vicar," it ran, "the most extraordinary scenes have been witnessed at St. Swithin's, Upper Chesham Street. The curate in charge, the Rev. Patrick Dombey, has, by a series of brilliant sermons, succeeded in attracting enormous crowds, so much so that last Sunday the queue at the church doors reached as far as Chesham Place.

"Many members of the congregation had walked from the worst slum districts in London to attend the service.

"The usual devotees and supporters, who are such warm admirers of the vicar, did not attend, but their absence was hardly noticeable, for there was barely standing room in the church; the pews and even the aisles were tightly packed. We predict a great future in store for this outspoken young clergyman, whose enthusiastic listeners are not confined to a single class, but to all sorts and conditions of men."

The eyes of the vicar of St. Swithin's narrowed as he read the article, and he flushed under his skin. He laid aside the newspaper and drummed with his fingers on his knee. This cocksure young curate had gone a little too far. He was making an unnecessary bid for popularity, and he would have to be stopped at all costs.

The Rev. James Hollaway rose from his chair in search of his hostess, but first he threw his newspaper carelessly into a wastepaper basket.

"Norah," he said, "I've given in to you too long, but now the time has come for me to leave you. The man must return to his harness, the shepherd must return to his flock."

He smiled down at her, running his fingers through his thick grey hair.

"Tell me," he said, "about the train service from here. I feel that tomorrow evening at the latest . . ."

The vicar leaned back in his chair, his eyes half closed, his finger tips pressed together. The curate stood before him on the hearth rug.

"Before I venture a word of criticism upon your conduct," began the vicar in smooth tones, "I want to remind you that when I left London six weeks ago I was a sick man. One of the best physicians in London had ordered me complete repose. It was only his insistence that persuaded me finally to accept the Duchess of Attleborough's offer of her house. I went, as you know, leaving all my responsibilities in your hands. You came to me at a moment's notice; there was no option but to accept your services. I need hardly say that I trusted you. What happens because of this trust? I am allowed no peace, no attempt to recover my health and strength. I am worried perpetually by my parishioners to return. And here you see me, barely convalescent as yet, obliged to take on my duties once more because you have proved yourself incompetent and worse."

He paused for breath, and the curate seized his opportunity to speak.

"I'm sorry you've been worried," he said. "I regret very much that anything I have said has disturbed your much-needed rest and quiet. At the same time, I am anxious to know how I have failed you. Incompetent, you say? May I know why?"

The vicar cleared his throat. "Certainly," he answered. "I have it on good authority that because of your first sermon, and the objectionable tone you took, and the expressions you used, not one member of the congregation returned the following Sunday. They were shocked; more than this—they were horrified. Superfluous to add that I received countless letters of complaint."

"And yet," said the curate quietly, "St. Swithin's has been overflowing every Sunday since."

The vicar looked mildly amused. "My dear fellow, I'm afraid a certain amount of ridiculous publicity has gone to your head. Of course, as a journalistic 'stunt,' your effort is to be congratulated. Finding the church empty, you were obliged to fill it as best you could. Merely the old parable of the blind and the halt, 'Go out into the highways and hedges,' and so on. I smiled to myself when I heard the news. 'This boy is absurdly young,' I said to the Duchess. 'He has possibly no idea of the harm he is doing. He fancies himself another Savonarola.' But I have the welfare of my church and my people at heart. I could not rest in Devon whilst St. Swithin's was becoming a vaudeville turn and my curate a laughingstock before the world."

The young priest turned white, and dug his nails into his hand.

"I think you have got your facts a little wrong," he said. "I don't know what you mean by a journalistic stunt. I came to St. Swithin's straight from one of the poorest parishes in the East End, where I have seen men and women die from hunger and cold, and stunted pale-faced boys and girls drink to prevent themselves from thinking. I tried not to make them hate me. Little by little they began to trust me, they realised I wasn't afraid. They asked me questions about Christ and I told them the truth. When I stood in the pulpit at St. Swithin's for the first time, it seemed to me that the church was a good imitation of a faked one at Hollywood. The crowd who made up the congregation were excellent supers. The women were very beautiful and the men well fed. I remembered the church in the slums that I had left. It was dark and unattractive. Nobody who came there ever washed. They were eminently suited to a religion that has for its God somebody born in a stable. Your congregation at St. Swithin's belonged to another world. They were there for an hour's amusement before a heavy meal. I took a tremendous pleasure in picturing Christ alive today, and being blackballed by all their clubs . . ."

The vicar struck his fist on the desk. "This is nothing less than blasphemy," he said.

"Oh, you can call it what you like," answered the curate. "That's what your parishioners felt when I told them the truth about themselves. As you said just now, they didn't come back. Their morning had been made too uncomfortable for them to face another. The following Sunday I expected to celebrate mass to an empty church, instead of which, it was filled with men and women from the slums. They had no wish to be flattered or amused. They came because they wanted to be told about God. I see now that I must have made a great mistake; it was foolish of me to speak in that way if I have any ambition to rise in the Church. You were quite right when you called me incompetent. Is there anything more you wish to say to me?"

The vicar rose to his full majestic height and pointed with one finger to the door.

"You had better leave the room before I begin to lose my temper," he said softly. "And I want you to understand one thing. Those ideas of yours are dangerous. One day you will regret them. And I am a very powerful man. You can go now. That's all."

The curate turned and went from the room without a word.

When he had gone, the vicar reached to the cupboard on the wall. He poured himself out a whisky and soda and lit a cigarette. Then he sat down, his chin in his hand, and began to think.

It was a quarter past eleven in the evening. The vicar of St. Swithin's, Upper Chesham Street, was returning in a taxi from the first night at the Frivolity Theatre. The piece, a light com-

edy, had been something of a flop. He had made no attempt to
go round and see Nancy afterwards. He hated to be tactless.

As the taxi drew into Lower Mallop Street, he remembered
that number 19 was the address of his curate, Patrick Dombey.
With a half interest he glanced up at the building and was
aware of a light in the front room, partially blurred by a thin
curtain. He supposed the fellow read socialistic tracts late into
the night. As the taxi drew past, he glanced once more at the
covered window. This time a shadow was reflected on the blind,
the shadow of a woman. For a moment the vicar remained motionless. Then he tapped on the glass to the driver. Three minutes later he was ringing the bell of number 19, a strange smile
of triumph upon his lips.

The door was opened by the curate himself. He seemed a little
shaken at the sight of the vicar.

"Is anything wrong at St. Swithin's?" he asked.

The Rev. James Hollaway brushed past him into the passage.

"No," he said. "The fact is, I was returning from the theatre,
and it struck me as I passed here that perhaps I had been a little
hasty with you this morning. I am not a man to bear malice.
Could we have a chat in your room?"

The curate hesitated a moment before replying. "I have somebody there," he said quietly.

"Oh! Pity. Couldn't you send them away?"

"Not very well."

Before he could be prevented, the vicar had glanced through
the crack in the door. He saw a woman standing in the corner of
the room. She appeared to have been crying. The tears had
blotched her make-up. She was cheaply overdressed. There could
be no doubt as to her profession.

The vicar raised his eyebrows and closed the door gently.
"Rather a late visitor," he murmured. Then, as the curate made
no reply, he laid his hand upon his shoulder. "I think you owe
me some explanation for this, Dombey," he said.

The young priest looked into his face.

"I have told her she can stay here tonight," he said steadily.
"She's frightened; she doesn't know where to go. She is a thief,
you see. She isn't much good at it, either. She tried to steal a
watch from an old man in Piccadilly. She was nearly caught. She

took hold of my arm in a desperate attempt to save herself. She was shaking all over with terror, and it was impossible for me to betray her. I pretended she was with me—I brought her back here. I don't believe she'll ever steal anything again. If I'd given her up they would have sent her to prison; she'd have become a hardened criminal in time. No—I'm not going to send her away."

The vicar whistled softly to himself. "My dear fellow," he began, "don't bother to tell me all this. After all, I've been young myself once. I know what temptation is. We are human, are we not? But you cannot possibly keep her here any longer. Somebody may have seen her."

The curate flushed all over his face. "You deliberately misunderstand," he said. "You know I've not brought her here for myself. She's like a frightened little cat that has lost its sense. Haven't you any idea of common humanity?"

The vicar's face hardened, his eyes narrowed. "If you persist in lying, I see myself forced by my conscience and my duty towards God to treat this matter seriously. You have committed a grave offence, Dombey. Have you anything further to say?"

The curate shrugged his shoulders. "You will be able to make out an excellent case against me, won't you? You realise that my conscience won't allow me to betray this girl as a thief. Therefore I stand convicted. Good-bye to ambition and all that. That's what you mean, I suppose? Rather an ugly story—the young curate and the fallen woman. No, I've got nothing more to say."

The vicar turned and opened the front door of the lodging house. "I shall do what I believe to be right," he said slowly. "You are suspended from further duty, Dombey. This is a matter for the bishop alone."

Ten minutes afterwards he was back in the library of his own house. He lay in his chair, his eyes closed, a faint smile playing upon his lips.

Suddenly the telephone rang at his elbow.

"Hullo," he said. "Yes, Nancy, my dear, speaking. . . . Oh! don't be absurd. You were wonderful, quite wonderful. . . . I didn't come round because I feared a crowd. . . . Yes, the play needs tightening up, of course. . . . Depressed, you say? What utter nonsense! . . . Unhappy? . . . My dearest child, is there anything I can do? . . . What, now? Isn't it rather late?" He glanced at his clock. The hands pointed to five minutes to midnight. "Nancy, you naughty little girl, you know you can get anything you want. . . . Stop crying at once, dear child. . . . Yes, I'll come round right away. . . ."

St. Swithin's was itself again once more. Gone were the slum crowds who had debased its holy atmosphere for six weeks. Gone were the rough-tongued men and women, the ill-fed, unwashed children. Gone was the plain-featured curate who had brought shame upon the house of God. Once more the waxen lilies breathed a pure air, once more the deep-toned organ throbbed its message to the rafters. The pews were filled with the devout, with the very faithful. The sweet-voiced choirboys swayed in time to the music. The candles glittered, and the incense floated upon the air.

When the vicar leaned from his pulpit it seemed as though he waited for applause. The shepherd had returned to the flock. He spread out his arms, he threw back his magnificent head, and spoke to them in the soft tones they loved.

"For there has been a wolf amongst you," he told them; "there has been a wolf amongst the lambs."

Tears came into the eyes of his listeners. They remembered the hard-voiced curate and his bitter sayings, they remembered his evil-smelling followers from the slums.

"My house has been called a house of prayer," cried the vicar, "but he has made it a den of thieves."

How appropriate were the words he used. How beautiful were the sentiments he expressed. Later, as he chanted before the high altar, it seemed to the vicar that his very voice had purified the air. His beloved congregation were with him again. There was a duchess in the front pew, an earl and a couple of actresses immediately behind.

The slum dwellers had left no trace of their lamentable presence. St. Swithin's and her worshippers remained as symbols of eternity.

"Therefore, with Angels and Archangels, and all the glorious company of Heaven, we praise and magnify Thy Holy Name . . ."

Indiscretion

I wonder how many people's lives are ruined by a moment's indiscretion? The wrong word at the wrong time—and then finish to all their dreams. They have to go on living with their tongues bitten a second too late. No use calling back the spoken word. What is said is said.

I know of three people who have been made to suffer because of a chance sentence flung into the air. One of them was myself; I lost my job through it. The other fellow lost his illusions. And the woman . . . well, I guess she did not have much left to lose, anyway. Maybe she lost her one chance of security. I have not seen either of them since. The curt, typewritten letter came from him a week later. I packed up then and came away from London, leaving the shreds of my career in the wastepaper basket. In less than three months I read in a weekly rag that he was claiming a divorce. The whole thing was so needless, too. A word from me—a word from her. And all through the sordid little street that runs between Shaftesbury Avenue and Leicester Square.

We stood at the door of the office, he and I. It was icy, it was December. I had a cold in the head, and I did not want to think about Christmas. He came out of his private office and gave me a genial clap on the shoulder.

"You're no advertisement for the time of the year," he said. "Come out and have a bite of lunch."

I thanked him. It is not every day, or every Christmas for that matter, that one's chief broadcasts his invitations. We went to his favourite restaurant in the Strand. I felt better once I had a plateful of beef before me, listening to his easy laugh, watching his familiarity with the waiter. He had the audacity to place a sprig of holly in his buttonhole.

"Look here, chief," I said. "What's the big idea? Are you going to play Santa Claus at a kids' party?"

He laughed loudly, a spot of gravy at the corner of his mouth.

"No," he said, "I am going to be married." I made the usual retort.

"I'm not joking," he went on. "I'm telling you the truth. They all know at the office. I told 'em before I left this morning. Kept it a secret up till now because I didn't want a scene. Aren't you going to congratulate me?"

I watched his smug, self-satisfied expression.

"Hell!" I said. "You don't know what I think about women."

He laughed again, his mood was ridiculous.

"This is different," he told me, "this is the real thing. I've found her at last—the only girl. You know, I'm fond of you, my dear fellow, I'm glad you came along to lunch."

I made some sort of noise of sympathy.

"It's all very sudden, of course," he said, "but I believe in that. I like everything cut and dried. None of your hanging about. We're going to Paris this evening, while this afternoon there will be a short ceremony at a registry office." He pulled out his watch. "In exactly an hour's time," he said, "I shall be a married man."

"Where's your bride?" I asked.

"Packing." He smiled foolishly. "I only decided on this trip yesterday evening. You'll have a tremendous amount of work at the office, I'm afraid, with the Christmas rush."

He leant forward, patronising, confidential. "I have a great deal of faith in you," he said. "I've watched you these few months. You're going to do big things. I don't mind saying"—he lowered his voice as though people listened and cared—"I don't mind saying that I shall depend on you in the future to work like blazes. You'd like a rise, wouldn't you? Might think of getting married yourself?"

I saw his friendly beam without emotion, and remembered with cynicism a proverb about "a little something makes the whole world kin." I thought of a word that would fit. "That's extremely good of you," I said, "but I shan't marry."

"You're a cynic," he said. "You've no illusions. You see all women in the same pattern. I'm twice your age and look at me—the happiest man alive."

"Perhaps I've been unlucky," I said. "Maybe I've struck the wrong type."

"Ah!" he said. "A bad picker. That's fatal. I flatter myself"—he opened his mouth to admit a forkload of food—"that I have chosen well. You young men are so bitter about life," he went on, "no romance."

Romance! The word conjured a vision in my mind of a dark night, with the rain falling, and a small face turned to me, weeping, her hat pulled over her eyes. The last taxi driving away from the Empire Cinema; men and women in evening dress, hurrying, bent under umbrellas.

"Romance!" I said. "That's funny." Funnier still the way I caught hold of one word. It would have been so easy to let it go.

I thought for a moment, turning it over in my head. "The last time I heard that word," I said, "was from the lips of a girl. I'm not likely to forget it in a hurry."

He glanced at me enquiringly, surprised at the note in my voice.

"More bitterness?" he suggested. "Why don't you tell me about it? You're such a silent fellow, you never give yourself away."

"Oh! It's a dull story," I said, "scarcely worth listening to! Besides, you're going to be married in an hour's time."

"Come on," he laughed, "out with it."

I shrugged my shoulders, yawning slightly, and reached for a cigarette.

"I ran up against her in Wardour Street," I said. "Queer sort of place for an adventure, if you come to think of it. Almost too obvious, perhaps. It's scarcely a beat of mine, anyway. I'm a retiring sort of a chap, as you know, don't go out much. Hate meeting people, and that kind of thing. Never go to theatres, never go to parties. Can't afford it, for that matter. My life is spent between the office and my rooms in Kensington. I read a lot, hang around museums on Saturdays. Let's admit it, I'm damn dull! But the point is I scarcely know the West End at all. So Wardour Street was unfamiliar to me. About six months ago I came back from the office feeling fed up with the world. You know how one gets, nervy, irritable, thoroughly dissatisfied with life in general.

"I hated my rooms suddenly, and I felt that any moment my landlady would come in and tell me about her sister who was 'expecting' again. It occurred to me out of the blue, then, this idea to go to the West End. I took the tube to Leicester Square.

"There's an organ that throbs a sentimental tune, and when you're soaked with this and rubbing knees with your next-door neighbour, they fling a picture on the screen calculated to send you soft inside. That night I was in the right mood. They kept on giving close-ups of the blonde heroine; she seemed to be staring right at me. The usual theme, of course. Lovely innocent girl in love with handsome hero, and the dark blackguard stepping in and trying to ruin her. You're kept on tenterhooks as to whether he ruins her or whether he doesn't. He doesn't, of course, and she finishes with the handsome hero. But even then it leaves you unsatisfied. I sat through the show twice, and stumbled out of my seat at twelve o'clock still living in a land of make-believe.

"When I got outside it was raining. Through a haze I saw people crouching under umbrellas, whisking into taxis. I saw all this as a dream; in my mind I was watching the blonde heroine shut the opening of that tent in the desert. Turning up my collar, I began to walk, my head low, hating the rain.

"So I found myself in Wardour Street. I remember glancing up at the name on the corner. A few minutes later somebody bumped into me. It was a girl. Thinly dressed, I noticed, not carrying an umbrella.

"'I beg your pardon,' I said. She looked up at me, a little white face under a hat pulled low over her brow. Then to my horror she burst into tears. 'I'm most frightfully sorry,' I began. 'Have I hurt you? Is there anything I can do?' She made as if to brush past me, and put her hands to her eyes. 'It's nothing,' she said, choking over her words, 'it was stupid of me.' She looked to the right and left, standing on the edge of the pavement, apparently in some hesitation as to which way she should go. The rain was streaming down, and her little black coat was clinging to her. Half consciously I remembered the blonde heroine of the picture I had just seen. The tears were still running on her cheeks. I saw her make some attempt to brush them away.

" 'Gosh! How pathetic,' I thought, 'how utterly rotten. And here am I dissatisfied with my life for no reason.' Acting on an impulse, I touched her arm. 'Look here,' I said, 'I know it's no business of mine. I've no right to speak to you at all. But—is anything the matter? Can I help you? It's such a filthy night . . .' She pulled out a wretched little end of handkerchief and began to blow her nose.

" 'I don't know what to do,' she said, 'I don't know what to do.' She was crying again. 'I've never been to London before,' she said, 'I've come up from Shropshire. I was to be married—and there's no address. There's nothing—he's left me. I don't know where to go. There's a man been following me,' she went on timidly, glancing over her shoulder, 'he tried to speak to me twice. He was horrid. I didn't understand . . .'

" 'Good heavens!' I thought, she was scarcely more than a child.

" 'You can't stand here,' I said. 'Don't you know of anywhere? Have you no friends? Isn't there a Home you could go to?' She shook her head, her mouth worked queerly at the corners. 'It's all right,' she said, 'don't bother.' It was no use, I couldn't let her go, not with that frightened gleam in her eyes, in the pouring rain.

" 'Listen,' I said. 'Will you trust me to look after you—just for the moment? Will you come and have something to eat? Then we will try to find a place for you to go.' She looked up at me for a moment, straight in my eyes, and then she nodded her head gravely. 'I think I can trust you,' she said. She said this in such a way—I don't know, it seemed to go straight to my heart. I felt very old and very wise, and she was such a child.

"She put her hand on my arm, still a little scared, a little doubting. I smiled at her. 'That's the way,' I said. We turned back again down Wardour Street. There was a crowd of people in Lyons. She clung tight to my arm, bewildered by them. She chose eggs and bacon and coffee. She ate as though she was starving.

" 'Is this your first meal today?' I asked. She flushed and bit her lips, ashamed.

" 'Yes,' she said. I could have cut my tongue out.

" 'Supposing you tell me,' I said, 'just what it is that has happened.'

"The food had pulled her together, she had lost some of her shyness; she was no longer tearful, hysterical.

"'I was to be married,' she told me. 'Back in Shropshire he seemed to be so fond of me, so attentive to me and my mother. Why, he was quite a gentleman. We live on a little farm, Mother and I, and my sister. It's quiet, you know, away from the big towns. I used to take the produce to Tonsbury on market days. That's where I met him. He was a traveller from a firm in London. He had a little car, too. Nothing poor or shabby about him —constantly with his hand in his pocket. He was always coming to Tonsbury for his firm, and then he would visit me. Then he started courting me—he was ever so handsome. It was all so proper, too. He asked Mother for her consent, and the date and everything was arranged.

"'Last Sunday he was up at home as usual, laughing and teasing, saying how soon we would have a home of our own. He was to give up travelling and get a settled job on the firm, and we were to live in London. He insisted on the wedding being in London, too, which was the one upsetting thing, as my mother and sister couldn't leave home.

"'Yesterday was to have been my wedding day.' I saw she was ready to burst into tears again. I leant across the table and patted her hand.

"'There, there,' I said stupidly.

"'We motored up on Tuesday in his little car,' she went on, 'and we came to London yesterday. He had taken rooms at some hotel.' Her words trailed off; I saw she was looking at her plate.

"'And the blackguard's left you,' I said gently.

"'He said we were to be married,' she whispered. 'I thought it was all right.' The tears sprang in her eyes. 'He went this morning, early, before I was awake. The people at the hotel were cruel—I found out then that it was a bad place.' She fumbled for her handkerchief, but I gave her mine.

"'I couldn't go back there, I daren't ask them for a thing,' she told me, 'and I've been looking for him all day, but I know it's no use now. How can I go home? What will they say? What will they think?' She buried her face in her hands. Poor little thing! She couldn't have been more than eighteen. I tried to keep my voice as gentle as possible.

"'Have you any money?' I said.

"'I've seven and eightpence,' she said. 'He told me I wouldn't need much.'

"I felt that this was the most impossible situation that had ever happened to anyone at any time. And there she sat looking at me, the tears in her eyes, waiting for me to suggest something.

"Suddenly I became very matter-of-fact. 'You had better make shift at my lodgings for tonight,' I said, 'and in the morning I'll buy you a ticket and pack you off to Shropshire.'

"'Oh, I couldn't,' she said awkwardly, 'I don't know you.'

"'Nonsense,' I said firmly. 'You will be perfectly safe with me.'

"We had some slight argument, of course, but finally I persuaded her.

"She was tired, too. I took her home in a taxi—she nearly fell asleep with her head on my shoulder. My landlady had gone to bed; nobody saw us come in. There was a bit of a fire left in the grate. The girl crouched in front of it, spreading her hands to the feeble flame. I remember looking down on her and wondering how I should explain her presence to the landlady in the morning.

"It was then that she looked up at me from the fire, and she smiled without fear for the first time. 'If I wasn't so unhappy,' she said, 'this would be like a romance, wouldn't it?'

"Romance! Funny. It was you saying the word 'romance' just now, chief, that brought this story back to me."

I squashed my cigarette in the ashtray.

"Well, go on," he said. "It's not finished yet, is it?"

"That was the finish of the romance," I said.

"How d'you mean?" he said. "Did she go back to Shropshire?"

I laughed. "That girl never saw Shropshire in her life," I told him. "I woke next morning and she had gone, of course. She had my pocketbook with all my worldly goods."

He stared at me in amazement. "Good Lord." He whistled, blowing out his cheeks. "Then you mean to say she was deceiving you the whole time? There wasn't a word of truth in her story?"

"Not a word!"

"But didn't you put the police on her tracks? Didn't you do something, make some effort?"

I shook my head. "Even if they had found her, I doubt if I could have legitimately retrieved my worldly goods."

"You mean you suspected her story before you left Lyons?" he asked.

"No," I said. "I didn't suspect her once."

"I don't understand," he said. "If she was nothing but a common swindler, why not inform the police?"

I sighed wearily. "You see, chief, the point is I didn't walk the streets all night, nor did I sleep on the sitting-room sofa . . ."

For a few minutes we sat in silence. He looked thoughtful, he stroked his chin. "You were a damn fool, and that's all there is to it," he said. "Ever go back to Wardour Street?"

"No," I answered, "never before and never again. My only visit."

"Extraordinary how you were so easily mistaken," he said. "I can spot that type of girl a mile off. Of course, it's the sort of thing to make you steer clear of women, I agree. But they're not all like that, my dear fellow—not all." He smiled. "Sometimes you find a really genuine case of a young, unsophisticated girl, with no money, let down by some blackguard."

"For instance?" I enquired.

"As a matter of fact, I was thinking of my own girl," he confessed, "the girl who has consented to become my wife this afternoon. When I met her six weeks ago she was quite new to London. Left an orphan quite suddenly, poor kid, without a bean. Very good family, she's shown me letters and photos and things. She was making a wretched living as a typist in Birmingham, and her swine of an employer made love to her. She ran away, scared to death. Thank heaven I came along. Someone would have got hold of her. First time I met her she had twisted her ankle going down that filthy moving stairway on the Piccadilly tube. However, that's not the point." He broke off in the middle of his speech and called for the bill. "If you could see her," he began again. "She's the loveliest thing."

Into his eyes crept that blue suffused haze of the man who has not yet loved, but will have loved by midnight.

"I guess I'm the happiest man alive," he said, "she's far too good for me." The bill was paid, we rose and left the room.

"Tell you what," he said, "come and see us off by the four o'clock train at Victoria. The good old Christmas spirit, eh?"

And because I was idle, because I was bored, because there was no reason to do it at all, I consented.

"I'll be there," I said.

I remember taking the tube to Victoria, and, not finding a seat, swinging from side to side, clinging to a strap.

I remember standing in a queue to buy a platform ticket, and being jostled by a crowd of pushing, feverish people. I remember walking senselessly up and down a platform, peering into the windows of first-class carriages, yelled at by porters. I remember wondering why I had come at all. Then suddenly I saw him, his big, red, cheerful face, smiling at me from the closed window of a Pullman car. He put up his hand and waved, shouting something through the glass I could not hear. He turned and moved down the car, coming to the open door, at the entrance.

"Thought you'd given us the miss," he shouted. "Good boy—turned up after all."

He pulled the girl forward, laughing self-consciously, scarlet with pride and satisfaction.

"Here's the bride," he said. "I want you two to be great friends. Show yourself, my darling."

I stood motionless with my hat in my hand. "A happy Christmas to you," I said. She leant from the window staring at me.

Her husband gazed at us both with a quick, puzzled frown. "I say, have you two met before?" he said.

Then she laughed affectionately, and, putting her arms round his neck, she flung into the air her silly little gesture of bravado, mistress of the situation, but speaking without forethought, reckless, a shade too soon. The guard waved his little green flag.

"But, of course, I know your face," she said. "Didn't we run up against each other once in Wardour Street?"

Fairy Tale

The room was hardly more than a garret. High up, at the very top of the building, there was nothing between it and the sky but a thin roof, and the walls were all outside walls, exposed to every breath of air. There was one large window on the left, and through this could be seen the ugly chimney pots and the slate roofs of other houses, stretching forever, as far as the eye could reach, with no trees to break the monotony, and a ceaseless stream of smoke rising from the chimneys into the leaden sky.

Because of its nearness to the roof, in summer the heat was unbearable, but now it was winter, and even with the window tightly shut the icy-cold air from outside penetrated the room. The atmosphere was freezing, even the walls and the bare boards of the floor were chilled—it was as if the room could never be warm again, not until the spring came once more and the sun shone.

Opposite the window, beside the door leading into the tiny bedroom, was a fireplace where no fire was laid. A little bundle of sticks stood in the grate, waiting their turn, kept preciously until the cold should prove beyond human endurance, when they would be kindled two by two, the poor flame showing a pretence at heat.

The walls of the room were brown, and high up by the ceiling large discoloured stains marked where the damp had forced an entrance.

The furniture was scanty. A table in the middle of the room, rickety on three legs, and two chairs, while near the fireplace was a large mat worn threadbare and a bench which seemed a rough imitation of a sofa, covered as it was by an old rug and boasting a faded velvet cushion. Close to the door leading to the landing there was a cupboard half open, and on the shelf stood a loaf of bread.

From the bedroom came the sound of a woman coughing, irritating, persistent, a dry hard cough repeated at regular intervals, and this would be followed by a sigh of exasperation, suggesting mingled fatigue and distress. Once she raised her voice and called to the room: "Aren't you back yet? Is there nobody there?" And she would realise by the silence that the room was empty, and then she would cough again. Because of her coughing she did not hear the sound of a low knocking at the door, and not until the door opened and someone stood inside the room could she have realised that she was no longer alone.

"Is that you?" she called. "Are you back at last?" The intruder waited a moment before he answered. He was an old man with a long shabby coat reaching almost to his ankles. His hands, wrapped in thick woollen mittens, were folded over his full protruding belly.

He shrugged his shoulders, passing his tongue over his lips. "It is I, madam," he said, turning his head in her direction, "'ave you not been expecting me all the day?" He smiled as he heard her stifled exclamation. "No, your 'usband he 'as not returned," he said, "maybe he will not come for a long while. But that makes not the leetlest bit of difference to me, no. You know why I 'ave come."

He waited, and then her voice came to him, tearful, hurried, with a suggestion of fear.

"I tell you I haven't got the money. It's no use. Even if you stand there and threaten me with murder, I can't give it to you. Why can't you wait—why can't you give us a little while longer? It can't mean much to you—to wait. He will be home soon, he may give it to you then. But I can't do anything, weak and helpless here."

The man's eyes narrowed, he glanced around the room as though seeking some solution, he even peered into the cupboard, bare save for the loaf of bread.

"I cannot wait any more," he said harshly. "I tell you last time, today was the limit of my patience. This morning the money was due—out of the goodness of my heart I wait till now.

How do you think I am to live? I must 'ave now what you owe. I do not go away till you give it me."

"But wouldn't I keep my promise if I had the money?" she cried. "There is nothing here, I tell you, nothing in either of the rooms. I haven't eaten all day—there's a stale loaf in the cupboard for my husband when he returns. What can I do? In bed, sick—"

The man spread out his hands. "I could let those rooms for double the sum you owe to me. Even now there are people ready to pay me, who wait only to take possession. I cannot any more afford to give the charity to paupers. You will either give me that money or I put you out in the street."

He could hear her crying in the adjoining room.

"You wouldn't do that?" she cried. "Not even the most brutal of men would act in such a way. I'm helpless here. For pity's sake wait until my husband returns."

"Your husband will not pay me," said the man, "he is a gambler, a wastrel, a good-for-nothing. He plays cards while you cry for food. Why should I be kinder to you than he? No—I will not wait. I shall call my son to aid me—we shall put these sticks of furniture into the street and you too—on the doorstep. There you can wait for your husband." He stood on the threshold of the bedroom, watching her eyes.

"Get up," he said, "it is all pretence, this illness. It is part of your deceit. Put on your clothes."

There was quiet for a minute. Then she stood beside the bed, a thin shawl over her shoulders, leaning against the framework to give herself strength to stand.

She spoke pleadingly, the terror rising in her voice. "No, no! You cannot do this, you cannot! My husband will kill you—you're a devil, wicked, inhuman!" She was choked by a paroxysm of coughing.

"Put on your clothes," he said.

She leant back, panting, exhausted. "Stop!" she said. "I've lied to you. I have some money. But nobody knows—I haven't told a soul, not even my husband. Because if he had known he would have gambled it away. So I kept it from him, hidden, my last wretched little stock, saved for such a moment as this. I've prayed to God the moment would never come. But you've won—you've beaten me."

He did not move; he suspected she was lying. "Show me your hiding place," he said.

"Go to the fireplace," she told him. "You will find a loose board, under the grate. Rock it slowly from side to side and it will come away in your hands. Feel down into the hole and you will touch a small wooden box. The money is in the box."

Still incredulous, shrugging his shoulders, the man obeyed her directions and, kneeling beside the fireplace, he felt for the loose tile as she had told him. After working at it for a moment it came away and, uttering an exclamation of surprise, he put in his hand and drew out a wooden box.

"You 'ave spoken the truth for once," he said. "How does it open?" He turned the box over in his hands.

"Bring it in to me," she said, her voice shaking. "I have a little key that will fit it."

He went into the bedroom. There was a pause while she struggled with the lock.

"It must be jammed somehow," she began; and then she called out in horror, realising the truth. "Good God!" she cried. "The lock is broken—it's been forced open. There is no money inside. It's gone—stolen!"

The sound of his voice rose above hers, furious and high-pitched. "You lie!" he screamed. "There was never money there. You wish to play me a trick—you think to deceive me. Liar, liar!"

"I swear I told the truth!" she said in terror. "My husband must have discovered it—he has stolen the money!"

The man came out of the bedroom, his face scarlet, shaking his fist in the air.

"You go out into the street," he shouted. "This is the end; you go now, this minute. By force I will make you—I will fetch my son!"

He flung open the door, crashed it behind him. From where she lay, exhausted, across the bed, she could hear the sound of his footsteps clattering down the stairs. He must have been interrupted halfway, because there rose the clamour of voices in argument, the noise of men shouting, and then a sudden silence.

"What is it?" she cried. "What is it?"

A light footstep sounded on the landing outside, then the door opened once more and a man came into the room. He wore a coat buttoned up to his chin, and a cap on the back of his head. Round his throat was knotted a rough scarf. He came in on tiptoe, a smile on his face.

"What's the matter?" he said. "I could hear you calling as I came up the stairs. Is your cough worse?"

Her only answer was a torrent of weeping.

"You've stolen my money," she sobbed. "Like a thief you took it, never telling me, creeping out of the house. And there's nothing left, nothing. He's been up here, threatening me. It's the end. There's only the streets left for us now!"

Still he smiled, his eyes dancing. "Yes, I took the money," he said. "I was a thief, I stole it. Aren't you going to forgive me?"

He heard her sigh, he heard her move restlessly.

"What have you done with it?" she asked wearily.

"I took it weeks ago," he confessed. "I put it in a lottery."

He rubbed his hands in delight as he listened to her exclamation of dismay.

"But you are mad!" she cried. "You have no sense of anything at all. Don't you realise it was the only thing that stood between us and starvation?"

"I know," he said. "I took a gamble—and I lost. It's no use going over it all now. I've just been talking to the old chap below. We can stay for tonight, so you needn't worry any more. Tomorrow something may turn up—who knows?" He looked through the bedroom door, laughing at her.

"You're hopeless," she said, "hopeless."

"I know I am," he said, "and you don't mind, really, do you? You wouldn't have me any different?"

He must have made her smile, for she answered: "No, I wouldn't change you for anyone in the world."

He came back into the room and stood looking about him as though it were strange to him.

"D'you know what we're going to do?" he said. "We're going to play a game of pretence. Somehow this last night has got to be passed, and as there's nothing to eat but a stale loaf, and it's too cold to sleep, it's not going to be very cheerful. So we'll pretend to ourselves we've won the lottery—and I'll make up for you a story of all the things we would do."

He cocked his head on one side, waiting for her reply.

"You're a boy," she told him; "you're nothing but a little child."

"Very well," he said, "but you've got to listen to my story."

He tiptoed across the room and threw open the window. He leant far out, beckoning down into the street. Then he drew back —he listened—but she had not heard. He opened the door onto the passage and waited.

"What are you doing?" she called.

"I'm just thinking how to start my story," he said. As he spoke he moved aside from the door, and with his finger on his lips he admitted some half dozen men into the room. They trod softly, in stockinged feet, their arms laden with packages, and as he moved amongst them, signing directions, he continued his rapid monologue to the bedroom.

"I think we'd begin with a fire, don't you?" he called, and as he pointed to the grate a man knelt down and proceeded to stack the fireplace with logs, and lumps of coal, and paper, to which he put a match. "Yes, we'd begin with a fire, and soon it would be burning brightly, throwing tongues of light onto the ceiling, filling the room with warmth. And as there is something so luxurious about a fire, we would think to ourselves that we ought to do away with our sticks of furniture and arrange the room in a new way."

While he was speaking the men, following his orders, carried the rickety table and chairs, the poor bench, the cupboard, the torn mat, out onto the landing, and brought back with them, swiftly, as though by magic, the things he was describing to her.

"At last we could afford some curtains," he said, "heavy blue velvet curtains, reaching to the floor. The pole is there all ready, it doesn't take a moment to hang them in place.

"And we'd want a blue carpet to match. You know, those carpets that cover a whole room, and when you step onto it your feet seem to sink right into it. We'd lay that right across the floor, and it would be exactly the same colour as the curtains. Then—well, let's admit it—we just couldn't bear to live any longer with these stained, brown walls. It takes a long while to have the room repapered, we'd have to make shift with something. I have it! Screens. We'd place screens against the walls, right round the room, and they would keep out the draught too. Don't you think it a good idea?"

And the curtains were hung, and the carpet was laid, and the screens were standing against the walls.

"Next we'd have to think about the furniture," he said. "I rather fancy one of those long, low divans next to the fireplace. You would be able to rest there, you see, propped up by cushions, and I should sit in a large armchair opposite you, so as to be near whenever you wanted anything. At the end you would have a bookcase packed tight with books, close against the screen, and whenever you cared to read you would only have to stretch out an arm. Do you like that? Aren't you pleased?"

Like a miracle, the room was being transformed under his directions, and he stood rocking on his heels, pointing here, pointing there.

"I must say I am pleased with our dining-room table," he said. "It's a genuine antique, and so are the chairs that go with it. We've got rather a superior dresser as well. You once told me you would love to have a dresser full of pots and pans.

"The thing that worried me most was the lighting. You see, up in this garret we aren't fitted with plugs for electricity. We haven't any gas either. D'you know what I think would be the best thing to have—in fact, the only way to get over it at all? Old standing lamps, and instead of electric light we'll have candles. You've no idea how nice it's going to look. There won't be a glare at all, but a soft shaded light. We'll have one lamp in a corner of the room and another by your divan. And on the dining-room table we'll have six tall candles.

"I tell you there's never been such a room as this." He had taken off his cap and coat by now; the scarf, too, was gone. Underneath he had been wearing a new suit of clothes. He ran his fingers through his hair.

"We'll hang a mirror over the mantelpiece, on the nail where we used to stick last year's calendar," he said, "and for ornaments—upon my soul, I don't think we can do better than a Dresden shepherd and shepherdess."

He stepped back from the fireplace, he glanced at the whole effect—the room was furnished.

"Nothing matters, now, but the fact that I'm ravenously hungry," he said. "We shall have to set the table for dinner. Plates, knives and forks, glasses. I don't mind admitting our dinner service is pretty good. What are we going to eat, though, that's the main thing. I'd like—I'd like—by Jove, what would I like? Roast chicken? Any objection to roast chicken? No, passed, settled. Right, we'll have roast chicken. It smells good, it smells damned good. And the vegetables aren't so dusty, either.

"I think we might pile the table high with fruit—peaches, grapes, tangerines, bananas, every sort of fruit under the sun. We'll drink champagne, of course. Let's be gluttons while we can. And—I say, you said just now I was a child. Well, would you think it terrible if I went on being a child and we had crackers? After all, it is a sort of a fête, and we ought to celebrate. Besides, they look so jolly on the table. There, I don't know that I can think of anything else.

"Wait a minute, keep quiet. I may have forgotten the most important thing of all. Yes, I knew it. The most important. We've just got to fill the room with flowers. Wherever there's any space we'll put flowers. Roses are still your favourite, aren't they? There are so many roses in the room that I'm practically suffocated. It's like a garden that will never come true."

He paused, he looked around the room once more. No, there was nothing to add now. Everything had been arranged and placed as he had described. The room was ready for her. He nodded to the men, and they went from the door gently, on tiptoe, just as they had come in.

"That's the end of the story," he said softly. For a moment there was no answer, and he heard her catch her breath, as though she would prevent herself from crying.

"It was beautiful," she said at last, "beautiful. How did you think of it? Did it all just come into your mind as you said it? I feel as though I'd woken up from a lovely dream. And I wanted the dream to go on—and on. It was cruel of you in a way, wasn't it?"

"Perhaps it was," he said.

"Your voice sounded happy and gay as you were telling me,"

she said, "and I pictured you standing in the middle of that bare, lonely room, your hands in your pockets, your collar turned up because of the cold. I was wondering, would it be very terrible to light those few sticks and make a tiny, tiny fire?"

"They couldn't make any difference to this temperature," he said, his eyes laughing.

"No," she sighed. "I suppose not." She was silent for a moment, then she said: "Are you frightfully hungry?"

"Frightfully," he nodded.

"What about the remains of the loaf of bread?" she asked him.

"I shan't eat anything unless you come and join me," he told her.

"It's so freezing in there," she said, "and I'm so empty. I want food so much that the bread will choke me after the story you've been telling me."

She was ready to break down again.

"Please come," he said, "even if the room is cold, even if there's nothing but half a loaf of bread and we're starving, and miserable, and the old chap is going to fling us into the streets, can't we be happy together?"

He waited, and then he said: "Besides, you haven't forgiven me yet for stealing your money and throwing it away in a lottery."

Then her voice called to him, gentle, tired: "I'll come."

He could hear her getting out of bed and fumbling for her shoes, the bed shaking slightly as she leant against it.

"D'you want any help?" he asked.

"I think I can manage," she said. "I didn't realise I should feel so weak. And I'm frightened of the cold. Shall I get a terrible shock when I come in?"

"I'm afraid you will," he said.

She sighed, he heard her walk slowly across the bedroom towards the door.

"Wait a minute," he said. "Tell me first you aren't angry with me any more! Tell me you've forgiven me?"

He heard her laugh helplessly.

"You know I've forgiven you," she said.

And she came into the room.

The Closing Door

He felt as though he had become part of the room. It was too well known to him. The soft, heavy carpet and these deep leather chairs, even the folds of the curtains discreetly hiding the light of the day—perhaps the room was furnished as a reminder that life was already a dead thing, waving a hand in farewell behind the closed door. The furniture had been chosen with care, calculated to soothe the weary body and ease the jaded mind.

He lay back in one of the deep chairs and gazed steadily at the electric fire. He had only to shut his eyes and surely he would sleep soon, surely he would be carried away to some unconscious place of slumber, where there were no thoughts, no work, no love. The room was silent too. The taxis hooting outside in Harley Street and the distant traffic rumbling in Marylebone Road; they belonged to another era and another time.

Hanging on the wall above the fireplace was a portrait in oils of a child in a rose-coloured frock with dark curls hanging down her back. Her hat was slung off the back of her head and attached to her neck by a piece of ribbon. Wherever he sat in the room he could not escape her eyes, or the challenge in them, or the bright unnatural smile.

He hated the picture and the staring child, yet he knew it was a friend, an old friend, and they were all bound together, he, the child, the deep chairs and the room, they could none of them escape. Automatically he stretched out his hand and found a copy of *Punch* within his reach. There was something of horror in the realisation that *Punch* had always been there, had never been anywhere else. *Punch* was there for eternity. The room knew this too, the room mocked him for his knowledge but shared his horror with a strange sympathy. "We are here to make things easier for you," whispered the room, "easier for you. Lean back and relax, that's the main thing, to relax."

But the little girl in the picture swung backwards, forwards, backwards, forwards, her cheeks the same colour as her frock, and "Look at me," she shouted, "look at me."

He settled deeper in his chair, his head sunk in his shoulders, his fingers restlessly turning the pages of *Punch,* whose jokes had been stamped upon his mind so long.

Like clockwork, as his eyes fell upon the features of an ex-Prime Minister caricatured as a farmyard animal, the door opened and the butler stood upon the threshold of the room, his voice toneless yet gentle, as though he knew: "Will you come this way, sir?"

He rose at once and, crossing the room, he followed the butler along the carpeted passage to the other room at the end, with the mahogany door.

Now the butler was gone, now the door was closed behind him, now he stood in the high wide room lined with books, and lamps with green shades, a roll-top desk, and a sinister settee like an operating table in one corner of the room. He felt stronger in this room because, although dreading it, loathing it, he was at grips with life, he was no longer waiting in silence.

Besides, someone was here. He came forward from behind his roll-top desk and held out his hands.

"Good morning. What a wonderful day, eh? Spring at last, and I believe we've got it for good. Sit down, my dear boy, sit down. Did you walk here?"

"Yes."

"Then it's more than I did. You may not believe it, but I'm an incredibly lazy man when it comes to physical exercise. In fact, I'm a very bad example to my profession."

He smiled, he shook his head.

Surely if he smiled it meant that there was nothing wrong? Or was he false, concealing behind his mask of assurance the subtle flash of cruelty? It must have been this, because he continued the conversation blandly, smoothly, his hands behind his back, pacing before the bookcase; while the other waited in his chair, swallowing from time to time, his fingers twitching foolishly at his trouser knee, his face upturned.

"I saw that new play they're talking so much about last night," continued the voice. "Didn't think much of it. That fellow is getting old, you know. Time he gave up. Suppose he can't afford to, poor beggar. Has to go on working, like all of us." The other murmured in response, and with his fingers still tapping on his knee he watched the light from the green lamp play upon the ceiling. The room seemed larger than before, and he himself a cramped indefinite thing lost in space, subject to strange torture. Still the voice continued talking.

"Wouldn't mind a holiday myself. Somewhere with a blue sky and the sun. A complete change. That's what everyone needs, a complete change. Pity is that not many people can afford it."

Was it his imagination, or was the voice talking because it was afraid of coming to the point? Afraid of having to tell the truth?

In a second the great figure lost his power, he shrank perceptibly, he dwindled to a sorry figure with human failings, powerless and absurd. He ceased from pacing before the bookcase, he stood still, his hands behind his back.

"Now you," he said abruptly, "could you afford to take a holiday?"

His victim summoned a smile, his mouth working.

"I don't know," he stammered, "I've never thought about it. Fact is—I've been trying to save lately. Various things crop up— you know how it is. A holiday is such a waste of time unless it's absolutely necessary."

"Yes. Well, it is necessary."

It had come. No more waiting, no more pretence. Hold on, can't you?

"Then . . . ?" It was difficult to frame words into a sentence. It was as though he searched for phrases in a foreign language.

"You see, I want to make things easier for you," said the voice. And it was gentle now, too gentle. Kinder if it had been bitter and harsh. "Miracles very seldom happen, I know that, and so do you. But a different climate, a warm climate, has been known to work wonders. I can't promise anything definite, my dear fellow, I only wish to heaven I could. But there might be a chance."

Powerless, with all his books behind him, all his knowledge, and those bottles in the laboratory! The man in the chair pitied him, felt that something must be said.

"If you could explain—vaguely—" he began.

"You remember I warned you last week," said the voice, "I warned you so that you could prepare yourself, be at least ready. I did not want it to come as a shock. But then I was not sure, I had not completed the final tests. Now there is no doubt, no doubt whatever. Those last X-ray photographs have shown me what I feared."

The man blinked stupidly. He wanted things explained to him as though he were a child. "You called it some long name before," he said. "It's a sort of paralysis, isn't it? That's what you mean, isn't it?"

"Yes, that is the form it takes. Paralysis. Of course, technically, the—"

It did not matter, though, what worked technically. It did not matter what ate its way into his bones, sapped his vitality and his life. He wanted to know what was going to happen to him.

"How long does it take?" he asked.

"It all depends."

The voice was evasive, the figure shrugged its shoulders.

"In your particular case it's rather difficult to say. It might be three months—it might be three years. I can't be definite about that. You will, of course, follow a certain treatment I shall prescribe. As I said before, though, another climate."

Never mind the other climate. Who the hell cared about that?

"I want to know what happens. Does it come suddenly—in a night? Do I wake up and find I can't move? Is that it? Or does it creep slowly, so that one is never quite sure? Gradually an arm getting weak, feeble—and my back more bent—can't you tell me, can't you explain?"

"No, a sudden paralysis attacks some as the result of a stroke, of having lived too hard. You are very young, you don't drink and you live quietly. No, it will not come as a shock."

That was worse, though, surely that was worse. He wondered what was the use of following a treatment if he could not be cured. Perhaps it was the usual method of making things easier to bear. Like the deep chairs in the waiting room below. Childishly he tried to remember what paralysed people did. Did they lie on their backs? Did they have some sort of employment? Perhaps they had to go to a Home. Surely most paralysed people were beggars, humped in a little chair with a cap outstretched before them. He cleared his throat nervously, watching the doctor's eyes.

"Shall I be—well, sort of absolutely helpless?" he asked awkwardly, sorry for him who had to answer such a question.

The voice did not come for a moment, obviously it was searching for the gentlest phrase.

"Not until the final stages," it said at last. "That would not be for some little time, needless to say. But before that—you will, of course, be considerably handicapped. That is to say, any physical exertion would be out of the question, sport, er—your work—well—my dear boy, I don't have to tell you how extremely painful it is for me to have to break all this to you. Every mortal thing that can be done for you I shall do, you know that. Sympathy is a wretched thing to offer—I—well."

He put his hand on the shoulder of the other, he shook it gently to show what he felt. And the other wished he would take his hand away, he wished that voice would not hold so much pity.

"Oh, it's all right!" he said with a smile. "It's all right. Don't worry—I mean, I don't mind at all. It's quite all right." He got up from his chair, he pushed it away. "Thanks terribly for all you've done. You've been marvellous to me." He waited for a moment, wondering how to go. "I mustn't keep you," he said, "you must be frightfully busy."

Already the doctor was elbowing him to the door, glad for him to be gone, relieved that he had taken the news so well.

"Will you come along at twelve on Tuesday? Then we can draw up your regime and a definite routine. I don't want to worry you any more today."

"Right. I'll be here on Tuesday. Thanks awfully."

"Tuesday."

The door closed, the voice was silent. The great figure would relax now that he had gone. He would light a cigarette and glance at the clock. After all, it was not he who was going to be paralysed. The butler was standing in the hall, the hat and gloves ready.

"Thank you," said the man who had been sentenced, smiling to show that everything was all right, but avoiding the butler's eyes.

As he crossed the hall he saw through the open door of the waiting room the picture of the little girl swinging backwards and forwards.

"I told you so," she shouted. "See you Tuesday."

The front door slammed behind him and he stood upon the steps, his hat at the back of his head, the clean cold air fanning his forehead, and he looked up at the sun. It seemed far away, shining brightly and indifferently in a glazed blue sky. And the houses were carved against this sky like frosted buildings on a Swiss postcard, hard and clear. As he walked, people bumped against him laughing, their cheeks glowing, glad that the day was fine. There was something breathless in the air, happy, intoxicating, like a whisper of spring, and because of it everyone must walk quickly, lightly, scarcely brushing the pavement with their feet. Even the horns of the taxis were high-pitched and tuneful, and the rumble of the traffic mellow, absurd. There were two girls sitting on the top of a bus without hats. The sun shone on their hair, the light wind blew it over their faces, and they rocked with laughter. A boy skipped along the pavement bowling a hoop, and a little white terrier ran at his heels yapping excitedly, worrying at his shoes.

It seemed almost that there was a shimmer of green on the trees in Regent's Park, as though at last the tight buds would unfold, relax, opening themselves. On a patch of grass gleamed the first crocus, yellow and fat. Somewhere a bird was singing. Then the man called a taxi and, climbing into it, he crouched back in the corner, his hat over his eyes.

She kept him waiting as usual. Ten minutes, a quarter of an hour, he did not bother to count. As a rule he would be restless, impatient, bringing out his watch every few minutes, getting up, pacing about. Today, though, it did not matter. For the first time in his life he wished she would not come. He wanted there to be a telephone message saying she could not get off today after all, or even a wire to tell him she had gone away. Because he knew when he saw her he would not be able to be strong. If she were not there, he could forget about everything. He would not think, he would not mind. But when she came and was with him, and they were together—then it was different, then he was weak. He remembered the deep leather chairs in the doctor's waiting room, and he wanted things to be made easier for him.

It would be easier if he did not have to see her. Perhaps there was a chance that she might say to him today: "I don't love you any more. It's over, our thing. Let's stop seeing each other."

For however much she would hurt him, it did not matter so long as he did not have to hurt her. She would be able to go off, careless, unmindful, nothing mattering any more, finding new people and new places, but she would not be hurt. He could keep his trouble to himself. She would not have to know. Then everything would be all right, then he would not care. Because, anyway, he had got to give up caring about things now.

Only, if she came today the same as she always was, then he was lost.

He did not know how he would tell her. She would not understand. She would look at him with eyes wide and bewildered. "But, darling—but, darling, it can't make any difference to us, it can't." And she would not see that every word was a fresh torture thrusting itself deeper, twisting and turning like a knife.

He knew her so well. He knew how she would think for a moment, biting her lip, making a picture of it all to herself, not understanding, young, romantic, absurd.

"I'll look after you—I'll never leave you. We'll go away together." She would pull at his arm, eager and impatient. "It will be all right, won't it?"

She would not be able to grasp the truth of what had happened, of what was going to happen. She would paint it in false colours, because she was ignorant, because she was feminine, because she loved him.

She would shut her eyes and dream a dream of a sunny land, and mountains and a lake, and him lying in a deck chair with her beside him, giving him grapes. She would lean over him, proud of her strength, loving his helplessness, seeing him as a child. He knew her so well, and that this would be her picture.

For him—he painted no portraits, he saw the truth, naked, sordid and uncoloured. There was nothing beautiful in it. He saw an existence that was a living death—dependent on charity, unable to give protection—or love—or life—and he knew.

He lifted his eyes and he could see that she was coming along the street, half running, knowing she was late. She waved her hand, even from a distance he saw that she was laughing.

She carried a muff. Small, curly and ridiculous, like a woollen toy. She wore fur at her throat, too, and a fur cap on her head. The tip of her nose was pink from the cold, and her eyes were a robin's eyes, round and inquisitive. She looked like a little bird sniffing at the air. She ran up to him, breathless, squeezing his arm.

"Darling—if you knew," she began, "if you only knew. I've had such a time getting here. Endless shopping, and I had my hair done, and then I had to go to a fitting for a new dress. Have you been waiting *ages?*"

He shook his head, smiling.

"What?" she said, not waiting for his answer. "But the thing is *I'm* late because I would not take a taxi. I just insisted on walking. It's such a lovely, lovely day. It's made me feel—now, I wonder how I can explain it to you? It's made me feel as though life were something so beautiful that I want to hold it close, very close, and shut my eyes and breathe very deep like this. Oh—" She took a long breath, and bit her lip, and looked up to him and laughed. But he did not say anything. He just watched her, smiling stupidly. "Oh, you think I'm mad!" she said, shrugging her shoulders. "Come on, let's walk, I'm ravenous, I want my lunch. But don't you see what I mean about the day? Don't you feel it too? When I woke up this morning the sun was shining straight through the window onto my pillow, and there was a beam of light full of a million flecks of dust, gold dust. There was a smell coming from the trees in the square. Do you know the smell? Of tight buds, and very fresh green leaves, and sunlight on a white pavement?"

He guided her through the stream of traffic because she never looked where she was going. Still he did not say anything.

"I thought to myself that this was a very special day," she went on, "a day when everything seems good, and people are nice, and to be alive is the most *wonderful* thing in the world. Darling, people can't be unhappy on a day like this, can they?

Just to see, and to breathe, and to feel, and to smell, that ought to be enough for everyone, don't you think?"

They waited on an island while a stream of traffic passed. High in the sky there was an aeroplane like a golden arrow poised against the sun. They lifted up their faces to look at it, and the far, faint drone came down to them as the hum of a bee in a distant garden. As he watched he thought of the beauty of moving things. That golden arrow of a plane, wending across the sky like a flash of light, the loveliness of ships, the freedom of horses on a stretch of moorland, and riding with the wind in your face. Walking with dogs over a deep ploughed field, or alone in a wet wood, the leaves dark and still, or running on the beach as a child, the sand beneath your feet.

He, too, closed his eyes and breathed deeply, and then he opened them again and smiled and said: "Yes, it's wonderful being alive, wonderful, isn't it?"

The traffic was blocked again and they passed across the street.

"Perhaps we're only feeling like this because it's the beginning of spring," she said, "perhaps it's only for a moment, perhaps it's not going to last. What do you think?"

"I don't know," he said.

"I'm holding it here," she said, "close to my heart, so that it can't escape. It's fluttering, like a bird that wants to fly away. Feel it, feel it."

She pulled his hand to her heart. "Do you hear him beating his wings?" she laughed. "D'you hear? He's so difficult to hold, but we won't let him go, we won't, will we?"

"No," he said.

She tugged at a bunch of violets at her waist.

"I didn't show you these," she told him. "I bought them just before I saw you. They were wet and glistening. I imagined I had picked them in a field with the dew still on the petals. Look, you've got to smell them." She held them up to him, and he buried his face in them deep.

"Doesn't it make you think of summer," she said, "and bathing, and the sea, and woods? Tell me you love them, tell me this beastly horrible winter is over and that spring has really come, never to go again?"

"They're lovely," he said, "lovely," and he went on walking

and swinging her hand, and he was thinking, "Anyway we shall have had this, this moment, the street and the sun. They can't take this from us."

The buses rumbled past, red and shining, and open cars, and somebody laughing and somebody without a hat.

"What is it?" she said, smiling up at him. "Everyone is crazy mad today. They none of them care what happens at all. Isn't it glorious, isn't it fun?"

In spite of himself he felt drawn into her mood, into the mood of that moment and that day. Perhaps he had thought too seriously about it, perhaps after all it was not true. Maybe he had seen too darkly, and really it was better to paint pictures as she painted, dream visions as she dreamed, of blue sky and the sun.

Suddenly, as they came to the edge of the pavement, he saw propped against the wall of a building the crumpled figure of a man, his legs twisted under him, his arms folded horribly, his limp fingers drooping from his white hand. He wore no hat and his glazed eyes, idiot's eyes, watched the passers-by without comprehension, a fixed dull stare.

At his feet his cap lay open, and into this one or two people had dropped a copper. By the side of the cap lay a pile of matchboxes. There was a little slate behind the boxes. On this was written in white chalk:

"I AM COMPLETELY PARALYSED."

His mouth moved and words came from it, inarticulate and strange. Perhaps he was asking people to buy matches. For a moment they both stood before him, blocked in a little crowd, and then she breathed quickly, smothering her nose in the violets, drawing away from him, whose face, without her having noticed, had grown so pale and stern, whose hands strayed mechanically to his pockets in search of sixpence.

"Oh, don't look at that *frightful* man," she said. "Turn away, quick. It will spoil our day if we think about him. Such people ought not to be kept alive, it's absolutely criminal."

He peered into her face as they stood on the kerb. The colour had flamed into her cheeks, a dark curl had slipped from beneath her fur cap. Suddenly she looked like the child in the picture.

Then she smiled, she tugged at his arm, brushing her face against his shoulder.

"Darling, it's good to be alive, isn't it? We're going to be happy, you and I, happy—happy."

The Lover

It was ten-thirty on a wet morning in January. The telephone boxes were empty on the Piccadilly Circus subway, empty save for one at the right-hand corner by the entrance to Shaftesbury Avenue.

A woman stood there, her lips pressed close to the mouthpiece, the pennies clutched in her hand. She moved impatiently and flung a glance over her shoulder, and rattled the receiver.

"But I've repeated the number three times already. I tell you I want Gerrard 10550—Gerrard 10550." She bit her lip and tapped her foot nervously on the floor. "Of course there is somebody there. Will you please ring them again?"

He turned over in bed and reached for a cigarette. He yawned, stretched himself, and fumbled for his dressing gown. Then he flung aside the bedclothes and strolled over towards his dressing table.

He ran the comb through his hair and peered at the dark shadows beneath his eyes. His hand wandered towards the bottle of Bromo Seltzer. When the telephone rang he frowned and, making no attempt to answer it, wandered into the bathroom. The steaming water foamed from the taps; his dressing gown slipped to the floor.

He lay back in his bath, a large sponge pressed to his chest, and watched his pale limbs beneath the water, flabby and mushroom-coloured. The smoke from his cigarette curled towards the ceiling. Still the telephone continued to ring on the little table beside the bed.

"Yes, Gerrard 10550. Can you clear the line again? There must be some mistake."

The woman's voice was very weary now, flat, with an added note of supplication. She raised her eyes and read once more the rules for the public telephone service.

He wrapped himself in a large warm towel and lit another cigarette. The rain splashed against the window. What an infernal row the telephone was making! He padded with bare feet into the bedroom.

"Hullo, what is it? Speak up; I can't hear a word."

The woman tilted her hat on the back of her head; her bag fell from her hand and crashed on the floor, spilling her change.

"At last! Oh, heavens, what a morning! Do you know I've been waiting here nearly half an hour? Were you asleep?"

"I suppose I was. What a time to ring, anyway! What d'you want?"

"What do you imagine? Don't you realise I have crept out of the house in this pouring, filthy rain, dressed anyhow, caring for nothing, husband and children waiting at home—only to speak to you? And then because I've wakened you up from sleep you snap at me in this beastly way . . ."

"Listen," he said quickly, "if you want to make a scene, go and make it to somebody else and not to me. I mean to say—life's too short . . ."

"Oh! you don't understand what I am going through because of you! I'm miserable, miserable. I haven't seen you for five days, and you don't apparently care."

"My dear, it's ridiculous to work yourself into such a state. You know perfectly well I'm terribly busy. I've not had a single moment."

"Where were you last night?"

"I worked until late, if you must know, and then went to bed."

"How do I know that you're speaking the truth?" Her voice was hard, suspicious. She could imagine the shrug of his shoulders.

"Oh, hell! If you're in that sort of mood, good-bye."

"No, no! I didn't mean it! Don't go! I am a fool." She clung to the receiver as though she was with him.

"Well, damn it! You make things so difficult. What do you think I did?" There was a pause.

The woman fumbled for her handkerchief; she felt her mouth drag at the corner.

"What—what are you doing today?" she began desperately.

"Literally haven't a moment today," answered the voice briskly. "I'm up to my eyes in work. I've got to finish a story for an American paper."

"Couldn't I—couldn't I come and sit with you?"

"No. I can't work with anyone around; you must know that by now."

"What about this evening, or a second for lunch today? I've kept it absolutely free, thinking we should be together. I'm going off my head these long, empty days—this endless rain, this never seeing you for one single moment."

"I'm afraid it's impossible."

How far the voice sounded, how distant! If only she could be with him now!

"If you only knew how much I love you!" she said.

He moved restlessly and glanced at the clock on the mantelpiece. "Listen. What's the use of all this? I've got to do some work."

"Then we aren't going to see each other at all today? I might just as well go away, go abroad, go right away from you. You don't care if you never see me again; you hate the sight of me; you . . ."

The senseless words poured from her mouth.

He closed his eyes wearily and yawned. "Why go into all that now? You know how I hate scenes—discussions. Why are you complaining? After all, we've had a good time; it's been good fun; we haven't hurt anybody. What's the point of all this tangle of nerves?"

"I'm sorry. I didn't mean to be tiresome, only it's never seeing you, never hearing you. Swear you aren't angry—promise you aren't angry. You see, I've been so unhappy. I'm loathsome, selfish—and you have your work. But if perhaps—loving you as I do—you . . ."

"Well, look, I'll ring sometime later in the week. Good-bye."

She jabbed furiously at the receiver. "Wait—wait! What are you doing tomorrow at half past three?"

But there was no reply.

She straightened her hat and wandered uncertainly away.

He lifted the receiver again and waited until the hotel exchange answered. "I say, if anyone rings again, say I'm working and can't be disturbed."

He stood before the window and watched the rain. What an effort it was, this continual lying. If one told the truth for one moment there was the devil to pay. Women were a cope—a decided cope. Still, difficult to live without them—one way and another.

He glanced at the letter that had arrived with his breakfast.

". . . And I'm so anxious for you to meet him, because he really is the most important publisher today. Naturally, a genius like you will find your feet anyway, but it does help to get in with the right people. Anyway, lunch at one as usual at the same place. No one will recognise me there. Isn't convention vile? I would like to shout about us from the housetops, and we have to sneak to our meetings as though we were ashamed of the most marvellous thing in the world.

"Darling, when I think of last night I . . ."

Good Lord! There were three—no, four pages of this. What a woman!

He placed the letter carefully in his notecase. One never knew. . . . All the same, she must not shout things from the housetops. Sort of damn silly thing a woman would do. Still, she did not yet telephone him every hour of the day like the last one. She was very lovely—and very useful.

He wound up the gramophone that she had given him. He supposed he would be able to use her car again today. Impossible to walk a step in this rain. She had suggested giving him a car of his own.

Yes, she really was rather wonderful. He lounged in the chair while the record whispered in his ear:

And that's why Chinks do it . . . Japs do it . . .

"Oh, but you look marvellous!" he told her. "Marvellous! Shall we take this little table in the corner?—and then there will be no chance of anyone seeing us. Isn't that a new hat? But, of course, I adore it; I adore everything you wear."

She felt for his hand under the table and sighed.

"You know, sweetheart, when you talk to me like this I feel like chucking up everything and just going away with you. After all, what does scandal matter? We love each other. I don't care about losing my money; we could live in a garret, in a tent."

He forced a laugh. "Aren't you wonderful!"

Surely she would never dream of losing her head to such an appalling extent! Women had no sense of proportion at all.

"Just think, you and I starving in a garret," she went on dreamily.

"Yes, but it would be the action of a cad," he said quickly. "I should never forgive myself. How could I be so brutal as to drag you away from all your comforts and luxury! It would be criminal." He struck his fist upon the table. Rather dramatic, this. He almost believed it himself. "No," he continued gently, "we must try and content ourselves with things as they are. One day—oh, one day . . ."

He looked into her eyes. He could say this so many times, and it invariably rang true.

"You know," he said, as he glanced down the menu and chose mixed grill at 1s.9d.—she might expect him to pay—"you know, I don't believe any two lovers have ever understood one another as we do. I can't explain; it's something that comes from the depths of one—a sympathy, a mutual form of self-expression . . ."

"I feel it too," she answered breathlessly. "I'm sure people have said this before, but they've never meant it."

"Never meant it," he agreed gravely.

"Whereas, with us, everything is completely natural; neither of us has to pretend," she told him.

"That's what is really so marvellous," he said. "Have some iced water, darling; the wine here is terrible. No, what I was saying is that no two people have ever loved the same way as we have. It's so much more than just sex, you know. Sometimes I feel I could be completely happy if I didn't touch you, if . . ." He saw the cloud come over her face, so he changed his phrase with great presence of mind. "If only one didn't have a bodily existence it would be comparatively simple; you and I would never go through our agonies of separation. As it is I suffer tortures when we are apart."

"I know; that's why we ought to go away," she broke in.

"No, no—you must not. I will not muck up your life." He spoke firmly, and stuck his fork into his mixed grill. "After all, we are happy in our fashion, aren't we? We see each other every day; we love each other; and there is no danger. No one will find out."

"Yes, it's perfect—but somehow—and since just a few days ago —I want to do so much for you. I want to slave for you; I want to be with you always!"

He had an uneasy pain in the pit of his stomach. Must she still harp on the subject? Was this affair going to be the same as the last one, all over again?

"God! If only I had some money of my own," he said gloomily. He stuck out his jaw and frowned.

"Money! What does money matter?" she said impatiently. "I hate money! I'd like to give it all away, and you and I to go away on some old dirty ship."

He smiled weakly without enthusiasm.

"One day soon we will," she said.

His spirits sank rapidly. "Of course there's no kick in being rich," he remarked carelessly, "but there's no doubt it does mean something in this callous world. One gets tired of striving and fighting, and sometimes one thinks, why write? Why go on? To what end? It's agony, being poor."

"But, darling, you know that you need never want for anything now you have me. All I have is yours, anything you care to ask for."

He wondered if she had forgotten about the car she had promised him.

"I can't go on taking things from you," he muttered. "You don't know how it hurts, how terrible it makes me feel."

"Now you're silly, you forget we are 'us,' and not two other people. Loving each other as we do, these things become so simple and so natural. I mean, if our positions were reversed you'd do the same for me. Besides, I adore helping you."

"Do you? If only I wasn't so confoundedly proud."

"Oh! But you're a genius—no one expects you to understand money. You're above the sordid material things of life."

"Um—I suppose I am." He frowned and drummed with his fingers on the table.

"Poor lamb," she thought, "how artistic he is, how temperamental."

"You will let me help you, won't you?" she pleaded.

He shrugged his shoulders and pushed away his plate. "If you must," he said sullenly.

He decided that the time had come for a change of mood.

"Let's forget money, work, everything but that we are together," he said, smiling. "After all, there is nothing else in the world, is there?"

"Nothing," she agreed.

"If only these people were not here and we were quite alone—like yesterday. D'you remember last night?"

"Remember—what do you think?"

Once more she felt for his hand under the table. "Tell me, that woman you told me about, do you ever see her now?"

"Good Lord, no; besides, there was nothing in it, nothing at all. She was never anything more than a friend. She's gone abroad, I believe, with her children." He bent to light a cigarette. Then he closed his eyes and waved aside the smoke. "I want to kiss you for twenty-four hours without stopping."

She revelled in the old, worn words. "Shall we go?" she murmured.

There was a slight awkwardness with the bill. She insisted on paying and he protested. Then, as he looked away, the distasteful moment passed.

To make up for this he hailed a taxi, aggressively rattling the change in his pocket. "But of course I'm going to see you home," he said reproachfully as she held out her hand. The taxi bumped amidst the traffic, and their kisses, though ardent, were unsuccessful.

"If we could be like this always," he lied.

She smiled in ecstasy and fumbled for her powder puff.

He leant back with his feet on the opposite seat and prodded the floor with his stick.

"By the way," he began, "about that car you mentioned. I've been thinking it over . . ."

The party had been dull, tedious, and after all the man had never turned up. Only his daughter, a young unsophisticated girl, red elbows in evening dress. Not unattractive in profile, but too young, much too young. Still, he had made the most of his time. After all, her father was an important man. It never did to let opportunities like this occur merely to pass them by.

He spoke to her early in the evening, and towards the end he was still by her side. "Do you know, I swear I am not flattering you, but the moment I saw you I said to myself, 'There is some-one who will understand.' It was something about your eyes, I think."

The girl gazed at him, flushing. "Oh! but nobody has ever talked to me like this before. You see, being my father's daugh-ter, they expect me to echo his remarks, and they don't seem to imagine for an instant that I have a mind of my own."

He laughed scornfully. "Absurd! After five minutes with you one realises—so much more than the ordinary thing. I admit I was disappointed not to meet your father this evening," he went on, "but you have made up for it—more than made up for it."

"Of course, you simply must meet him," she exclaimed, "I'm quite sure you would get on famously together."

"You dear thing, that's very sweet and adorable of you. But listen—tell me more about yourself."

She held on to her evening bag with hot, sticky fingers. "Oh! there's nothing, nothing."

"Nonsense. Anyway, I feel we are going to be friends, real friends." He held out his cigarette case and smiled. "You don't smoke? How refreshing. One gets so tired of these women with their eternal cigarettes."

The girl's eyes wandered towards the figure of her hostess, sur-rounded by a little group of men and women. "She's lovely. Do you know her well?"

"Oh! one comes across her from time to time," he answered carelessly. "But luxury has never appealed to me, I like simple things, books, being alone, or with somebody who understands."

"So do I." They smiled at each other.

"I can talk to you about anything," he said softly, "not only books, but things that matter. It's marvellous to be able to dis-cuss sex with a girl of your age and not feel self-conscious, not be aware. You're so lovely, too, which makes it all the more rare and astounding. You've been told so hundreds of times."

"No—never—"

"But that is absolutely remarkable." He moved closer to her, pressing her knee.

Then his hostess moved from her group towards them. He rose to his feet and made an excuse to the girl.

"For the last hour I've been driven nearly mad," he whispered rapidly. "I haven't seen you for a moment alone. Always surrounded by that infernal crowd. And I've been sitting here, chatting to this little schoolgirl, watching you. Gosh—you look wonderful—wonderful."

"My poor darling—and I imagined you were enjoying yourself."

"As if I ever think of anything but you for a single moment," he said.

She put her finger on her lips. "Hush—someone may hear. Be reasonable and remember tomorrow."

He started, feigning astonishment. "Tomorrow? I don't think I can manage tomorrow."

"But you said at lunch . . . ?"

"Yes, I know, only when I got back I remembered there was an article that must be written."

"Naturally your work comes first. But in the evening?"

"Yes, of course, in the evening."

"Good night, my beloved."

"Good night."

He wandered down into the hall and saw the girl step into her car. He ran bareheaded down to the pavement. He arranged the rug carefully over her knees.

"I can't tell you what it's done to me—meeting you," he said. "I'm going back to work. I shall think of you."

"How—how wonderful," breathed the girl.

He glanced up at the house behind him, and then bent forward intimately and took her hand. "Listen—are you doing anything tomorrow between five and seven?"

It was midnight when he let himself into his room at the hotel. After all, he had not wasted his time. He flung off his clothes and slipped into his dressing gown. Then he prepared the room for work. Five cushions on the sofa, and on a stool beside it the gramophone and a case full of records. A box of cigarettes, matches, whisky, and a soda siphon on the floor within reach.

He lay down upon the sofa, settled the cushions behind his head, started a record, and balanced a sheet of foolscap against his knee.

The room filled with smoke and the gramophone played, but the sheet of foolscap remained white and untouched.

Suddenly the telephone rang sharply, screamingly, in his ear. With a grunt of annoyance he stretched out his hand. A woman's voice came across the wire, whispering, pleading.

"Is that Gerrard 10550? Is that you? Oh! forgive me, but you made me so miserable on the phone this morning. I'll try and be patient about not seeing you—but tell me, do you love me as much now as you did in September . . . ?"

Leading Lady

He stood in the passage, his hat on the back of his head, a cigar hanging from his mouth. He pulled out an enormous watch and stamped his foot impatiently.

"Look here," he shouted, for all the world to hear, "I'm not accustomed to be kept waiting. Doesn't Miss Fabian know I've arrived? What the hell is everybody doing?"

The doorkeeper peered at him timidly. "I'm sorry, sir; it will only be a few moments. What name was it, sir?"

Damn it all, this fellow hadn't even recognised him! He looked at the doorkeeper steadily, waited so that he should grasp the full significance of his reply.

"Paul Haynes," he said superbly, and turned away. A frightened dresser appeared at the bottom of the stairs.

"Will you please come this way, sir?" She knew who he was all right. Hers was the proper subservient attitude to take. Good God, once he got this theatre under his control he'd change the whole damn staff. The doorkeeper would be the first to get the sack.

He strode after the dresser along the passage, swaying from side to side like a turkey cock, spilling ash as he went. He stood on the threshold of the dressing room, his legs wide apart, his hat still on the back of his head.

She was sitting before the looking glass, patting her hair into place. She turned round with a little cry of distress.

"Oh, but can you ever forgive me for having kept you waiting? Those appalling film people never leave me alone for a moment—keep pestering me to go to Hollywood and offering me stupendous sums. Lewisheim has been on the telephone for twenty minutes." She waited a moment to allow her words to sink into the man's brain. She murmured something unnecessary to her dresser and then turned back to him with a smile. "However, let's forget about that—it's something quite apart. Now, please sit down—forgive this untidiness everywhere, but you know what it is, the last few days of a long run. First of all, I must tell you, I went yesterday afternoon to see your new revue. Oh, it's the most marvellous thing I've ever seen—but the most. I can't speak about it. I've never enjoyed anything so much. Those girls—the whole production! Of course you're an absolute genius; there's no one to touch you!" She shrugged her shoulders almost impatiently.

He did not attempt to conceal his smile of satisfaction. So she liked it? H'm. Lewisheim's productions would never hold a candle to his. This woman had sense, after all. She was looking more beautiful than ever, too. Pity, perhaps, she wore so little jewellery. Only a chain round her neck. It wasn't impressive; much too simple altogether. He would like to see her in a mass of diamonds.

"Yes, it's a good show, and I don't mind admitting it," he said loudly, blowing a great cloud of smoke into her face.

Her manners were exquisite; she didn't even wave it away with her hand.

"I spend more money on my productions than any other manager in London," he went on. "None of your skimpy, shoddy stuff for me. No painted scenery."

She made a little sound in her throat and shook her head for sympathy.

"Where you spend money you draw money," he announced, "and that's always the way I do things. If you and I put on this play of yours together, I'm going to see that you have the very best of everything. No—don't thank me." He spread out his large fat hand. "You're a businesswoman, you know what you're about when you join forces with me. My dear, you're going to have a real big success, and you're going to make a packet of money."

She said nothing for a moment. What a conceited fool the man was! Talking to her as if she were some pathetic little actress striking out on her first venture. He didn't know anything about the theatre either. Because he was rich he managed to surround himself with people who did, that was all. He was lucky, and they flattered him, but it was only his money they wanted. Then she leant back in her chair, as if defeated.

"I think you are quite the most wonderful man I know," she said softly. He looked at her, and put away his cigar. Once more he bent towards her.

"I'm going to tell you something," he began in a slow, impressive tone, "and it's something that I don't say to many people, because I'm a very difficult man." He waited a moment as though to prepare her for some stupendous announcement. Then: "I like you," he said. "I like you very much," he went on. "There's no nonsense about you. You look a man straight in the face and tell him the truth. I'm a great believer in truth myself. If I say a thing I mean it. If I didn't like you, I'd be perfectly frank and tell you so. My frankness brings me many enemies, but I'm not afraid of any of 'em. They know what to expect. In fact, the words 'to be as frank as Paul Haynes' have become a common expression, so they tell me. If a fellow wants to hear the truth about himself, or someone else, let him come along to me."

"Oh, but I admire you for that," she broke in impulsively. "It shows such strength of mind, and such a superb indifference to what the world thinks of you. They matter so little, don't they?— all the people we meet in this profession. I have my few friends —my books, my child." She turned with a wistful smile at the photograph on her dressing table. Half unconsciously she pushed the snapshot of a famous boxer out of sight behind a powder box.

"You are quite unique, my dear," he continued. "If you were not, I shouldn't be sitting here now. You know I've got a whole lot of ideas about the theatre that I think would interest you. I'm a bit of an idealist in my way, you know."

The fatuity of this man! She glanced at her watch, shading her eyes with her hand.

"Tell me about yourself," she begged.

"I want to change the present conditions," he shouted. "I want to get a different atmosphere into the theatre altogether and, by heaven, I'm going to do it. I've started with my own revues, and I want to do the same with the straight plays. Do you know my revues are the cleanest in England? There's not a single line in my new show that would make a man blush. But

that's not the point; that's not what I'm getting at. I'm going to
put a stop to what goes on behind the scenes—all these dirty little love affairs, all this promiscuous stuff in dressing rooms. I'm
going to make it my business to find out the private life of every
actor and actress who works for me. I'll make a clean sweep of
the rotters. I'm a powerful man. If I find out that any man or
woman hasn't got a fit record, I'll see to it they don't get another
job on a London stage."

He leant back, exhausted with his eloquence.

"Of course, you're quite right," she said without hesitating. "I
suppose I'm weak. I shut my eyes to things. And I hate to get
anyone into trouble."

He went on, pleased with her reply. "Do you know, you are
one of the few actresses who has never been divorced. Of
course, you're a widow, but even if your husband had lived, it
would have made no difference. Someone told me that five years
ago, when you went about a lot with John What's-his-name—the
fellow who left his wife and went out to Australia. Whether it's
true or not, you showed great wisdom in cutting him out of your
life. They tell me he's gone entirely to pieces—out of work,
drinks like a fish. Now that's the type of thing I'm going to put a
stop to; and I want you on my side. You and I together, my dear,
will be practically an unbreakable force. What do you think?"

She looked him straight in the eyes. "I agree with every word
you say," she told him.

He took her hand and patted it. "Partners—what?" he said,
controlling his smile. "About the cast," he went on, clearing his
throat. "We've decided on everyone, I think, except the other
man. Is there anyone you fancy for that part?"

She began to polish her nails carelessly.

"You know Bobby Carson, the boy who has been playing my
brother in the present play? He's really charming, and very capa-
ble. Not a bit expensive either."

"H'm. It requires more than capability, you know. It's a
striking emotional part. The second act is almost entirely in his
hands, if you remember. I don't care a damn about the expense.
Now, the chap I want in the part is this young Martin Wilton.
Have you seen him?"

"No." She turned to the dressing table, frowning ever so slightly.

"His play comes off next week, so we might be able to get him. Come along Friday afternoon; they have a matinee. I think he's the finest natural actor I've seen for years. Quite young, quite unspoilt. Doesn't know how good he is. See what you think of him, anyway. He can rehearse the part on trial."

"Yes, yes, of course." She had heard too much already of this Martin Wilton. People were raving about him. The critics were almost nauseating in their praise.

"Friday, then." She smiled. "How exciting! I shall adore it."

A few minutes later Haynes leant back in his taxi with a smile of satisfaction. He decided he had made a great impression on her. Well, it was not surprising. After all, he was rich; he had brains; he was under sixty. He felt that she had probably never met anyone quite like him before. He admitted that her husband had been a remarkable man, but no doubt very dull to live with, always wrapped up in his work, seeing her only as a character in one of his plays. He couldn't have known how to make a woman happy. Good thing he had died when he did.

Idly he wondered whether she was lonely. You never heard her name coupled with anyone—not since that fellow went to Australia, all of which was undoubtedly malicious gossip. Well, she had seen eye to eye with him over his ideas for the theatre. It was a wonderful scheme of his, to launch a great purity campaign. With the *Daily Recorder* to back him up, he would get tremendous publicity. He would be known as the Man Who Cleaned Up the English Stage. And Mary Fabian would help. Her beauty and his brains would make a great combination. He supposed she must be well in the thirties by now, with a child growing big. She wasn't everybody's money. Jove, what a figure, though! He would like to see her in a diamond necklace and with a little less on. This next play was going to be enjoyable in many ways. . . .

Back in the dressing room, Mary Fabian was cursing him for having kept her so long after the performance. He hadn't even apologised. What an appalling man! All that frightful twaddle about his clean revues, while he smacked his lips at her as though she were butchers' meat.

"Tell Mr. Carson I'm alone now," she said to her dresser.

It was past midnight, and she wanted her supper. She threw off her clothes impatiently and began brushing her hair behind her ears.

"Bobby," she called through the wall. "Bobby, my sweet."

She sat in the stalls on Friday afternoon without moving a muscle of her face. She was alone, after all; Paul Haynes had been called to Manchester. She thanked heaven for his absence. She could not have borne with his enthusiastic remarks, his eager concentration upon the stage. She drew her fur coat more closely around her; she buried herself in it as though she did not wish to be seen.

This Martin Wilton was good, far too good. His personality stuck out a mile, with his vivid face and tawny hair. Not her type at all, of course; but that was not the point. Even had he been attractive to her, she would not have considered him. Not for a moment. It was much too dangerous. It would be fatal to have him in the new play; he would run away with it entirely. She would become a secondary figure, her part would not matter at all.

And she had reached an awkward moment in her career. The slightest slip, the smallest mistake, and attention would be drawn away from her. People would say she was becoming monotonous, she was overplaying herself. No, this boy was too good. Already she could imagine the first night, with Martin Wilton getting the applause. She would have to stand in the background and efface herself, pushing him forward with a smile. And the papers next morning would be a paean of praise. "Mr. Martin Wilton gave the finest performance of the evening." And so on, and so on . . .

Something had got to be done. He must be prevented at all costs from playing the part. She would have to be careful, though; it was not going to be too easy.

Mechanically she wrote a note to Martin Wilton after the matinee.

"Your performance quite marvellous. Never seen anything like it. I want you to come and be with me in my next play. Will send it along for you to read tonight. Wonderful part for you. Forgive me for not coming round. I've got to dash away."

She felt she could not face that boy now, and his probable insufferable conceit. She drove home, racking her brains for some solution to the problem.

On the morning of the first rehearsal, when Martin Wilton was to read the part for the first time, she received a wire from Haynes. "Detained Manchester. Impossible to attend rehearsal. Rely on your judgement entirely *re* Wilton."

She crushed the wire in her hand and went onto the stage, sensing victory.

"Mr. Haynes is in Manchester and can't get away for the rehearsal. Is everybody here? Then we'll begin at once."

At eight o'clock, when they had finished for the day, she flung herself down in her chair, exhausted. Things had gone exactly as she had feared; the boy had been wonderful—never seemed to make a mistake, and his technique was uncanny. How she hated him!

She sat in front of the mirror and began to make up her face very carefully. She cast her mind back to the night last week when Paul Haynes had voiced his grotesque plans for delving into the private lives of actors and actresses, and the germ of an idea came into her mind. "Will you tell Mr. Wilton I should like to see him?" she said to her dresser.

In a few minutes the boy knocked at her door. "May I come in?" he said shyly. She gave him a dazzling smile; she held out her hands. "We've got so much to discuss," she told him. "Are you doing anything this evening?"

The boy flushed all over his face. "As a matter of fact, I was going back to my wife, but if it's important I can easily ring her up."

She gave a little cry of astonishment. "Married! But you're far too young. What do you mean by it?" She shook her head at him in mock reproof. "Ask her to spare you for a few hours," she pleaded. "We've got to talk about this second act."

In half an hour they were having dinner together in her flat. At first he was painfully shy, he would scarcely say a word.

Completely unself-conscious on the stage, in private life he was nervous, clumsy, aware of his hands and feet. She pretended not to notice; she smiled encouragement, she spoke softly, using all her old tricks mechanically. Soon he began to warm to the influence of the room, her voice, the excellent food, and his second glass of burgundy. He could scarcely believe he was sitting here alone with Mary Fabian.

She sat with her face in her hands, a cigarette between her lips. The fire cast great shadows on the ceiling and played about her profile. Her hair shone dully like an old coin. She was so human, so open with him; and he loved the room, with the heavy curtains, the shaded light, and the smell of the queer stuff she burnt on the fire. He was happy and at peace; she seemed to understand him so well. He had never found anyone who could listen to him like this, not even his wife.

"I want you to sit by the fire, and smoke a cigarette, and tell me all about yourself," she had said.

He found himself speaking to her as if he had known her for years, explaining all the worry of those early years, how he had fought and struggled with his family.

"You seem to understand things about me that nobody else has ever dreamt existed," he said. "The serious side of me. What I really feel about life. Because I do feel things, you know, tremendously. People have often told me that when they first meet me I seem horribly shy. All my life it's been the same. My mother, bless her, could never understand my passion for the stage. You're so awfully sympathetic." He gazed at her with worship in his eyes. "You'll think me absurd," he went on, gaining confidence, "but the one ambition of my life, ever since I first went on the stage, was to act with you. I've dreamt of it for years, grinding away in the provinces."

"No, no—you're joking!" She smiled.

"I promise you it's absolutely true. I saw you first about five years ago, and I remember thinking to myself: 'There is somebody worth while, who spends her time giving happiness to other people.' Oh, you were simply wonderful. You became my ideal, my sort of guiding star, my good angel. I judged everything by what I imagined your standards to be. I guessed you would never put up with the second rate in life, or in acting. You would only accept the best. I love it more than anything in the world—the theatre, I mean."

She stirred slightly, and reached for his hand. "You dear," she murmured; "you dear quixotic person." Then she leant back in her chair, pillowing her cheek against a cushion.

If he went on much longer she felt she would scream. It was incredible that anyone should talk so much. What a fool he was! She turned her rising yawn into a smile. "You know, you remind me of myself," she told him. "Oh yes, quite a lot. All your ideals and beliefs. I so appreciate your outlook on life. All for Art, and the world well lost. Ah, how well I understand! I adore my work passionately. I couldn't live without it. One doesn't care about money, people, or success—it's just the longing to achieve something, isn't it?"

"Yes, yes!" he said eagerly, the light of a fanatic in his eyes.

"To create a living character out of a mass of words, to breathe life into it, to—to—" She made a little gesture with her hands, uncertain how to continue. "Oh, how marvellously you understand!" she ended, and: "We're going to be such friends, you and I."

She slipped from her chair to the floor, crouching, her hands spread to the blaze of the fire. Her head was aching; she had had a tiring day. She was longing to go to bed and to sleep. What on earth was he talking about now?

"Hamlet," he was saying. "I want to play Hamlet as no one has ever dared to play it before. There is something terrific about him, misunderstood, suppressed. You remember, in the beginning of Act Three, when he is with Ophelia, when she starts, 'My lord, I have remembrances of yours,' you know . . ."

"Yes, wonderful, wonderful!" she murmured. Oh, God, not Shakespeare, not at this hour! She made no attempt to listen. She was wondering what time Paul Haynes arrived back from Manchester. He was certain to ring her up. The boy mustn't be here then.

"It will almost break my heart if I don't play this part with you," said Martin Wilton. "It's the chance of a lifetime. It's going to be hell until it's settled. Supposing Haynes thinks I'm no good?"

She broke from her thoughts with an effort. "Of course, you

are young," she said gently, "a little too young. Personally, I
think it makes the part all the more sympathetic, and I shall tell
him so. Paul Haynes is a very difficult man, but I think I can per-
suade him. Unless he gets some absurd idea into his head. He's
very thickheaded and obstinate, and once he has made up his
mind, nothing in the world will make him change it. But I am
sure he will like you; he is bound to agree with me."

He seized hold of her hands and kissed them. "You are being
an angel to me," he said, flushing. "I can't ever forget this."

She smiled at him sadly; she ran her hand through his hair.
"You remind me of someone I used to be fond of . . ." she
began, and then broke off, as though emotionally moved. He
cursed himself for his lack of tact. Of course, her husband was
dead. It must be terrible for her. How brave she was, facing life
alone like that! No one to look after her.

"You must go soon," she whispered. "It's getting late. And I've
got to say good night to my little girl. She won't sleep until I've
tucked her up myself." The child was with a nurse in lodgings on
the east coast, but he would never know that. He had probably
seen pictures of her soon after she was widowed, holding the
child in her arms. When she appeared the first time after her
husband's death, in one of his plays, carefully made up, allowing
herself to look a little wan and pale, the audience had gone
nearly mad. The publicity had helped her enormously at the
time.

"She is the only thing I have left," she said gently.

He stroked her hand awkwardly, like a clumsy animal. "I wish
I could help," he began. "I hate to think of you like this. . . . I
had no idea . . ." He fumbled with the bangle on her wrist. She
seemed very young suddenly, very pathetic. He wished he knew
how to comfort her. The world who watched her act would
never guess that off the stage she was this sweet, simple woman,
brokenhearted, her life empty.

"It's all right," she was saying, "but sometimes one gets so
frightfully lonely . . ."

Awkwardly he put his arm round her, patting her shoulder as
though she was a child. She reached for her scrap of a handkerchief, turning her face from him, blowing her nose and laughing
shakily.

"I feel so ashamed," she said. "I've never let this happen before."

He brushed the top of her head with his lips, at a loss for words, and then, impulsively, "Look here—you ought to meet my wife; she's the most sympathetic person in the world. I know you'd like her; she has a sort of gift for killing depression; she's an absolute angel. We've only got a tiny flat in a mews, but she'd adore to meet you. Come round now—it's not too late. She said she would go to a film when I rang her before dinner, but she'll be back by twelve. And we've got some wonderful records I'd love you to hear. A Beethoven concerto, César Franck . . ."

"No, no, you mustn't tempt me like that; it isn't fair. I've been foolish tonight. I can't understand myself. And I should love to meet your wife, some other time. . . . But I'm tired now; we are both tired; and you must go. Bless you for being so sweet to me."

"Good Lord! I've done nothing. I've just blundered on about myself. It's been the most marvellous evening. You've brought back all my old ideals and faith in the theatre; you've made me feel that everything's worth while. Any success I make I shall owe to you."

He stumbled out of the flat, not looking where he was going, his head in the clouds, his mind filled with the glorious, impossible future.

Thanking God she was alone at last, she sank into a chair, a cushion behind her head, a cigarette between her lips. Five minutes after he had gone the telephone rang. It was Paul Haynes.

"Hullo," he said. "I'm only this minute back from Manchester. Have you gone to bed or can I slip round for two minutes?"

"No, I'd love to see you," she lied. "Come along at once."

She powdered her face a little whiter than usual, using no colour, but shadowing her eyes. She looked very beautiful, but tired, strained.

"Now, I'm not going to keep you up," he said as soon as he came into the room. "You've had a long day, and so have I. We can't afford to burn the candle at both ends in our profession, eh? Got to have beauty sleep." He smiled broadly, showing large gums. "Well, just tell me how it went. Everything go off all right without me?"

"Marvellous—considering. You know what first rehearsals are."

"Tell me—how did they all seem?"

"Splendid, on the whole. I don't think we need make any change."

"And what about young Martin Wilton? Is he going to be good?"

"He was very much all there. Knew exactly what to do. He won't require much producing. His technique is marvellous in anyone so young. I can't understand where he's learnt it all."

"He's not too young, is he?"

"No—not really, I don't think. I hope not. We don't want to make a blunder, though. Oh, how I wish you'd been there!"

"Yes. I could have told you what I thought as soon as I'd clapped eyes on him. How did he strike you personally? Did he seem a nice chap? Not conceited? Will you like having him in the theatre?"

She did not reply for a moment, and then laughed a little self-consciously. "He's very good at his job—I've said so already. What more can I say?"

"Look here, you're keeping something back. Don't pretend with me. Part of our bargain is to tell the truth. Martin Wilton was rude, bad-mannered?"

"No, no. Please don't ask me any more. Let's forget about him."

"I don't forget, and I shall worry you until I've had this out with you. Come on, my dear; what was the trouble?"

"It's so unfair to the boy," she protested. "He probably didn't realise what he was doing. He's young, and I suppose mixes with a crowd of awful people. I know the type—half drunk and very promiscuous."

"What are you driving at? Wasn't he sober? What did he do to upset you?"

"Well, he—he tried to make the most violent love to me, that's all." She laughed and shrugged her shoulders.

Paul Haynes looked at her in amazement. "Good God! What on earth do you mean?"

"My dear, I assure you I was never more embarrassed in my life. Those sort of things don't happen to me. However, let's forget it."

"No, by heaven, we won't forget it," he said savagely. "I want to get to the bottom of this. What did he do, the little swine?"

"I asked him back here to talk over the second act and he stayed on and seemed to expect dinner. Perhaps he drank a little too much—I don't know. But he started talking the most frightful nonsense about being here alone with me, and said he'd been waiting for this for years. He tried to kiss me and was, well, rather rough. I was so surprised that I wasn't prepared, you see, and—Oh, I hate telling you all this!"

"Go on," he said.

"I think he must be very unbalanced and rather peculiar. So many young men are, nowadays, don't you think? I feel so sorry for his poor little wife."

"Do you mean the little rat is married?"

"Yes—that's the awful part about it. He seized hold of me and said would I go to his flat—his wife was out—wouldn't be back till late. He was quite uncontrolled; it was revolting. Finally I quietened him down and managed to get him away. He'd been gone only a few minutes when you rang up. That's why I'm looking so exhausted. I suppose he lost his head for the moment—probably took advantage of my being here alone. Promise me not to think any more about it."

"I'm very sorry," he said slowly. "But you remember what I told you the other day? It's just that type of thing I'm out to smash. It's vicious and disgusting. How he dared try it on with you, that's what gets me! He's probably stiff with drugs. An out-and-out rotter. And to think I was going to offer him the chance of his life! But, my dear, you weren't going to tell me. That's carrying chivalry a bit too far, isn't it?"

"But I hate making trouble," she broke in.

"Trouble? Don't talk such nonsense. If I let that boy play the part it would go against all my principles; it's one of my great ambitions to break up that gang of degenerates and I'm going to start right now. Young Mr. Wilton is going to get the surprise of his life. He'll be finished in six months. As for the part, I'd rather give it to a stage hand than to him."

She shook her head hopelessly. He moved towards the door.

"Well, you're dead beat, my dear, and must go to bed. You've been through a very trying time."

Then, as he reached for his hat, "What's the name of the chap who played your brother?"

"What?" she said carelessly. "Oh, Bobby Carson. Why?"

"We'll get on to him in the morning. Tell him to be down at the theatre for rehearsal at eleven o'clock sharp. Good night, my dear."

Nothing Hurts for Long

She had the window flung open as she dressed. The morning was cold, but she liked to feel the sharp air on her face, stinging her, running like little waves over her body; and she slapped herself, the colour coming into her skin, the nerves tingling. She sang, too, as she dressed. She sang when she took her bath, her voice seeming rich and powerful as the water fell and the steam rose, and later, before the open window, she bent and swayed, touching her toes with her fingers, stretching her arms above her head.

She permitted herself the luxury of fresh linen. Conscious of extravagance, she drew the neat pleated little pile, straight from the laundry, out of the drawer beneath her dressing table.

Her green dress was back from the cleaner's. It looked as good as new and the length was quite right, although she had worn it last winter as well. She cut the disfiguring tabs from the collar and sprayed the dress with scent to take away the smell of the cleaner's.

She felt new all over, from her head to her shoes, and the body beneath her clothes was warm and happy. Her hair had been washed and set the day before, brushed behind her ears without a parting, like the actress she admired.

She could imagine his face as he stared at her, his funny smile that ran from one ear to the corner of his mouth, and his eyebrow cocked, then, his eyes half closing, and holding out his arms—"Darling, you look marvellous—marvellous." When she thought about it she felt a queer pain in her heart because it was too much. . . . She stood before the window a moment, smiling, breathing deeply, and then she ran down the stairs singing at the top of her voice, the sound of her song taken up by the canary in his cage in the drawing room. She whistled to him, laughing, giving him his morning lump of sugar, and he hopped from side to side on his perch, his eyes beady, his tiny head fluffy and absurd after his bath. "My sweet," she said, "my sweet," and pulled the curtain so that the sun could get to him.

She glanced round the room, smiling, her finger on her lip. She pummelled at an imaginary crease in a cushion, she straightened the picture over the mantelpiece, she flicked a minute particle of dust from the top of the piano. His eyes, in the photograph on her desk, followed her round the room, and she paraded before it self-consciously, as though he were really there, patting a strand of her hair, glancing in the mirror, humming a tune. "I must remember to fill the room with flowers, of course," she thought, and immediately she saw the flowers she would buy, daffodils or hard mauve tulips, and where they would stand.

The telephone rang from the dining room. It was really the same room, divided by a curtain, but she called it the dining room. "Hullo. Yes, it's me speaking. No, my dear. I'm afraid I couldn't possibly. Yes. Yes, he comes back today. I expect him about seven. Oh! but you don't understand, there are tons of things to see to. I like to think I have the whole day. No, I'm not silly, Edna. Wait until you're married, then you'll see. Yes, rather, we'll go to a film next week—I'll let you know. Goodbye."

She put down the receiver and shrugged her shoulders. Really —how ridiculous people were. As if she could possibly go out or do anything when he was coming home at seven. Why, for the past fortnight now she had remembered to book nothing for Tuesday. Although he would not be back until the evening it did not make any difference. It was his day.

She crossed the absurd space known as the hall and went into the kitchen. She tried to look important, the mistress of the house, ready to give her orders, but her smile and the dimple at the corner of her mouth betrayed her.

She sat on the kitchen table, swinging her legs, and Mrs. Cuff stood before her with a slate. "I've been thinking, Mrs. Cuff," she began, "that he always does so enjoy saddle of mutton. What do you say?"

"Yes—he is fond of his mutton, ma'am."

"Would it be terribly extravagant? Do saddles cost a lot?"

"Well, we've been very careful this week, haven't we?"

"Yes, Mrs. Cuff, that's what I thought. And for lunch I can have a boiled egg and some of that tinned fruit, it'll be heaps. But this evening, if you think you could cope with a saddle—and p'raps—what does one eat with it? Oh! mashed potatoes, done his favourite way—and brussels sprouts, and jelly."

"Yes, ma'am, that would be nice."

"And—Mrs. Cuff—could we possibly have that kind of roly-poly pudding he likes with jam inside? You know—one is terribly surprised to see the jam."

"Just as you wish, ma'am."

"I expect he'll be frightfully hungry, don't you? I'm sure it's horrid in Berlin. I think that's all, don't you? It doesn't seem only three months, does it, it seems three years since he's been gone."

"Oh! It has been dull, ma'am. It will be a different place with him back."

"He's always so gay, isn't he, Mrs. Cuff? Never dreary and depressed like other people."

"Please, ma'am, while I remember it—we want some more Ronuk."

"I don't think I've ever seen him in a bad temper. What did you say, Mrs. Cuff? Ronuk? Is it stuff for swilling round basins?"

"No, ma'am—for cleaning the floors."

"I'll try and remember. All right, then, an egg for my lunch and the saddle tonight." She went upstairs to see that his dressing room was tidy.

> *"Someday I'll find you,*
> *Moonlight behind you,"*

she sang, and opened the cupboards in case the suits he had left behind, and might want to wear tomorrow, had not been brushed. The shabby old leather coat, not good enough for Berlin, still hung on its peg. She fingered the sleeve, and pressed her nose against the motoring cap that smelt of the stuff he put on his hair.

The photograph of herself swung crookedly from a drawing pin on the wall, curling at the corners. She pretended not to notice it, hurt that he had never bothered to get a frame, never taken it to Berlin. "I suppose men think in a different way from women," she said to herself, and suddenly she closed her eyes and stood quite still without moving, because it had come to her swiftly like a wave covering her from head to foot, a wave of the sea and the sun, exquisite and strange, the realisation that in less than ten hours he really would be next to her—they would be together again—and they loved each other, and it was all true.

She had filled the two rooms with flowers, and had even drawn the curtains separating the dining room aside, so that the space should be magnified. The canary still sang in his cage. "Louder, sweet, louder," she called, and it seemed that the house was filled with his singing—a high, joyous clamour straight from his small bursting heart—and it mingled in some indescribable fashion with the beam of gold dust shining upon the carpet, the last lingering pattern made by the setting sun.

She poked the fire and dusted the ashes in the grate, thinking as she did so how, in the evening, she would be doing the same thing, and would remember this moment. The curtains would be drawn then, and the lamps lit, and the bird quiet in his cage, and he lounging in the armchair by the fire, stretching out his legs, watching her lazily. "Stop fussing—and come here," while she turned towards him, smiling, her hand on his knee. And she would think, "This afternoon I was alone and now I'm looking back remembering it," and the thought would be somehow delicious, like a secret vice. She hugged her knees and stared at the fire, childishly excited at the memory of the large, expensive bottle of bath salts she had bought that morning and put on his dressing table, as well as the bowl of flowers.

When the telephone rang she sighed regretfully, unwilling to leave the fire, alter her position and be taken from the queer, lonely pleasure of her dreams to the conversation of someone who did not matter, forced and unreal.

"Hullo," she said, and there came from the other end of the wire a little choking sound, the pitiful drawn breath of one who is crying, who cannot control her tears.

"Is that you? It's May . . . I had to ring you. I—I'm so desperately unhappy," and the voice trailed off, choked, suffocated.

"Why," she said, "what on earth is the matter? Tell me, quick, can I do anything? Are you ill?"

She waited a moment, and then the voice came again, muffled and strange.

"It's Fred. It's all over—we're finished. He wants me to divorce him—he's stopped loving me." Then she heard a quiver and a sharp intake of breath, and the sound of sobbing, hideous, degrading, uncontrolled.

"My poor darling!" she began, amazed and horrified. "But how perfectly frightful. I can't believe it—Fred—but it's absurd."

"Please—please—come round and see me," begged the voice. "I think I'm going out of my mind—I don't know what I'm doing."

"Yes—of course. I'll come right away."

As she put on her things she brushed from her mind the selfish regret she felt at leaving the fire and the book she was reading, and the idea of making toast for tea, all the things that were part of the loveliness of waiting for him, and she gave her thoughts to May, broken and distressed, crying helplessly, her happiness gone from her.

She went in a taxi, because, after all, May was her greatest friend, and one and six was not so much; and that reminded her she had forgotten about the Ronuk. Oh well! Never mind. . . . And Mrs. Cuff seemed pleased with the saddle of mutton. . . . Was he crossing now? she wondered; how awful if he was sick, poor angel, how sweet . . . She must remember to think about May, though; Life was frightful, of course . . . And here she was at the door, thank goodness, only a shilling; still, she would go home in a bus, anyway. . . .

May was lying face downwards on a sofa, her head buried in a cushion. She knelt by her side, patting her shoulder, murmuring senseless little words of comfort.

"May, darling May—you mustn't cry like that, it's so weakening for you; it will pull you down—try not to, please, try and pull yourself together, darling."

And May lifted her head and showed her face, swollen, disfigured and blotched, so ravaged with her tears that it was shocking, something that should not be seen.

"I can't stop," May whispered. "You can't understand what it is—it's tearing at me like a knife, and I can't forget his face as he told me, so cold and different . . . it wasn't him at all, it was somebody else."

"But it's simply unbelievable, May! Why should Fred suddenly take it into his head to tell you he doesn't love you? He must have been drunk—it can't be true."

"It is true." May was tearing her handkerchief to little shreds and biting the ends. "And it's not sudden, that's the whole thing; it's been coming on for some while. I've never told you—I've never breathed a word to anyone. I kept hoping and praying it was only my imagination, but all the time I knew deep down that everything was wrong."

"Oh! my poor May. To think I didn't know . . ."

"Don't you understand that there are some things one can't tell, that are too intimate; that I was terrified to breathe, hoping if I kept silent they wouldn't come true?"

"Yes—yes—I see. . . ."

"And then today, when there was no longer any doubt, I suppose the agony and terror I had been holding inside could not stay silent any more; I had to give way."

"Oh, May—darling, darling May!" she said, looking round the room hopelessly, as though by getting up and moving a piece of furniture she could do some good.

"What a beast—what a brute!" she said.

"Oh, he's not that!" said May, staring before her, her voice weary from crying. "Fred's only a man like other men. They're all the same; they can't help it. I don't blame him. I'm only angry with myself for being such a fool to care."

"How long have you known?"

"Ever since he came back from America."

"But, May darling, that's eight months ago. You surely haven't been suffering all this time, keeping it to yourself? It's impossible!"

"Oh, my dear—it hasn't been eight months to me, but an eternity! I don't know if you can realise for one minute the hell that it's been. Never quite being certain, the awful bewildering doubt and pretending that nothing was wrong. Then the degradation of trying to please him, of not noticing his manner, of making myself a sort of slave in the hope that he might come back to me. Eight months of misery and shame . . ."

"Oh, if only I could have helped!" she began; and she was thinking, "But these things don't happen to people—they can't; it's only in plays."

"Help isn't any use," said May. "You have to go through it alone. I believe every moment has made its mark upon me, hurting and branding my heart—every moment from the very first until the last."

"But, May darling, why should America have made any difference?"

"Because going away does make a difference to men. Don't you see that when Fred wasn't with me he forgot about wanting to be with me, and once he forgot that he was ready to forget anything. And a different way of living, and seeing new things, and meeting new people."

"But still . . ."

"Directly he came back I knew what had happened. I can't describe to you the difference there was. Nothing marked or striking. But a queer, subtle change. Little things he said, his manner, even his voice—he talked louder, like someone who is trying to bluff a secret—can you understand? The very first day he was home I saw—and I pushed it aside but it hurt—and it went on hurting until today—and now I know at last what I've tried to hide."

"Is he in love with somebody else?" she whispered.

"Yes . . ." and the voice broke again, the tears welling up into her eyes, "yes . . . there is some woman, of course—behind it; but it's not only that—it's our life he doesn't want any more, this house—me—everything. He wants to break away altogether. He doesn't want ties, or a home—he talks of going back to America . . ."

"But Fred to behave like that—and all this time when I've seen you together, not a sign from either of you—my poor May!"

And though her words were full of pity and she held May close to her, trying to comfort her, she was aware that her heart could not hold any real sympathy, and that the sight of May's tears awoke even a sense of irritation and contempt which was difficult to banish, and she said to herself, with her eye on the clock, "I suppose I can't feel this because I know it couldn't ever happen to me."

"I haven't thought yet how I'm going to live," said May. "All I know is that it's impossible to suffer more than I have suffered already. Those terrible months—and then today."

"Don't cry, darling," she said, and she was thinking, "Oh dear! Is she going to begin all over again? It's really too much. Besides, it's getting late."

"Don't you think," she said gently, "that a large brandy and soda would do you good? And your poor head must be splitting. If you go upstairs and go to bed with a nice hot bottle—and two aspirins—and try to forget . . ."

May smiled at her through her tears. "If you think that is a cure," she said. "No—I'm all right . . . don't worry about me. You must get back, too . . . he's coming home tonight, isn't he? I've only just remembered."

"Yes," she said indifferently, trying not to parade her pleasure, and to make up for it she seized hold of May's hands and said, "Darling—if you knew how terribly I feel for you, if only I could share it. What a wicked shameful thing life is—God shouldn't let it happen—this horrid, miserable world, why were we ever born . . ." And the tears came into her eyes, too, and they rocked together on the sofa, and she was thinking, her heart fluttering with absurd joy and the image of his face before her, "Oh dear— I'm so happy!"

Finally she tore herself away, the hands of the clock pointing to half past six. "Of course I'll come tomorrow," and "Supposing his train is early," she thought, and she wondered how she could possibly keep from smiling before poor May. "Darling, are you sure you are all right left alone?" she said; and, not waiting for the answer, she was dragging on her coat and her hat, looking for her bag, trembling with the excitement which it was impossible to control any longer.

"Good night, darling," she said, kissing her fondly, patting the blotched, disfigured face which roused in her an insane desire to laugh. ("How vile of me," she thought.) She searched feverishly for some parting, consoling phrase; and because in half an hour she would be with him, blotted against him, losing herself, caring for no one, drunk and absurd, she said happily, her face radiant as she stood on the doorstep, "It's all right; nothing hurts for long."

For the fourth time she made up the fire, stabbing at the coal with the tongs, sparks flying onto the carpet, and she did not notice. She jumped up from her chair and touched the flowers, she sat down to the piano and played the bar of a tune, only to run across to the window and pull aside the curtain, thinking she heard a taxi.

She was not sure how she wanted him to find her. Crouched by the fire, perhaps, or lying in a chair, or putting on a record. The clock in the dining room struck eight. "Oh! but it must be fast," she thought wildly, and called to the kitchen, "Mrs. Cuff, what is the right time?"

"Past eight, ma'am, and the dinner is spoiling."

"Can't you keep it hot?"

"I can keep it hot, ma'am, but the joint is overdone and the vegetables are cooked. Such a pity. He's not going to enjoy it much."

"I can't understand why he is late, Mrs. Cuff. I've rung through to the station, and the train came in punctually at six forty-five. What can have happened?"

She walked from the dining room to the kitchen, biting her nails, wondering if she was going to be sick. Surely he would have let her know if he had been coming by a later train. "He'll be so ravenous when he does arrive he'll eat anything—if it's burnt to cinders," she said. She was not hungry herself; it would have choked her to touch the dinner.

"He's always up in the clouds," she thought, "he probably doesn't realise the time. That's the worst of being temperamental. All the same . . ."

She put on a gramophone record, but the noise grated; the voice of Maurice Chevalier sounded high-pitched and ridiculous.

She went and stood before the looking glass. Perhaps he would creep in suddenly and stand behind her, put his hands on her shoulders and lean his face against hers.

She closed her eyes. Darling! Was that a taxi? No—nothing.

"This wasn't how I imagined it at all," she thought. She threw herself in a chair and tried to read. Hopeless—what nonsense people wrote, anyway. Why was one supposed to take an interest in the life of someone who did not exist? She wandered over to the piano once more and began to strum.

"Someday I'll find you,
Moonlight behind you,"

she sang, but her fingers were heavy and her voice a poor thin
whisper of a thing that went flat and could not strike the right
note. The canary in the cage pricked up his ears. He started his
song and soon it filled the room, deafening her, shrill and absurd,
so loud that she flung the cover onto his cage in irritation.

"Be quiet, can't you, you horrid little thing!" she said. It was
so different from the morning, and as she poked the fire again
she remembered that moment during the afternoon when she
had smiled to herself and thought, "I shall remember this
minute."

And the chair was still empty, and the room looked lifeless
and dull, and she was a little girl whose mouth turned down at
the corners, who bit the ends of her hair, who wriggled with
hunched shoulders, sniffing in a hankie, "It isn't fair."

Soon she had to go upstairs again to do her face, because she
had dressed herself all ready for him at half past nine. Her face
wanted doing again. Her nose must be powdered, her lips lightly
touched (the stuff did come off so), and her hair brushed away
from her face in the new way.

As she took a final peep in the glass she thought how cheap
she was making herself—any girl waiting for a man—squalid, like
birds who paraded before each other, and it seemed to her that
the face that stared at her from the mirror, pretty and smiling,
was not the real she at all, was forced and insincere; the real she
was a frightened girl who did not care how she looked, whose
heart was beating, who wanted only to run out into the street
and beg him to come home to her. . . .

Then she stood quite still—because surely that was a taxi
drawing up to the front door, and surely that was the sound of a
key in the lock, and weren't those voices in the hall, suitcases
dumped down, and Mrs. Cuff coming out of the kitchen, and his
voice? For a moment she did not move; it was as though something rose in her throat, stifling her, and something crept down
into her legs, paralysing her—and she wanted to go quickly and
hide, locking herself somewhere. Then the wave of excitement
broke over her once more, and she ran out of the bedroom and

stood at the head of the staircase, looking down at him in the hall below.

He was bending over his suitcase, doing something with his keys. "You might take these things up right away, Mrs. Cuff," he was saying; and then he straightened himself, hearing her step on the stair above, and he looked up and said, "Hullo, darling."

How funny—why, he had got fatter, surely, or was it just his coat? And he must have cut himself shaving, because he had a silly little bit of plaster on his chin.

She went down the stairs slowly, trying to smile, but odd, somehow, shy.

"I've been so worried," she said. "Whatever happened? You must be absolutely famished."

"Oh! I missed my connection," he said. "I thought you would guess. It's all right, Mrs. Cuff, I had my dinner on the train."

Had his dinner? But that was not how she had planned it.

He kissed her hurriedly, patting her shoulder as though she were a little girl, and then he laughed, and said, "Why—what on earth have you done to your hair?"

She laughed too, pretending she did not mind. "I've had it washed—it's nothing, just a bit untidy." They went into the drawing room.

"Come and get warm," she said.

But he did not sit down, he lounged about, jingling the money in his pockets.

"Of course I would come back and find a lousy fog," he said. "God—what a country."

"Is it foggy?" she said. "I'd not noticed it." And then there was a pause for a moment, and she looked at him—yes, he was fatter, different somehow—and she said stupidly, "How did you like Berlin?"

"Oh! it's a grand place," he said. "London can't compare with it. The atmosphere, the life there, the people, everything. They know how to live." And he smiled, rocking on his heels, remembering it; and she thought how terrible it was that he was seeing things in his mind now that she would never see, going over things he had done that she would never know.

"Fancy," she said, and she knew she hated Berlin, and the people, and the life. She did not want to hear about it—and yet supposing he did not tell her, but kept it to himself, wouldn't that be worse? "Oh!" he said suddenly, striking his forehead, a stupid theatrical gesture—not impulsive but planned. "By Jove—I must telephone. I'd quite forgotten. Some people who are over here from Berlin."

"Telephone?" she said, her heart sick. "But, darling, you've only just come back."

"I promised, though, rather important," he said, and kissed her as though he were saying, "There, now—be a good girl," and already he had pushed aside the curtains and was lifting the receiver and giving the number. It tripped off his tongue, she thought, he did not have to look it up in the book.

She went and crouched by the fire, cold for no reason, and tired. She felt empty inside—perhaps it was because she hadn't had any dinner.

He had got on to his friends. He was talking German—and she did not understand. A flow of hideous stupid words, and he kept laughing—surely these friends couldn't be as funny as all that. Why was he laughing? She thought he would never finish. And then he came back through the curtain, red in the face, smiling.

"Well," he said, talking rather loudly, "tell me all the news." Perhaps he felt that after all it was her turn. She felt herself closing up, shy, stupid. She remembered May and her husband. No—she could not tell him about that, it was as if—as if it wasn't the right moment, it was too soon—besides . . .

"Oh! I can't think," she said. "There doesn't seem to be anything to tell."

He laughed, and his laugh turned into a yawn. "How's the old bird?" he said, glancing carelessly at the cage, not really wanting to know.

"He's all right," she said.

He sprawled in a chair, still yawning, his mouth wide open, and she knew as she looked at him that it was not just her fancy, it was not just imagination, but, besides being fatter, he was different in another way—altered, queer—*changed*.

He whistled softly, his eyes staring into space. Then he said slowly, "Gosh—time's a funny thing. To think that at this moment last night I was in Berlin."

She smiled nervously, anxious to please, but something stabbed her heart like a sharp little knife, twisting and turning—and into her mind ran the words over and over again: "It's all right, nothing hurts for long—nothing hurts for long."

The Rendezvous

Robert Scrivener noted, with some slight irritation, that his secretary had her eye upon the clock. He had made no engagements for the evening, in view of his early departure the following morning for Geneva, and she knew this, therefore her preoccupation with the passing of time could not be on his account. No doubt she had what was vulgarly called "a date." A secretary had no business with "dates" when her employer, a writer of Robert Scrivener's standing, had a mass of correspondence to clear before leaving the country.

"Judith," he said at last, raising his horn-rimmed spectacles and balancing them on his forehead, "you keep looking at the clock. Are you, for some reason, in a hurry?"

She had the grace to blush. "It's all right," she said quickly, "it's only that I'm going to the theatre later, and I rather wanted to change first."

So typical of the girl's mentality. To arrange a visit to the theatre on the one day of the week when she was likely to be kept late. He stared at her, baffled by her stupidity.

"What an odd thing to do," he said, "to choose tonight of all nights to go to the theatre. Does that mean you want to go at once, and leave these letters until I return from Geneva?"

She had flushed all over her face. Most unbecoming. "Of course not," she said. "I'm really in no hurry. It was just . . ."

"Youthful impatience to be free of your fetters," he declared, "to be done with all this tedious nonsense. I quite understand. May I go on? I'll make my letters as brief as possible."

He replaced his spectacles, and continued dictating his letters in measured tones. Robert Scrivener was a writer of renown and great integrity. He had first attracted notice in the literary world by his reviews in a liberal weekly, and later in a Sunday newspaper. These reviews showed him to be a man of wide culture; given neither to wild enthusiasms nor to damning condemnation, he showed appreciation of the finer, more polished writings of his contemporaries, of the scholarly biographies, of the books of travel in countries less known to the general reader. In fiction he was careful to praise books which were unlikely to sell, but which showed some constructive approach to world problems.

During the war—poor eyesight kept him from active service— he continued his literary criticism, with a slight bias towards the left in politics, but he gave his services to the censorship department of the War Office and received a small decoration in recompense. A pamphlet entitled "On Both Sides of the Fence," gently tilting at the poor organisation of certain wartime governmental activities, was always understood to have been written by Robert Scrivener. Then, the war over, he published a novel that was instantly successful and was not only praised by his fellow critics but bought by the general public. *Fortune Favours the Brave* was the story of a soldier who, horrified by war and its consequences, holds a spearhead on the Italian front against tremendous odds, and is subsequently captured. He tries to escape three times, but each attempt proves abortive. Finally he catches bubonic plague and dies, but not before giving a message on freedom to his fellow prisoners which is a model of exquisite prose, and for which Scrivener himself received an Italian decoration. The novel was, indeed, an amazing and deeply moving piece of work, coming as it did from someone who had never in all his life seen a shot fired.

His success was not a flash in the pan. The novel that succeeded the war book, entitled *Madrigal,* was the story of a man who, pursued by women, could find no peace or harmony within himself until he had acceded to their demands, and so impoverished his own spiritual integrity. Scrivener himself was unmarried, and was not known to possess intimate friends of the opposite sex, but his second novel was widely acclaimed. Here at last was someone who might restore some sort of standard to English fiction. Other novels followed, all exquisitely written, all throwing into relief the problems that so beset mankind during the present century, and Scrivener's income began to approach five figures.

Robert Scrivener did not permit himself to be spoilt by his success, and he was careful to tell his friends that he would never be tempted by offers from Hollywood to prostitute his work upon the screen. As a matter of fact no such offer came, but this was beside the point. Had it come, Robert Scrivener would have turned it down. He concentrated almost entirely upon his literary work, but he also gave lectures, and appeared from time to time on "Brains Trust." He had a good appearance and an agreeable speaking voice, and to those television viewers who were ignorant of his work as novelist and critic he suggested the law, a distinguished barrister, or even a youngish judge. Scrivener knew this and was not displeased. In fact he was determined to touch lightly on certain aspects of the law, as it concerned writers, during his forthcoming series of lectures at Geneva; but mostly he would concern himself with the integrity of the writer's Self and how, once dedicated to the perfecting of the written word, no writer who respected his profession should swerve from the high standard he had set himself.

Robert Scrivener continued to dictate his letters; although he was careful not to prolong the dictation, there was a certain deliberation in his voice, a formality of delivery, that warned the girl he considered her evening engagement unnecessary, and a breach of faith. Finally he removed his spectacles and sighed.

"That will be all, Judith," he said. "Don't let me detain you a moment longer."

The secretary, still uncomfortable, felt she had ruined Robert Scrivener's evening. Her own late arrival at the theatre, unchanged, did not matter.

"I'll get them typed at once, and bring them for signature," she said, pushing back her chair, and then, before leaving the room, remembered a letter, still unopened, on his desk.

"I'm afraid I forgot to open the one from Switzerland," she said. "It's there, on your blotter. It must be from that fan who keeps bothering you about some poem you promised to criticise. I think I recognise the handwriting."

Scrivener glanced at the envelope. "Very probably," he said. "In any case it can wait. I would not dream of letting you be late for the theatre."

His secretary left the room, and immediately she had gone

Scrivener reached for the letter. How careless of him, he thought, as he slit the envelope with a paper knife, not to glance through the pile before starting to dictate. He might have known there would be a letter, and even the scribbled "Personal" would not keep it sacred from the prying eyes of Judith.

Some few months previously Robert Scrivener had received a letter from a reader praising three poems that had appeared in a new quarterly. Nowadays he did not often contribute verse to literary periodicals, and when he did so it was a special favour, an intimate revelation, so he thought, of his more personal feelings, which he would have hesitated to make public but for his duty to Art and to Letters. The editor of the quarterly, whose own book of verse had recently been praised by Scrivener in the Sunday newspaper for which he still wrote, was pleased to publish his more famous colleague's group of poems, and they were, indeed, given pride of place when the quarterly appeared.

The writer of the letter said that never had any poems, save those of Rimbaud and Rilke, made such an instant and profound impression upon the reader. The reader's world, literally, had changed. The depth of wisdom, the cosmic understanding, the sheer tragedy of outlook—the poet, as it were, looking out upon a doomed world with a wry smile, yet giving this same world his benison—these things had made the reader review the whole of life in its totality, personal problems were forgotten, the reader—in a word—was reborn.

Robert Scrivener answered the letter. The signature was ambiguous, A. Limoges, and the address Zurich. Scrivener visualised a professor of psychology, or if not a professor—for surely such a one would have letters after his name—possibly a student, at any rate someone of great sensibility and intelligence.

A week later he received an acknowledgement. The writer had not slept the night after receiving it, but had walked the streets of Zurich. Scrivener replied to this letter too. He might not have done so had he not also received that day a press cutting from some obscure newspaper in the United States disparaging his last novel, *Taurus*, which, anticipating A.I.D., showed how the self-sacrifice of one man could be responsible for the birth of thousands. The reviewer called the novel "pretentious nonsense," and advised the author to inject himself with some genuine bull's blood. Scrivener threw the press cutting into the wastepaper basket; nevertheless the review pricked, and it would be irritating if his American friends should come across it. It was a relief to turn to the letter from A. Limoges. This time he let himself go, and discoursed for two pages on suffering, the inner man, and the existentialist approach.

There was silence for a week, and then a modest note came containing a poem by A. Limoges and asking for criticism. Scrivener read the poem indulgently. It was not bad. A little influenced, of course, by everything A. Limoges had ever read, but even so there was nothing glaringly faulty about it, or even amateur. Scrivener wrote back, enclosing his own signed photograph. He imagined the lonely professor, or lonely student, placing the photograph inside his copy of *Madrigal—Madrigal*, it appeared, was the most treasured of Scrivener's books, next to the poems—and then Scrivener dismissed the fellow, the "fan" as Judith insisted on calling him, from his mind. He was surprised to receive by return of post the photograph of a girl, signed Annette Limoges, and he realised, with a slight shock, that his correspondent and admirer was neither a professor of psychology nor a student, but sold nylon stockings in a large store in Zurich.

Scrivener's first reaction was to tear the photograph in two and throw it, with the letter, into his fire. Then the eyes of the girl, very large and liquid, stared up at him reproachfully. She was certainly lovely. Nothing cheap about her, or vulgar, and the letter enclosed with the photograph said something about a father, now dead, who had been a colonel in the French army. Scrivener locked the letter and photograph in a drawer in his desk where the inquisitive hands of Judith could not rummage, and it was only when yet another letter came, apologising for the presumption of sending her photograph, and declaring that the sender was so overcome by Scrivener's own photograph that she had, for the second time, walked the streets of Zurich by night, that the renowned author of *Fortune Favours the Brave* decided to acknowledge it.

It was following upon this exchange of photographs that a weekly correspondence was set up between Robert Scrivener and Annette Limoges. It made, so he told himself, a relaxation from the work he was engaged upon, a biography of Swedenborg. His letters varied. At times serious, at times amusing, he formed the habit of treating his unknown correspondent as a form of peg on which to hang his theories and his moods. A week that had gone well reflected itself the following weekend in the letter to Annette Limoges. The letter would be confident, even gay, containing scraps of gossip about his own friends of whom the salesgirl in the Zurich store had never heard. A week that had gone badly, with only a few pages of manuscript covered, resulted in a certain asperity of outlook, or perhaps a tirade against his muse, which had, for the time, forsaken him. The letters he received in return invariably commented on his feelings and his moods, making Scrivener feel that here, at last, was someone who understood, someone who, while making no sort of interference in his life, had yet become part of it, absorbing his confidences as blotting paper absorbed the ink blobs from his pen. Annette Limoges lived, it would seem, only to retain what Scrivener cared to send her, passing chills in London were her concern in Zurich, his laughter at noon her solace at midnight, his thoughts, his whims, his attitudes her spiritual food.

It did not occur to Robert Scrivener, when he accepted the engagement to give two lectures at Geneva, that this might give him an opportunity to meet Annette Limoges in person. He wrote and told her of his forthcoming visit, as he told her all his plans, but with no other thought in mind. It was Annette—and by now they were Annette and Robert—who wrote in great excitement saying that the dates he had booked for the lectures in Geneva happened, by a miracle, to coincide with her own vacation, and it would be the simplest thing in the world to take the train to Geneva and meet him at last.

Now it happened that Scrivener had, that particular week, attended the wedding of a friend and fellow author, a widower, who had suddenly decided to marry again. Although Scrivener had gone to the wedding in a spirit of mockery he found himself, during the reception, with the tables turned. The elderly groom, his young bride at his side, twitted him, Robert Scrivener, with being an old maid! There were standers-by who laughed. He even overheard a guest murmur something offensive to the effect that experts who wrote books called *Taurus* should practise what they preached. When he shook hands with his old friend, whose books he despised—they sold in ridiculous numbers—and congratulated him, his friend smiled, almost as if he were sorry for Scrivener, and said, "Don't you envy me, going off to Majorca with this?" And he looked at his bride and laughed.

The episode rankled: it was almost as though there was some disagreeable suggestion afoot that he, Robert Scrivener, was a fake, without the wide experience of life that his novels appeared to possess. Boldly he took up his pen and wrote, there and then, to Annette Limoges suggesting that she should come down to Geneva to meet him, and that he would reserve the necessary accommodation.

As the time for the encounter drew near Robert Scrivener was aware of mounting excitement. He felt ten, twenty years younger, and found it almost impossible to concentrate on his notes for the forthcoming lectures. The integrity of the writer, the perfection of the written word, these things took second place when he thought of the two connecting rooms at the Hotel Mirabelle, Geneva—he had been careful to make the reservations himself—and on this last night, before departure, he allowed himself the luxury of imagining the first meeting: Annette radiant and a little shy, smiling at him across a dinner table set on a terrace. The lecture was not until the following night, and his earliest engagement was luncheon with the Swiss man of letters who was organising the tour, therefore the first evening would be set aside for Annette alone. The letter he now opened, which had escaped the vigilant eye of Judith, was an ecstatic note telling him she would arrive in Geneva first, possibly the day before, and would be waiting at the airport to meet him. "If I'm not there," she said, "it will mean I don't want to embarrass you before the officials, and you will then find me at the hotel." This showed her discretion; she was not going to put herself forward in any way. And then . . . Image succeeded image, and Robert Scrivener could hardly wait for the necessary hours to pass before he left London airport for Geneva.

The flight to Geneva was luckily smooth—Scrivener disliked bumps, and a rough trip might have brought on migraine—and as the aircraft taxied up the landing strip he looked out of the window eagerly for a young girlish figure with a cloud of light brown hair. The time was late afternoon; the sun blazed, the

lake was a dazzling blue. A crowd of people had gathered behind the reception barrier to greet their friends, but he could see
no one resembling the photograph that he now knew so well.

Scrivener went through customs, collected his baggage and
hailed a porter. No official advanced to welcome him. This did
not bother him, although it might have been courteous. As for
Annette, she had warned him she might not come. It was disappointing, but discreet. The porter summoned a taxi, and very
soon it drew up before the Hotel Mirabelle, gay and inviting in
the bright sun, its windows and terrace overlooking the blue
lake. Scrivener's bags were seized by a page, and he went to sign
the register and collect his key.

It was a moment of apprehension. He had a foreboding that
after all Annette Limoges might not have come. Something could
have prevented her. Some mishap in Zurich. He heard himself
asking in an unsteady voice if there was any message for him.
The concierge turned to a pigeonhole and produced an envelope; it was in her handwriting. He stepped aside and opened it.
The message was brief. She had arrived safely, actually she had
been in Geneva two days. It had turned so hot in Zurich, and her
holiday had started, so it seemed foolish not to take the opportunity and give herself an extra day. The rooms were wonderful.
The flowers he had ordered to welcome her were exquisite. Geneva itself a paradise. She had gone to bathe, but would be back
at the hotel directly. Scrivener followed the page upstairs.

The first thing he did, after glancing round his room and ap-
preciating the window and the balcony, with the view over the
lake, was to try the communicating door. It was locked. However, that could easily be remedied. Feeling a little foolish,
he put his eye to the keyhole. He could see nothing. He
straightened himself and began to unpack. He had a bath,
changed, and went out onto the balcony. The waiters were already on the terrace serving drinks. Beyond the terrace was the
promenade, and beyond the promenade the lake. In the far distance he could see diving boards, and boats, and collections of
happy bathers sitting about bronzed and idle, or with bobbing
heads in the still water.

Scrivener telephoned for his floor waiter to bring him a martini, and as he sipped it, standing there on the balcony looking

down on the terrace, his anticipation of what the hours would bring him grew into a fever of impatience. Why was she late? It was not thus that he had imagined the start of their evening.

Too agitated to remain on the balcony, he went back into his room and, flinging himself in a chair, began to read over the notes for his lecture. It was no use, though. He could not concentrate. Then he had the idea that she might, after all, have arrived back at the hotel and gone to her room, lacking the courage to let him know. He crossed the room and tapped on the door. There was no answer. Possibly she was in her bath. He seized the telephone and asked to be put through to the room next door. There was silence, and after a moment or two the voice at the switchboard informed him that room 28—his own room was 27—was unoccupied.

"Unoccupied?" he said. "But there must be some mistake. I want to speak to a Mademoiselle Limoges, who has taken room 28."

"Monsieur is mistaken," replied the voice. "Mademoiselle Limoges occupies room 50, on the floor above."

Scrivener controlled himself with difficulty. The fools at the reception must have made some idiotic mistake. He had distinctly ordered the two communicating rooms. The mistake could no doubt be set right, but perhaps not tonight. He asked, with shaking voice, to be put through to room 50. The inevitable ringing tone followed, with the inevitable no reply. Scrivener swore, and replaced the receiver. Then he went down to the terrace and ordered another martini. People came out onto the terrace, in couples or in groups, some to drink and some to dine, and Robert Scrivener sat at his solitary table with nothing to do but watch the door leading into the Mirabelle restaurant. Even the solace of lighting a cigarette was denied him; he was a nonsmoker. A third martini did little to calm him; being a moderate drinker at all times, this sudden taking to spirits produced an intensity of fever. It occurred to him that some disaster might have overtaken her, cramp in the lake, anything, and it was only a matter of time before a grave reception clerk would appear through the restaurant door to break the news.

Twice the waiter had come to his table with the menu and had been waved away. Then, as he downed his last martini, he saw advancing towards him, half screened by a group of people dressed for dinner, someone in striped jeans and sandals, a vivid emerald shirt, and yes, it was she, it was Annette Limoges. She raised her hand and waved, and blew a kiss. Scrivener stood up. She was by his side, taller than he had expected, darker, the hair still damp from her swim and dishevelled, but lovely, undeniably lovely, people at the next table were staring at her.

"Can you ever forgive me?" she said, and the voice, attractive with its slight accent, was soft and low.

"Forgive you?" he said. "Of course I forgive you. Waiter . . ." and he turned to summon a passing waiter for another martini, but she put her hand on his arm. "No . . . no . . ." she said quickly, "you surely don't think I'm going to sit down like this? I'll fly upstairs and change. I'll be ten minutes. Order me a Cinzano."

She was gone before he had time to assimilate anything that had happened. He sat down again and began to crumple a roll, thrusting small pieces of it into his mouth. The photograph had led him to expect something attractive and warm, but the reality far surpassed the photograph, and indeed the images conjured in imagination. In fact . . . he was bowled over. He had seen himself being indulgent, a little patronising, while she sat listening with rapt eyes to his conversation, but now he was not so sure; hypnotised by the striped jeans and the emerald shirt, he felt suddenly at a loss, callow, as awkward as an undergraduate ordering his first dinner.

He was considering the menu in consultation with the maître d'hôtel when she returned—better than her word, the minutes were seven. She had changed into a strapless frock of some sort of spotted material, showing to great advantage the already bronzed arms and shoulders. The light brown hair, worn long when she first appeared, was now twisted into a knot behind her head, very chic, very becoming, and the touch of green eye shadow made the eyes themselves seem even larger and more lustrous. Scrivener felt himself outdistanced. Her appearance warranted a tuxedo, a buttonhole, and his grey suit somehow seemed out of place, more fitted to a doctor, a lawyer.

"You can't imagine," she said as she sat down, "what it means to me to do this. After the long hours in that terrible store, where

I care for no one and no one cares for me, to be transplanted, by the wave of a magician's wand. And you are the magician, you, sitting there in front of me, just as I imagined. Robert. Robert Scrivener."

He smiled, and made a little gesture of deprecation. "The Cinzano," he said, "is it iced enough for you, is it how you like it?"

"Perfect." She embraced him with her smile. "But then, everything is perfect. Geneva, the hotel, the lake; and you."

The waiter was at his elbow again, and Scrivener had to take his eyes away from Annette Limoges and concentrate upon another perfection, the final decision of what they should eat and drink. It seemed to him immensely important that he should not fail her in this, that their first dinner together should be as momentous as everything else had been to her.

"You are quite sure that is what you would like?" he asked for the third time, overanxious in his desire to please, and she nodded, and the waiter bowed and disappeared.

"Well . . ." Robert Scrivener looked across the table at his correspondent over so many months, to whom, indeed, he had bared his heart, released his innermost thoughts, and he found himself inarticulate, the fine phrases that rolled from his pen with such ease were non-existent.

"The wonderful thing about this," said the girl, "is that we know each other already. We don't have to break any ice. We might have been having dinner together night after night."

He wished he felt the same. The one thing that troubled him at that moment was that they had never dined before.

"I know," he lied, "it makes all the difference."

"Usually," said Annette, "there is some sort of restraint when two people meet for the first time. But not with us. You know that you can tell me everything. I know the same."

She had finished her Cinzano and was looking about her for another. Feverishly, he summoned the waiter.

"Another Cinzano for Mademoiselle," he said. It was all very well on paper, alone in his study, with a glance perhaps at the photograph, but now in reality, faced with this vision, with that face, those eyes, those lips, how much simpler it would be if they did not have to talk, did not even have to endure the performance of this dinner, but could go upstairs and let nature take its course. Forget conversation. Forget everything.

The business of eating helped, and with the wine, the blessed wine, his self-confidence returned, his aplomb, and he could not have seemed dull to her or disappointing because she laughed and smiled, accepting his smallest remarks as witticisms; it was just a momentary phase, he realised, that sensation of his own dumb idiocy. At any rate, she had not noticed it. Little flattering phrases fell from her tongue like crumbs of comfort. She asked him about the lectures he was to give, about the biography he was writing, every remark she made proving how often she must read his letters, and when the ritual of the dinner was over, and they sat over their coffee and liqueurs, Robert Scrivener felt himself bathing, as it were, in a kind of luminous warmth. He was being nourished and caressed by someone who was half the figment of his imagination and half the bodily presence of this beautiful entity before him.

"You know," he said, and he was aware now that his words were a little slurred, "you know, my dear, the fools have made a mistake about our rooms."

"A mistake?" She looked up at him, puzzled.

"Yes. I'm on the first floor. You are on the second."

"Oh, but that's my fault." She smiled across at him. "When I arrived I was on the first floor, number 28, I think it was, but it was such a little cubbyhole of a room, I asked to have it changed. Now I have a beauty. With a wonderful view both ways."

"Ah! That explains it."

He pretended to understand, but in truth he was taken aback. From what he had been able to glimpse of the room next to his—from the closed window on the balcony—it had not been a cubbyhole at all, but exactly similar to his. He had made a point of ordering communicating rooms of the same size.

"I hope they've given you a quiet room," she said. "You'll be working, probably, last thing at night and first thing in the morning. That's your usual routine, isn't it?"

"I don't work on holiday," he said.

"But the lectures," she said, "do you mean they are quite ready, no final polishing to give?"

"Any polishing," he told her, "will be done on the platform, as I speak."

She was surely being a little obtuse. He might have thought it natural modesty, had she been shy, but she was so certain of herself, with such innate sophistication, that this supposition that he would be working in the evening struck him as strange. He wondered whether he should be blunt, announce, with a laugh, "If there is one thing I detest, it's walking about hotel passages in a dressing gown," when she suddenly put out her hand across the table and took his. "This is the most wonderful part of all," she said, "that I can say anything to you, just anything. As though you were my twin. Other people think of you as Robert Scrivener, but not me."

The warmth held him deliciously. So much promise in the voice, such subtle strength in the pressure of the hand. After all, did it matter so much about the room on the second floor? The actual fact of separation might make the going to and fro the more intriguing.

"It's exciting," she said, "to be so terribly in love."

He returned the pressure of her hand, wondering how best to manoeuvre their departure from the terrace. Perhaps a stroll by the lake for ten minutes or so, and then . . .

"It happened so suddenly," she said, "you know how it is, it must have happened to you a dozen times, with your experience. You know how in *Madrigal* you made Davina walk into a restaurant and lose all account of time and space. It was like that with me. Directly I saw Alberto come out of the bathing hut yesterday I knew I was finished."

Scrivener let his hand stay where it was, in hers, but he felt his body stiffen.

"Alberto," he repeated.

"Yes," she said, "Alberto. It sounds like a hairdresser, doesn't it? In point of fact he's the bathing attendant on the Mirabelle plage, and the handsomest thing you've ever seen. Bronzed, a sort of sun god. We took one look at each other, and there it was." She laughed, and squeezed his hand again.

"I said I had no towel," she went on, "so we got into conversation, and then—he acts as swimming instructor too—he came in the water with me. Of course I swim like a fish, but it was fun to pretend, and it looked better, because of the other swimmers. Oh, Robert, I can't tell you how wonderful it was. I spent the rest of the day down there, on the plage, and again today, and of course that was the reason for my being late for dinner. I told him all about you and he was so impressed, he was quite embarrassed that you might be here waiting for me. I said he needn't worry. 'Robert Scrivener isn't an ordinary man,' I said. 'He's the most intuitive, the most understanding person in the whole world. That's why he is famous.'"

She withdrew her hand to light another cigarette, and he made a pretence of swallowing the dreg of liqueur left in his glass. Whatever happened, she must learn nothing from his face or from his voice.

"How very amusing," he said.

She wrinkled her nose as she lit her cigarette. "But I don't behave like this as a rule," she told him. "I'm very good, very sedate. This is just one of those things. As I said to Alberto this evening, 'How Robert is going to mock me when I tell him what has happened.' Alberto was not so sure. He thought you might be offended."

It was Scrivener's turn to laugh. The laugh sounded natural, but the effort he put into it cost him ten years.

"Offended?" he said. "Why on earth should I be offended?"

"Why indeed? 'It's just one more tiny bit of experience for Robert,' I said to Alberto. No, what is so wonderful for me is that you've made the meeting possible. Here I am, in this heavenly hotel, having the time of my life, and it's all owing to you."

Ironic phrases rose to Scrivener's lips. Bitter reflections such as, "Glad to be of use," or "Always willing to oblige," but he had the strength of mind to smother them. To show the faintest shadow of annoyance would be to lose face.

"Do I meet the paragon?" he asked lightly.

"But of course," she said. "As a matter of fact I told him to be at the bar near the railway station at precisely ten o'clock. Which it is now. We agreed the railway station was best, because no one would recognise us there, and it's always crowded. You see, if it was known that the bathing attendant from the plage was having a wild affair with one of the hotel visitors my beautiful Alberto might lose his job."

And rightly, thought Robert Scrivener. A dull anger had succeeded the first feeling of shock, but an anger which he could
not utilise. The futility, the indignity of the evening ahead, over-
shadowed action. One jibe and he was lost. One slip, and his
writer's integrity, the possession he had come to Geneva to lecture on, the balance, the understanding, would be forever
blemished.

"I'm ready if you are," said Scrivener, and she rose at once—no
attempt for courtesy's sake to disguise her eagerness—and led the
way from the terrace through the restaurant, a sensuous, alluring
figure, cool and lovely in the strapless frock, primed for the bathing attendant, but not for him.

The terrible thing was that there was no redress. To feign sudden fatigue, the excuse of work, indigestion, any of these excuses
meant total loss of prestige. What above all caused him anguish
was the consciousness of his own letters, week after week, the
letters of a friend, a confidant, baring his soul.

"Don't mind if Alberto's shy," she said as they walked through
the streets, humid now that darkness had fallen, languorous with
the softness of velvet, "he's only twenty-two, my age, and he
won't know what to say to you. Naturally he wants to come to
the lecture tomorrow. We thought we'd go together. He's never
met a well-known writer before."

"Have you?" The retort shot from him like a bullet from a
rifle, but she was too happy, or too temporarily insensitive, to
seize his tone.

"In Zurich, sometimes," she replied, "but I'm generally too
tired in the evenings to go out and enjoy myself."

"Yes. Selling stockings must be an exhausting business." How
apt, how cutting, could it be said; but pride forbade.

They came to a garish bar, fronting the wide street by the station, and Annette Limoges, confident and gay, pushed her way
through the knots of laughing people. "I hope you won't be
recognised," said Annette. "It would be too bad if the evening
was spoilt by some wretched official coming up and buttonholing
you."

Robert Scrivener felt it would be his one salvation. He would
have given much for some member of the International Society
of Letters to approach him at that moment, to touch his arm

with reverence, some stranger, however heavy, however deadly dull, to approach him and say, "It's Robert Scrivener, isn't it? We've been trying to get you at the Mirabelle. Do join us in a drink." Then, only then, after some such bald encounter, could he look across at Annette Limoges and say, "My dear, do you mind? Run along and find your Alberto. I have to join these friends." Pride would then be salvaged, the wreckage of morale restored. Nothing of the sort happened. Annette led him to a corner of the bar where, sitting upright on a high stool, was a bronzed young man with a great mop of curling hair. Good-looking, perhaps, in a flashy sort of way, but the ring on the little finger made Scrivener flinch. And Annette . . . Annette, who had seemed so entirely in place on the terrace of the Hotel Mirabelle, so full of savoir-faire, so desirable and truly lovely, seemed suddenly to lose caste before his eyes. The wriggle that she gave as she sighted Alberto—for Alberto it must be—was frankly . . . common.

"Hullo, darling," she said, and the "darling" was an offence to Scrivener, an outrage, "here we are. I want you to meet Mr. Robert Scrivener."

The young man put out his hand, and Scrivener touched it as he would an unclean substance.

"Pleased to meet you," said Alberto, sliding from his stool, and then the three of them stood there, falsely smiling, and Scrivener, the host, ordered the round of drinks.

The three of them sat at a small table, and the older man, who earlier that evening had been the girl's proud escort, the cynosure of other men's envious eyes, must now play the role of indulgent uncle or—worse—plain gooseberry. It seemed to Robert Scrivener that his sense of inferiority was deepened by an instinctive feeling that the bathing attendant was aware of his discomfiture, and as embarrassed as he was himself. A real vulgarian could have been despised, but Alberto, as retiring as Annette Limoges was brazen, kept his eyes fixed on his glass of beer, which apparently satisfied his modest wants; now and again fluttering his long lashes and glancing sideways at Scrivener with a semblance of apology.

The writer knew—and it was this knowledge that only made degradation more profound—that should Annette leave them for the space of a few minutes he could turn to Alberto and pass a note for a few thousand francs across the table, and the bathing attendant would understand his meaning without a word in reply. He would just disappear. Once out of the way, the girl would be Scrivener's once more. The shocking truth was that, could this only be achieved, Scrivener would still be willing to blot out from immediate resentment the events of the past two days, such was the fascination of the salesgirl from Zurich. Scrivener was not so blind as to assume that his own physical charms could be as compelling as those of Alberto; nevertheless the girl had come to Geneva to meet him, she was his guest, the guest of someone renowned in the international world of letters, who must surely command adulation from the most beautiful women in the world. But could he? Here was the secret stab. Everywhere there were men at this moment acting the part of husband or lover; sometimes they paid for the privilege, sometimes the services of their companion were given free, but in either case contact did at least take place. Yet Robert Scrivener, known the world over for his masterly diagnosis of the problems of the human heart, was obliged to seek out a shopgirl from a Zurich store who could not even wait for his custom.

"I tell you what, Robert," said Annette, breaking in upon his bitter train of thought, "if you don't have any engagement before the lecture tomorrow evening we could all three of us spend the day in the mountains. You could hire a car, and we could take a picnic. I'm sure the Mirabelle would put us up a packed lunch."

Oddly enough, this had originally been Scrivener's plan. Before the advent of the bathing attendant. He had visualised a drive to the mountains, or an expedition across the lake, after his luncheon with the Swiss men of letters.

"I'm afraid," said Scrivener, "that I am booked for luncheon."

"Oh, what a bother," said Annette, "but I suppose we could go without you. Alberto will be free after twelve o'clock." She squeezed the hand of the bathing attendant, as she had squeezed Scrivener's at dinner. "Darling," she said, "you'd like that, wouldn't you? Robert would arrange a car for us, and we could stay out until it was time to come back for the lecture. Then we could all dine afterwards."

Alberto, his bronzed skin flushing, looked apologetically at his host. "Perhaps Mr. Scrivener has other plans," he demurred.

"Oh no," said Annette Limoges, "you haven't, have you, Robert?"

The writer felt a sudden irritation at the constant use of his Christian name. Never had the surname Scrivener sounded so sweet in his ears, so full of dignity. He tried to remember when he had first given permission to the correspondent in Zurich to call him Robert, but it was too many months ago, they had slipped into the habit without realising.

"I have no plans at all," he said, "I am in Geneva to deliver two lectures. I'm really in the hands of the authorities concerned."

"Well, we can always arrange details in the morning," said Annette. "The thing is for us all to be happy. Alberto hasn't read *Taurus* yet, have you, Alberto, so he doesn't know that wonderful passage where Mark explains his philosophy of life—I'm going to buy him a copy tomorrow and you'll autograph it for him, won't you, Robert?"

"I shall be delighted," said Scrivener, and with the gallantry of Sir Philip Sydney he ordered another beer for the bathing attendant. The endless evening wound to its close. The bar emptied. And long before this, had it not been for fate and Alberto, Scrivener and Annette Limoges would have been clasped together in heaven knows what sweet, prolonged embrace in room 27 or 50 of the Hotel Mirabelle.

"The bartender," said Scrivener, "looks as if he wants to get rid of us." The three inseparables rose to their feet, Scrivener paid the bill for the final round of drinks, and they proceeded back to the hotel, Annette between the writer and the bathing attendant, holding an arm of each.

"This is what I call heaven," she said, "to be with the two men in the world who mean most to me."

Neither of her escorts answered. Whether coals of fire were heaped upon Alberto's head Scrivener neither knew nor cared. He himself was reminded of the remark of an Irish groom to the ecstatic purchaser of an unridable horse, "Faith, you're easy pleased."

Outside the steps of the Mirabelle Annette paused. She dropped the arm of Scrivener but still held that of Alberto.

"I'll walk with Alberto to the end of the promenade," she said, and Scrivener saw her glance towards the pontoons bordering the lake where stood the line of bathing huts, discreetly dark and silent, to which the attendant very probably possessed the key.

"Then I will bid you both good night," said Scrivener.

Annette Limoges embraced him with her smile. "It's been a wonderful evening," she said, "I don't know how I'm going to thank you."

Nor do I, thought Scrivener. Raising his hand in a salute of farewell, half benevolent, half fascist, he turned his back on both of them and, entering the Hotel Mirabelle, was borne upstairs to room number 27 by a yawning page. His bed was turned down, his pyjamas laid out upon the cover. How neat, how smooth, how virginal the room! The suit he had discarded hanging upon the wardrobe, the notes for his lectures folded on the table. Switching on the bedside lamp, he saw that the time, by his travelling clock, was a quarter to two. He crossed to the window and with a determined gesture drew the curtains close. He picked up the Penguin Turgenev he had been reading in the aeroplane and put it, with his spectacles, upon his pillow. Soberly, he undressed.

Scrivener did not see Annette Limoges until late the next morning. He telephoned her room at ten, and the sleepy voice that answered him was too heavy, too drugged with the delights of the preceding night, to make itself understood. Curtly he rang off, telling her he would ring again at eleven. He did so, having by that time bathed and dressed himself, breakfasted, and been out for a short walk. This time there was no reply, and the switchboard operator suggested that the inmate of room 50 was probably in her bath. Scrivener was due to be collected by his Swiss man of letters at midday, therefore he was ready and waiting in the hall of the Hotel Mirabelle at five minutes to the hour. At precisely three minutes to twelve Annette Limoges came out of the lift, dressed in her striped jeans and sandals and emerald shirt. Her hair was loose upon her shoulders. Her lips were a vivid red. She looked like a ripe peach that had just been plucked, and not, alas, by Scrivener.

"It's all arranged," she said with a huge smile. "I've ordered the car. I'm picking Alberto up at half past twelve."

As she was speaking a stout man in a grey suit, carrying a homburg hat, entered the hotel. He moved ponderously towards Scrivener.

"Mr. Robert Scrivener?" he enquired, his accent Swiss-German, his manner affable. "I am pleased to present myself, Fritz Lieber, secretary of the International Society of Letters. Welcome to Geneva."

"Thank you," said Scrivener, and after a moment's hesitation, "this is Mademoiselle Limoges." The stout man bowed.

"It's too bad, Herr Lieber, that you are taking Mr. Scrivener off to a solemn lunch," announced Annette gaily, "we had it all fixed for a day in the mountains."

Herr Lieber, puzzled, turned to the writer for confirmation. "I hope there has not been some misunderstanding," he began, and Scrivener, embarrassed, waved his hand. "No, no, of course not, our luncheon was arranged many weeks ago."

His companion for the day, anxious for the International Society of Letters to be all-inclusive in hospitality, murmured something about any friend of the guest of honour being welcome at the luncheon table. Robert Scrivener, seeing a momentary hesitation in Annette's eyes, quickly interposed. He sensed that such an invitation must also include the bathing attendant.

"Mademoiselle Limoges has already made other arrangements," he said and, turning to Annette, "I shall see you when I return. If you are back before me, leave a message at the desk," and, fearful that she might suggest a change in plans involving Alberto, he forced a genial smile upon the representative of the International Society and added, "Shall we go?"

As they stepped into the waiting car and drove away, Scrivener caught a glimpse of the distant mountains, the peaks snow-capped in spite of summer, and he thought of what might have been on some sun-baked plateau, or perhaps beside a glacial stream, but instead the formal luncheon inside the airless restaurant of a rival hotel. Guest of honour indeed, but the sales-girl from Zurich and Alberto of the Geneva bathing plage would enjoy, at his expense, the more varied delicacies of the afternoon.

"I regret very much," began Herr Lieber, "that you did not

tell me there would be others in your party. It would have been so simple to extend the invitation. The young lady . . . did you say, your niece . . . ?"

"An acquaintance only," said Scrivener coldly.

"Please to pardon me. The young lady, Mademoiselle Limoges, will surely require tickets for the lecture this evening, and tickets too for anyone else you care to bring?"

"I believe," said Scrivener, "that Mademoiselle Limoges has already booked her tickets."

"Good. Excellent. There will be refreshments afterwards, of course. Mr. Scrivener, I must apologise for certain difficulties that have arisen, I was unable to warn you in time, but owing to many people being on holiday at the moment and certain other factors beyond our control, we were unsuccessful in selling many tickets for the second lecture you were kind enough to suggest giving. For the first we are fully booked, but for the second . . ." He broke off, pink with embarrassment, and blinking behind his spectacles.

"I quite understand," said Scrivener. "You would prefer to cancel the second lecture?"

"That is, of course, for you to say," said Herr Lieber quickly. "It is just that the hall might be almost empty, it would not be very agreeable for you, Mr. Scrivener, and a waste of your valuable time."

"You must cancel it, of course," replied Scrivener, and he was aware of the expression of relief on his companion's face.

They arrived at the hotel, and within a few moments he was the centre of an earnest group of men and women, some twenty-five to thirty in number, to all of whom he was introduced before they filed into the restaurant towards a long table set at the end of the room, decorated with the flags of many nations.

Generally Robert Scrivener was pleased to discuss the merits of his novels with strangers. The finer passages of *Madrigal*, the philosophy of *Taurus*, even the possibly outmoded theme of his first success, *Fortune Favours the Brave*, these things made contact, as a rule, between himself and the less well endowed members of the reading public. Today, for no fit reason that he could give himself, the subject was dull as ashes. Why profess himself grateful to the pince-nezed lady on his right for being able to quote a whole paragraph from *Jason* without hesitation, and how did it profit him to know that the learned gentleman on his left had read *Taurus* a dozen times and himself proposed to lecture upon it, granted Scrivener's permission, to the university at Basle the coming winter? He heard himself answer courtesy with courtesy, platitude with platitude, and he ate his way through course after course of rich, substantial food, but his mind and his heart were elsewhere. Upon what ice-blue peak, he wondered, did the luscious entity of Annette Limoges disport itself with the sun-bronzed Alberto, what mountain strawberries fall into their mouths, what melting snow, what kisses?

"Yes, indeed," he answered his hostess on the right, "it is up to all of us, as writers, to fight the commonplace where we find it, to do battle continually against those philistines who would drag us all to their own level of mediocrity. I hope to touch on this very subject in my lecture tonight."

He shook his head as the waiter offered him a second helping of roast pork—strange choice for a June luncheon—and bent his ear to the neighbour on his left, who declared that the cinema had destroyed the values of the Western world.

"Even in Geneva here," declared his neighbour, "where we like to pride ourselves on gathering into our midst the best brains of Europe, your second lecture, Mr. Scrivener, must be abandoned through lack of demand for tickets. Yet two streets away the people fight to get into some nonsense from Hollywood. I call it murder of the intellect. There is no other word for it."

"No other word," agreed Scrivener, and, glancing furtively at his watch, he saw that the hands already stood at half past two, and the luncheon had been in progress since half past twelve.

His entertainers did not release him until after five in the afternoon. The luncheon over, he must visit the headquarters of the International Society of Letters and examine the array of manuscripts in their possession, usually kept behind glass, but today spread open upon a table in his honour. There were portraits, too, of other famous members of the Society, not present, unfortunately, to welcome Scrivener, but their letters of regret for absence were all read. Tea was produced at four, with luncheon not yet forgotten or digested, and with tea came a formal line of new arrivals, not considered of sufficient standing to attend the luncheon yet every one anxious to shake the hand of Robert Scrivener. It was nearing half past five when, warned that he had but two hours' respite before his lecture, due to start at half past seven, the writer returned to the Hotel Mirabelle.

The first thing he noticed on asking for his key was that it had gone. He was told that Mademoiselle Limoges had asked for it about an hour before, and, since it had not been given back, must doubtless still be there. Scrivener summoned the lift and hurried along the corridor to his room. Annette was lying on the balcony, changed from her jeans into brief enticing shorts. Large black glasses protected her from the sun.

"Hullo," she called as Scrivener entered the room, "we've had a wonderful day. Alberto's only just gone, but he'll be back again directly." Indeed, about his neat room were traces of recent occupation other than his own. A pullover flung on the bed. A tray of drinks. His books moved. And worse still, on the bathroom floor a wet towel.

"I thought you were going to the mountains?" he said, too taken aback to protest at this invasion of his room.

"We never went," replied Annette. "We lunched just outside Geneva, and then decided, as it was so hot, to go and bathe instead. The car took us to an enchanting spot Alberto knows, about fifteen miles along the lake. Then we came back here. I couldn't ask him up to my room, it would have looked odd, but I knew you wouldn't mind if we came up here instead. Alberto had a bath, and now he has gone off to change for your lecture."

She removed her black sunglasses and smiled up at him.

"I thought," said Scrivener, "that you did not care to invite your friend into the hotel for fear it should get him into trouble with the management?"

"Had he come to my room, yes," answered Annette. "I would never have suggested that. But as you can well imagine, Mr. Robert Scrivener can do no wrong. There are notices everywhere in the entrance hall about your lecture. Alberto and I are dying for it."

Dying, observed Scrivener to himself, so much that he could not even pick up the bath towel from the floor or stand the cork mat to dry. The splodgy marks of wet feet were still upon it. And the soap, the cake of soap he had brought from London, had been left in the bath. It protruded, half consumed, from the gaping waste hole. Murderous rage gripped Scrivener. It rose in his throat and nearly choked him. He turned away from the bathroom and went to the balcony and stared down at Annette Limoges, who was intent on anointing her toenails a vivid puce.

"You know what," she suggested, dipping the brush in the bottle of scented varnish, "how would it be if the three of us went dancing, when your lecture's over? There's a wonderful place, Alberto tells me, the other side of the lake, where one can dine and dance outside, and watch the floodlighting and the fountain."

"You've spilt some varnish on the balcony," said Scrivener.

"Have I? Never mind, the *femme de chambre* will wipe it off. Well, what do you say to my idea? You'd like some gaiety, wouldn't you, after the mental strain of the lecture?"

"Mental strain!" echoed Scrivener. "Mental strain . . . !" The laugh that came from him held an hysterical note.

Annette Limoges glanced up at him, surprised. "What is it?" she said. "Is anything the matter?"

And even now, he thought, even now, if she would only dismiss the bathing attendant for this once, he could forget his rage, forget her intolerable presumption and impertinence, swallow pride, swallow indignity, and be ready to continue where they had so disastrously left off.

"You're not nervous, are you?" asked Annette. "I assure you, there's no need to be. Only the people in the first six rows will hear what you say anyway. The acoustics are very bad, Alberto says. He knows someone who cleans the lecture hall."

Robert Scrivener clenched his fists. It seemed to him that there were two alternatives. One was to murder her at once. The other to seize her from the balcony and carry her to his bed. He lacked the courage to do either. The third alternative, miserable as it was, was the only course now open. He turned away from her, and, going into his bathroom, slammed the door and locked it. Presently he heard her knock. He took no notice and proceeded to run both taps. Then he sat with folded arms until the sound of a distant door told him that she had gone away. Scrivener then prepared himself for the lecture.

Punctually to the minute, at seven precisely, his host of the day arrived at the hotel to bear him away. Bulging from his stiff shirt front like a pouter pigeon, Herr Lieber once again expressed his apologies for the fact that the idea of the second lecture the following day must be abandoned, blaming, as had the neighbour at luncheon, the pull of the cinema over potential listeners.

"They are queueing in hundreds for this film across the way," he observed. "My wife and daughter have been twice. I never go to the cinema myself. Of course, when we arranged your lecture we did not know what was to be shown at the Elysée."

Had they known, wondered Scrivener, would they have written to him cancelling the first lecture as they had done the second? His thesis was ruined, as it was. The two lectures, planned to present a cohesive whole—on the theme of the essential purity of the poet, and his cosmic significance, acting as counterpoint to the novelist's duty to mankind—these headings that he had worked upon before leaving London had to be abandoned, or rather embodied into a single credo that would send his audience forth informed and satisfied. The task, he felt, was impossible.

As he sat on the platform, listening to the introduction of his person by the president of the International Society of Letters and looking down upon the rows of earnest faces, it seemed to Robert Scrivener that all he had worked for hitherto had been in vain. *Fortune Favours the Brave, Madrigal, Taurus, Jason,* all being lauded at this moment by the president of the Society, and presumably familiar to the audience below, had been set at nought through a sequence of events which he had been powerless to control. His journey to Geneva had been ill starred, and even now, when he should be gathering the threads of his wasted material together, part of his mental process was composing a telegram to Judith, warning her that after all he would be returning to London the following day. For what use was it now to consider getting hold of a car and driving up the Rhône Valley, if the hoped-for companion of his travels was not worthy of her hire?

"And so I have much pleasure in introducing the famous nov-

elist, poet and critic, Mr. Robert Scrivener." The president of the
Society bowed towards him, and Scrivener rose to his feet.

Integrity, he supposed afterwards, integrity and training
brought him through the ordeal. The appreciative silence of the
audience, interrupted only occasionally by the coughing of those
who should have remained in sanatoriums, and the generous applause at the conclusion, followed by a buzz of conversation and
the congratulations of fellow members of the Society upon the
platform with him, these tributes proved to him that he had not
failed. He was, however, exhausted. He had spent himself for literature. Not for his own fame had he stood there for the full seventy minutes of his lecture, but to place on its true pedestal, out
of reach of the vulgar, the trivial-minded, the prostitutes of art,
the sacred vessel he had dared to call his Muse. Let the lesser
breed defile it if they so willed, the essence would remain untouched in the hands of himself and others like him.

Almost fainting as the result of his own eloquence, Scrivener
allowed himself to be led into the room behind the platform,
where he was given chicken sandwiches and sweet champagne.
This, he understood, was the culmination of hospitality that had
begun for him that morning at half past twelve. When he had
sufficiently cooled his parched throat, and shaken the remaining
hands extended to him, he would be a free man, without even a
car or Herr Lieber at his disposal. For this, he was grateful. Further expressions of international good will would have slain him.
He made ready, therefore, for his departure, giving as excuse a
belated supper with friends who awaited him even now at the
Hotel Mirabelle.

Just as he was about to leave, a note was put into his hands by
Herr Lieber. Scrivener recognised the handwriting of Annette
Limoges, and put the note into his pocket. A final handshake, a
final bow, and he made his escape from the Society of International Letters.

A steady rain was falling when he came out into the street.
One of those brooding thunderstorms that hover over the Jura
and finally break upon the lake of Geneva had evidently burst
during the course of his lecture. Here was the aftermath. And he
could see no taxis. He stood for a moment, looking to right and
left, and then remembered the note in his pocket.

Dearest Robert [he read], you were marvellous. Alberto is quite overwhelmed. We left early, so as not to be trampled in the crush. I expect you will be having supper with the Society and won't be back at the hotel until after midnight, so this is just to let you know I shall take Alberto up to your room and we will have supper there, as we are both feeling too tired to dance. Looking forward to seeing you later on, and congratulations once again,

Fond love,
Annette

P.S. You had better knock on the door before coming in!

Robert Scrivener crumpled the note in his hand and dropped it down a convenient drain. Then, with his collar turned up, he hurried along the street to find a taxi. But if he found one, he wondered, where should he go? Annette and Alberto were even now making free of room number 27. His head low, because of the rain, he found himself brought to a standstill by a crowd of people. Were they all looking for taxis too? Glancing about him, he realised that he had, through the mischance of not looking where he was going, got himself jammed into a cinema queue, and now, unable either to proceed further or break from it, he was forced to advance with the queue towards the auditorium. The one advantage in this form of motion was that he was now sheltered from the rain. Slowly but steadily he was borne towards the box office. Useless to try to explain that he had no wish to visit the cinema; simpler to let circumstance defeat him. He wanted, above all, to sit down, to relax.

Scrivener felt in his pocket for change, and as he passed the box office exchanged his few hundred francs for the small slip given him in return. He was propelled on once more, and, stumbling in the darkness over legs that seemed thrust out purposely to trip him, blinded by a torch flashed in his eyes, he groped his way to the humble seat answering to the number on his ticket. The picture, whatever it was, had begun. Galloping horses chased one another across a wide screen. Music sobbed from the sound track. Robert Scrivener was very tired. The sweet champagne had numbed, for the moment, his taut nerves, and a sad self-pity, a nostalgic *à quoi bon*, had turned his mood to one of resignation.

He sat back on his hard cheap seat, hemmed in and breathed upon by his neighbours, and lifted his eyes to the screen. Little by little the thread of the story became plain. The leading character was a man of middle age whose life had turned sour and who, in a moment of drunken folly, had killed his wife. He then fell in love with his stepdaughter. As Scrivener followed the denouement and watched the leading character, who might have been himself, wander across an endless prairie, deserted not only by his stepdaughter but by his horses too, he was aware of a terrible sensation of despair. Tears came into his eyes and began to roll slowly down his cheeks. This wretched man was himself. The stepdaughter was Annette Limoges. And the horses, the horses which the man had driven with such confidence and power at the beginning of the story and which now ran from him, scattering with thundering hooves across the wild prairie, these horses symbolised for Scrivener those works that he had written and that were now lost to him, lost across the wasted years of his own dull, empty life.

He sat there in the cheap cinema seat and wept. He had no interest now in the past or in the future. The thought of the return flight to London, the resumption of his biography of Swedenborg, was odious to him. He took out his handkerchief and blew his nose, as indeed did those around him, while the words "The End" flashed upon the screen. Only then, reading through the titles repeated before him, did he realise that what he had been seeing, and what had moved him so much, was the adaptation of that best-selling novel he had always despised, that unworthy potboiler written a year or so ago by the fellow writer whose wedding he had attended such a short time before. Robert Scrivener replaced his handkerchief and, rising to his feet, shuffled his way through the departing queue, and so out into the damp streets of Geneva. His cup was full.

East Wind

Nearly a hundred miles west of the Scillies, far from the main track of ships, lies the small, rocky island of St. Hilda's. Only a few miles square, it is a barren, rugged place, with great jagged cliffs that run steep into deep water. The harbour is hardly more than a creek, and the entrance like a black hole cut out of the rock. The island rises out of the sea a queer, misshapen crag, splendid in its desolation, with a grey face lifted to the four winds. It might have been thrown up from the depths of the Atlantic in a moment of great unrest, and set there, a small defiant piece of land, to withstand forever the anger of the sea. Over a century ago few knew of its existence, and the many sailors who saw its black outline on the horizon imagined it to be little more than a solitary rock, standing like a sentinel in mid-ocean.

The population of St. Hilda's has never exceeded seventy, and the people are descendants of the original settlers from the Scillies and Western Ireland. Their only means of livelihood used to be the catching of fish and the cultivation of the soil. Today things are greatly changed, owing to the monthly call of a coastal steamer, and the installation of wireless. But in the middle half of the last century, years would sometimes pass without communication with the mainland, and the people had degenerated into quiet, listless folk, the inevitable result of intermarriage. There were no books then, no papers, and even the small chapel that had been built by the original settlers had fallen into disuse. Year in, year out, the life remained unchanged, with never a new face or a fresh thought to break the monotony of the days. Sometimes, on the horizon, the faint glimmer of a sail would be seen, and the people would gaze with wonder in their eyes, but slowly the sail would become a far-off speck, and the unknown ship pass into oblivion.

They were peaceable folk, these natives of St. Hilda's, born to a quiet, untroubled existence as monotonous as the waves that broke against their shores. They knew nothing of the world beyond the island, they saw no more momentous happenings than birth and death and the changes of the seasons. Their lives were untouched by great emotions, by great sorrows; their desires had never been lit, but lay imprisoned within their souls. They lived blindly, happily, like children, content to grope in the dark and never to search for the something that lay beyond their darkness. Some inner sense warned them that in their ignorance dwelt security, a happiness that was never wild, never triumphant, but peaceful and silent. They walked with their eyes to the ground; they had become weary of looking upon a sea where no ship came, of lifting their faces to a sky that seldom changed.

Summer and winter passed, children grew into men and women—there was no more in life than these things. Far away lay the other lands dwelt in by strange people, where the life was said to be hard and men had to fight for their existence. Sometimes an islander would sail away, shaping his course for the mainland and promising to return with news of the rest of the world. Perhaps he was drowned, or picked up by some passing ship; no one could say, for he never came back. No one who left the island returned. Even the few ships that so rarely visited St. Hilda's came once only, and passed not again.

It was almost as if there were no such place, as if the island were a dream, a phantom creation of a sailor's brain, something rising out of the sea at midnight as a challenge to reality, then vanishing in surf and mist to be forgotten, to be half-consciously remembered years later, flickering for a bewildered second in a dusty brain as a dead thought. Yet to the people of St. Hilda's the island was reality, the ships that came and went were their phantoms.

There was only the island. Beyond it lay the ghostly, the intangible; the truth was in the seared rock, in the touch of the soil, in the sound of the waves breaking against the cliffs. This was the belief of the humble fisherfolk, and they cast their nets during the day, and gossiped over the harbour wall at evening with never a thought of the lands across the sea. At dawn the men set off to fish, and when their nets were filled they would return to the island and climb the steep path that led to the fields, to work with stolid patience at the soil.

The group of cottages was clustered together at the water's edge, with seldom more than two rooms to contain an entire family. Here the women bent over their fires, cooked, and darned their men's clothes, talking peacefully from dawn till dusk.

One cottage stood apart from the others, built high on the cliff and looking down upon the creek. Today only the site remains, and instead of a cottage stands the ugly wireless station; but sixty years ago this was the home of the chief fisherman of St. Hilda's. Here Guthrie dwelt with his wife Jane, living as children, content in each other, unmindful of desire, ignorant of distress.

Guthrie stood on the cliffs at twilight, watching the sea. Below him in the harbour the fishing boats rocked, moored for the night. The men gossiped over the harbour wall and the sound of their voices rose to him, mingled with the thin cries of children. The little quay was slippery with spray and blood and the scales of dead fish. The smoke curled from the chimneys, a thin blue column, twisting and turning in the air. From the door of his cottage came Jane, her hands to her eyes, searching for him. "Come away down!" she called. "The supper's been ready an hour since. Ye'll find un spoilt, as likely as not." He waved his arm and turned, pausing to glance at the horizon for the last time. The sky was speckled with white loose-flocked clouds, and the sea, changing from the oily smoothness of the day, was running past the harbour in a low swell. Already there was a wash upon the rocks, at the eastward entrance. A soft humming sound came to his ears, as the sea gathered force, and a cool breeze played with his hair. He ran down the hill to the village, and cried to the fishermen who were standing by the wall.

"'Tis the East Wind startin'," he told them. "Can't ye see the sky like a fish's tail, and the big lumpin' sea awash on the rocks? Before midnight there'll be a gale to blow your heads off, and the sea angrier than the devil himself. Look to the boats."

The harbour was sheltered from the wind, yet the vessels were moored securely fore and aft to prevent the possibility of their breaking adrift.

After he had seen that everything was safe for the night, Guthrie climbed the path to his cottage on the cliff. He ate his supper in silence. He felt restless and excited; the quiet atmosphere of the cottage seemed to oppress him. He tried to occupy himself in mending a hole in one of his nets, but he could not give his mind to the task. The net slipped from his hands; he turned his head and listened. It seemed as if a cry had risen out of the night. Yet there was nothing, only the low hum of the wind, and the sound of surf breaking upon the rocks. He sighed and gazed into the fire, oddly disturbed, his soul heavy within him.

In the bedroom, with her head by the window, Jane knelt, listening to the sea. Her heart beat strangely, her hands trembled, she wanted to creep from the cottage and run onto the cliffs where she would feel the true force of the wind. It would strike upon her breast and sweep the hair from her face, she would hear the singing of it in her ears, she would smell the salt tang of the spray as it stung her lips and her eyes. The longing came upon her to laugh with the wind, to cry with the sea, to open wide her arms and be possessed by something which would envelop her like a dark cloak and prevent her from straying far away on the lonely cliffs amongst the tall grass. She prayed for the day to dawn, not gently as was its custom, but fiercely, with the sun burning the fields and the wind sweeping the white-edged seas, bringing destruction. She would stand and wait upon the shore, feeling the wet sand beneath her naked feet.

A footstep sounded outside the room and she turned with a little shiver from the window. It was Guthrie. He gazed at her solemnly and bade her shut out the sound of the wind. They undressed quietly and lay beside each other in the narrow bed without a word. He could feel the warmth of her body, but his heart was not with her. His thoughts left his form, imprisoned there at her side, and fled into the night. She felt him go, yet minded not. She put away his cold hands from her, and gave herself to her own dreams, where he could have no entrance.

Thus they slept together in each other's arms, yet separately; like dead things in a grave, their souls long vanished and forgotten.

When they awoke the dawn had broken in the sky. The sun

shone blindly from a blue heaven, scorching the earth. Great seas, tipped with foam, crashed against the cliff and swept the rocks outside the harbour, and all the while the East Wind blew, tossing the grass, scattering the hot white sand, forcing its triumphant path through the white mist and the green waves like a demon let loose upon the island.

Guthrie went to the window and looked out upon the day. A cry came from his lips and he ran from the cottage, unable to believe his eyes. Jane followed him. The folk in the other cottages had risen too and stood staring at the harbour, their hands lifted in amazement, their excited voices filling the air with sound yet fading away, indistinguishable from the wind. For there in the harbour, dwarfing the little fishing boats with her great spars, the sails stretched upon her yards to dry in the morning sun, lay a brig at anchor, rocking against wind and tide.

Guthrie stood on the quay amongst the crowd of fishermen. The whole of St. Hilda's was gathered there to welcome the strangers from the brig. Tall, dark men they were, these sailors from beyond the sea, with narrow almond eyes and white teeth that gleamed as they laughed. They spoke in a different tongue. Guthrie and his fellows questioned them, while the women and children surrounded them with gaping mouths, gazing into their faces, feeling their clothes with timid, wondering hands.

"How did ye find the entrance to the harbour," cried Guthrie, "with the wind an' the sea in league together against ye? 'Tis the devil himself that hath sent ye here maybe."

The sailors laughed and shook their heads. They could not understand what he said. Their eyes wandered beyond him and the fishermen to the women. They smiled and spoke amongst themselves, happy at their discovery.

All the while the sun beat down upon their heads and the East Wind blew, scorching the air like a breath from hell. No man went forth to fish that day. Great mountainous seas thundered past the harbour mouth and the fishing boats remained at anchor, small and insignificant beside the strange brig.

Something of madness seemed to fall upon the people of St. Hilda's. Their nets lay neglected and unmended beside their cottage doors, the fields and flowers remained untended on the hills above the village. There was no interest in their lives but the sailors from the ship. They clambered upon the brig, leaving no part of her unvisited, they touched the strangers' clothes with excited, inquisitive fingers. The sailors laughed at them, they hunted in the sea chests and gave the men cigarettes, they found bright scarves and coloured kerchiefs for the women. Guthrie led them out upon the cliffs, swaggering a little like a young boy, a cigarette between his lips.

The fishermen threw wide their cottage doors, jealous of one another's hospitality, each one desirous of extending the greatest welcome. The sailors soon explored the island; they thought it a poor, barren place, without interest. They descended to the shore and formed themselves into groups on the quayside, yawning, idle, hoping for a change of weather. The time hung heavily upon their hands.

Still the East Wind blew, scattering the sand, turning the earth to dust. The sun blazed from a cloudless sky, the big seas swept round the shores, green, foam-flecked, twisting and turning like a live thing. The sun set streaky and windswept, pointing orange fingers to the sky. The night came, warm and alive. The very air was restless. The sailors found the disused chapel at the end of the village and encamped there, fetching tobacco and brandy from the brig.

There seemed to be no order amongst them. They had no discipline, they obeyed no rules. Two men only remained on the brig to watch. The fisherfolk wondered not at their conduct; their presence on the island was so wonderful and rare a thing, nothing counted but this. They joined the sailors in the chapel, they tasted brandy for the first time. The night rang with cries and song. The island was a new place now, broken of peace, swayed by suggestion and filled with strange desires. Guthrie stood amongst his companions, his cheeks flushed, his cold eyes bright and foolish. He held a glass in his hand, he swallowed the brandy with deep, contented draughts. He laughed with the sailors, wildly, without reason; what did it matter if he could not understand their words? The lights swayed before his eyes, the ground sloped beneath his feet, it seemed as if he had never lived before. The wind could shout and the sea thunder and roar, the world called to him now. Beyond the island lay the other lands, the homes of these sailors. Here he would find life, and beauty, and strange, incredible adventures. No more would he bend his back, toiling at the useless soil. The songs of the sailors rang in his ears, the tobacco smoke blinded his eyes, the brandy seemed to mix with the blood in his veins.

The women danced with the sailors. Someone had found a concertina, and a fiddle with three strings. Crazy tunes broke into the air. The women had never danced before. They were whirled from their feet, their petticoats flying out behind them. The sailors laughed and sang, beating the measure with their feet upon the floor. The fishermen lolled stupidly against the walls, drunken, happy, careless of time. A sailor came across to Jane and smiled, holding out his arms. She danced with him, flushed, excited, eager to please. Faster, faster went the music, and faster flew their feet around the room. She felt his arm tighten round her waist, and was aware of the warmth of his body against hers. She could feel his breath upon her cheek. She raised her head and met his eyes. They looked into hers, seeing her naked, and he moistened his lips with his tongue. They smiled, reading each other's thoughts. An exquisite shudder, like the touch of a cool hand, ran through her. Her legs felt weak beneath her. She lowered her eyes, conscious of desire, and turned to see if Guthrie had noticed, guilty for the first time.

And the East Wind blew against the church, shaking the roof, and the surf broke and thundered on the shore.

The next day dawned the same, hot and relentless.

The wind did not weaken in its power, nor the sea lessen in its fury. The brig still rolled at her moorings amongst the fishing boats. The fishermen leant with the sailors against the harbour wall, drinking and smoking, without thought, without energy, cursing the wind. The women idled at their cooking, neglected their mending. They stood at the doors of the cottages, new scarves round their shoulders, scarlet handkerchieves upon their heads, impatient with the children, restless, waiting for a smile.

The day passed thus, and another night, and yet another day. The sun shone, the sea shuddered and crashed, the wind blew. No one left the harbour to fish, no one worked on the land. There seemed no shade on the island, the grass lay brown and withered, the leaves hung parched and despondent from the few trees. Night fell once more and the wind had not ceased. Guthrie sat in the cottage, his head between his hands, his brain empty.

He felt ill and tired, like a very old man. Only one thing could prevent the sound of the wind from screaming in his ears and the heat of the sun from scorching his eyes. His lungs were dry, his throat ached. He staggered from the cottage and went down the hill to the church, where the sailors and the fishermen lay in heaps upon the floor, the brandy running from their mouths. He flung himself amongst them and drank greedily, senselessly, giving himself to it, forgetting the wind and the sea.

Jane closed the cottage door behind her and ran out onto the cliffs. The tall grass bathed her ankles and the wind leapt through her hair. It sang in her ears, a triumphant call. The sea flung itself upon the rocks below and loose flecks of foam scattered up towards her. She knew that if she waited he would come to her from the chapel. All day his eyes had followed her as she walked amongst the sailors by the harbour wall. Nothing mattered but this. Guthrie was drunk, asleep, forgotten, but here on the cliffs the stars shone upon her, and the East Wind blew. A dark shadow appeared from behind a clump of trees. For one moment she was afraid. One moment only.

"Who are you?" she called, but her voice fled to the wind.

The sailor came towards her. He flung off her clothes with deft, accustomed fingers; she put her hands before her eyes to hide her face. He laughed, and buried his lips in her hair. She stood then with arms outstretched, waiting, naked and unashamed, like a white phantom, broken and swept by the wind. Down in the chapel the men shouted and sang. They fought amongst themselves, mad with drink. One fisherman threw a knife and pinned his brother against the wall. He writhed like a serpent, screaming with pain.

Guthrie rose to his feet. "Quiet, you dogs!" he shouted. "Can you not drink in peace, and leave men to their dreams? Is it like this you wait for the wind to change?"

Jeers and laughter drowned his voice. A man pointed a trembling finger at him. "Aye, talk of peace, Guthrie, you weak-limbed fool. With your wife even now shaming your bed with a stranger. We'll have new blood in the island, I reckon." A chorus of voices joined in, laughing, and they pointed at him. "Aye, Guthrie, look to your wife!"

He leapt at them with a cry of rage, smashing their faces. But they were too many for him, they threw him from the chapel, flinging him onto the rough quayside. He lay stunned for a moment, then shook himself like a dog and rose to his feet. So Jane was a wanton. Jane had deceived him. He remembered his wife's body, white and slim. A haze of madness came over him, mingled with hatred and desire. He stumbled through the darkness, up the hill to the cottage. There was no light in any of the windows; the rooms were empty.

"Jane," he called, "Jane, where be ye hidin' with your damned cur lover?" No one answered. Sobbing with rage, he tore an axe from the wall—a great clumsy tool, used for chopping firewood. "Jane," he called once more, "come out, will ye?"

His voice was powerless against the wind that shook the walls of the cottage. He crouched by the door and waited, the axe in his hands. Hours passed and he sat in a stupor, awaiting her return. Before dawn she came, pale and trembling, like a lost thing. He heard her footfall on the path. A twig snapped under her feet. The axe uplifted.

"Guthrie," she screamed, "Guthrie, let me alone, let me alone." She spread her hands in supplication, but he pushed them aside and brought the axe down upon her head, crumpling her, smashing her skull. She fell to the ground, twisted, unrecognisable, ghastly. He leant over her, peering at her body, breathing heavily. The blood ran before his eyes. He sat down by her side, his senses swimming, his mind vacant. He fell into a drunken sleep, his head pillowed on her breast.

When he awoke, sober, himself again, he found her dead body at his feet. He gazed at it in horror, not understanding. The axe was still upon the floor. He lay stunned, sick and frightened, unable to move. Then he listened, as if for an accustomed sound. All was silent. Something had changed. The wind. He could no longer hear the wind.

He staggered to his feet and looked out upon the island. The air was cool. Rain had fallen while he slept. From the southwest blew a cool, steady breeze. The sea was grey and calm. Far on the horizon lay a black dot, her white sails outlined against the sky.

The brig had gone with the morning tide.

MEMORIES

INTRODUCTION

The ten prose pieces which follow are not articles in the strict sense of the word, for I have never been a journalist but a writer of novels, stories and biographies, including one book of childhood and adolescent memoirs. The reader will have understood how the fiction arose out of the unconscious, coupled with observation but above all with imagination.

The pieces in the present section have nothing to do with my imagination, but with the conscious self, the person who is Me. This may sound, and probably is, conceited, but I make no apology for it; they were written at different times throughout my life because I felt strongly about the various subjects, and so was impelled to put my thoughts on paper.

The first three are about my grandfather, my father and my cousins, and I place them at the beginning because my family counted tremendously when I was young and as I matured, and still does in the latter half of my life. The only apology here is that I have not, as yet, written about my own children and my seven grandchildren.

The next three, again written at varying times throughout my professional career, express what I felt about three very different subjects, and here the reader may sense a certain cynicism of outlook which reflected my attitude to those matters at that particular moment. It is possible that my outlook has changed, perhaps developed, but this is not for me to say, because I cannot be sure.

"Death and Widowhood" was written with deep sincerity and emotion, coupled with a desire to help others who have suffered in similar fashion.

The last three follow in chronological order, and bring the reader and myself up to date. Have I changed, matured, or sunk into senility? It is for the reader, not for myself, to judge!

The Young George du Maurier

When George du Maurier died in October 1896, at the age of sixty-two, he was mourned not only by his family and his friends but by a wide circle of people who had come to know him through his drawings and his novels, and who felt, although they had never met him, that here was an artist and a writer who had expressed for many years all the graces of the world they knew. If the characters that he drew and wrote about were a little larger than life—the men almost too tall, the women more than beautiful—this was seen not as a fault but as a virtue; for du Maurier was a man who worshipped beauty and was not ashamed to put his ideals upon paper, which was something that his generation understood.

To him, as to his contemporaries, beauty was an end in itself. Whether it was the turn of a woman's head, her smooth dark hair parted in the centre with the low knot behind, and the curve of her shoulder; or the way a man stood, the way his shoulders were set; the sudden smile of a child, and the quiet, grave patience of old people—these were things to be revered and loved, and later reproduced with tenderness. Even when pulling jokes and poking fun—and as a humorous draughtsman for nearly thirty years he had full measure of this—du Maurier was never malicious or unkind. He mocked at many, but with a twinkle in the eye. Never from him the sneer, the acid half-truth behind an innuendo, the damning Judas-thrust that passes for modern wit. He laughed at people because he loved them, because he understood and shared their little weaknesses, their foibles; their snobbery was his snobbery, their sudden social gaffes and faux pas were misfortunes committed all too often by himself, a bohemian at heart on the fringe of high society. The mistress of the house caught unexpectedly in disarray by unwelcome

callers; the precocious child who faces a visitor with great innocent eyes and lets fall a blast of candour; the odd man out at a
dinner party far above his milieu, the one cricketer among musi-
cians, the one musician among cricketers, the bore who talks too
much, the dullard who talks too little, the woman who laughs too
loudly and too long—all these were targets for his pencil in those
pages of *Punch* some sixty and seventy years ago, and no one ap-
preciated the fact more than the delighted butts who recognised
themselves.

It was the fashion once to decry the late Victorians, their pictures and their novels. They seemed hidebound and intolerant to
a later age that promised freedom. Not so today. We have learnt
our lesson. Looking back, separated from them by more than
half a century, the years they graced and the world they
delighted in appear to us now as things lovely and precious, lost
by our own fault. I do not mean the mere picture postcard
charm of crinolines and carriages, which du Maurier drew with
his pencil and saw with his own eyes. Nor the lamplight that he
knew, and the unbusy streets. Nor the houses new-painted for a
London season, the window boxes gay, and the water cart that
came early on a June morning to sprinkle the fresh sand. Not the
croquet that he played on a summer afternoon, nor the leisurely
lawn tennis. Not the young man that he sketched who would be
leaning on his croquet mallet asking a question of someone
whose muslin dress swept the ground, and who smiled for one
brief moment under her sunshade and then turned away. Nor
the small boys in sailor suits, nor the little long-haired girls in
pinafores, nor the husband and wife reading aloud in turn, upon
a winter's evening. Nor the grandmother and the unmarried
sister living in the same house, or written to each day and visited; nor the new baby that came every spring. These things
were as natural to du Maurier and to his contemporaries as the
air they breathed and the ground they walked upon. But with
them went deference and courtesy, fidelity and faith, a belief in
a man's work and the pride that goes hand in hand with that belief. These fundamental standards wove the pattern of a Victorian day, and the writers and artists of that day became part of
the pattern and echoed it in print or upon canvas, stamping it
with their individuality, their own genius, creating an era that

was at once warm and colourful and prosperous, an age away from our present world of meagre mediocrity.

We who are offered today a so-called wealth of literature from the bookstalls of stations and airports, pulpy pages known as digests or potted shorts, find it hard to understand the part played by *Punch* in the latter half of the nineteenth century. It stood alone, the only weekly paper of its kind. A gibe at the government from *Punch* in 1870, and worried members of Parliament would be discussing the fact in the lobbies the same day. A cool criticism of a picture or a poem, and the luckless author hung his head in shame. Only the best draughtsmen of the day contributed to *Punch*, and with them the wittiest writers, the ablest critics. A successful future was assured to whoever was lucky enough to obtain a permanent place on the *Punch* staff. And George du Maurier was so lucky. When the well-known illustrator Leech died in 1865 he succeeded to his place, although only thirty-one years old. His weekly drawing on the left-hand side, beside the cartoon on the right, soon became the most talked-of page in *Punch*, and had he ended his days as a draughtsman only, he would long have been remembered and loved for this work alone.

But in late middle age he wrote two novels, *Peter Ibbetson* and *Trilby*, which somehow found their way into the hearts of his contemporaries in a way few novels have done before or since. The word "hearts" is used intentionally, because the critical mind cannot admit that George du Maurier was a great novelist, in the sense of a Dickens or a Thackeray. As a writer he was careless, and knew little of style or form, and the plots of his novels can be called fantastic, melodramatic, even absurd. Yet these two stories sounded such an echo in the emotions of the men and women of his day, both in this country and throughout the United States of America, that they were read, and reread, and thumbed again, year after year, down to our own time; and not only read, but in some inexplicable fashion deeply loved. When a novel can affect the human heart in such a way it seems to mean one thing only: not that the tale is exceptional in itself, but that the writer has so projected his personality onto the printed page that the reader either identifies himself with that personality or becomes fascinated by it, and in a sense near hypnotised.

It so happened that the personality of George du Maurier, though never forceful in a strong or domineering way, held great attraction. He radiated a kind of warmth that made people turn to him on sight with sympathy, and as they came to know him better this quality of warmth caught at their hearts, just as his novels caught at their readers'. It is true to say he had no enemies. He was a man well loved. His charm—most wretched word, too often overdone—was never forced, and never insincere. It was a gift from God.

His feeling for family was deep and strong and very French. Not only his affection for his wife and his five children: to him the ties of blood stretched far beyond, to nephews, nieces, cousins and second cousins, so that any who needed help were not afraid to come to him. Ancestors, long buried in French soil and never known, were dear to him; and dearer still the grandchildren and the great-grandchildren he did not live to see.

He was a man of very simple tastes. He loved his home. He had no wish to travel, except to France, or to the Yorkshire fishing port of Whitby, and when his novels made him famous he found himself embarrassed by his fame. "Perhaps Papa will now put electric light in the lumber room," said Gerald, his younger son, when success burst upon his father; but the lumber room remained unlit. George du Maurier saw no reason to change his way of living because he received hundreds of letters every week from perfect strangers. He smiled to himself, and thought it all very peculiar, and went for a long walk on Hampstead Heath: and when he returned he rolled a cigarette and went to his easel in the studio, and continued drawing, or writing, with the continual clatter about him of his family or his friends.

If the fortune he received from *Trilby* remained unspent upon himself, it was because he had the forethought to set it all aside for those who came after him. He remembered his own early days, in Paris and in London, and he saw no reason why his descendants should suffer want if, by the success of his own efforts, he could make provision for them. His own father, Louis-Maturin Busson du Maurier, had not been able to make provision

for him, or for his mother, brother and sister, and they had
suffered much in consequence. His father had been a delightful,
engaging man of many talents, with a beautiful singing voice
which his son inherited. Although he was a scientist by profession his inventions always failed, in spite of which he lived with
unfailing confidence and good humour until the day of his death.

He married Ellen Clarke, the daughter of the notorious Mary
Anne Clarke whose liaison with the Duke of York at the beginning of the century had caused so much scandal. Possibly the
memory of those early days had left a permanent strain upon the
daughter, because she possessed a more difficult character than
her husband Louis-Maturin. She was by nature nervy, anxious
and highly strung. Disappointed in the ability of her husband to
make a success of life, she concentrated upon her elder son, loving him fiercely and possessively, a love which he returned with
real feeling, but fortunately for himself without a sense of strain.

There were three children born of the marriage. George, who
was never known as George but always as Kicky, a nickname
which he carried to the end of his days, was the eldest, and was
born in Paris in 1834. He was brought up there, with his younger
brother Eugene, nicknamed Gyggy, and his sister Isobel. His
happy childhood and his schooldays he described in *Peter Ibbetson* and in his third, not so successful, novel, *The Martian*.

In spite of his later fame, and his real contentment with his
life in Hampstead, he looked back upon those early Paris days
with deep nostalgia and almost passionate regret, as though in
the depths of him there was a seed of melancholy, a creature un-
fulfilled, who, longing wistfully for what-was-once and cannot-
be-again, comes to the surface with the written word and
vanishes, unseen.

That happy childhood was a memory he clung to all his life,
all the more so because his adolescence and early manhood were
not so blest. The reason for this was that his father, still seeking
the fortune that eluded him, left Paris with his family and settled
in London, in Pentonville, and for the next few years, until his
father died in 1856, young Kicky, to please him, studied chemistry, a subject which he detested and for which he had no apti-
tude. The younger boy, Gyggy, neglected and misunderstood,
had the sense to run away and return to France, where he joined

the French army; but his character was lighter and more irresponsible than his brother's, and he never had the energy to rise above the rank of corporal, to the shame of his parents and the indifference of himself.

When Louis-Maturin died, Kicky persuaded his mother to let him return to Paris and study art in the studios of the Quartier Latin. He and his brother and sister had drawn brilliantly from an early age, and Kicky felt strongly that unless he could develop this gift freely, without restriction, in the city he loved so well, he would never make anything of his life, but would drift into failure, like his father before him. His mother understood him well enough to know that this was true, so Kicky, her firstborn and best-beloved, was given her blessing to follow the career he had chosen for himself.

Back in the Paris he loved, young George du Maurier spent eighteen happy months amongst his fellow students, living the life that Little Billee lived in *Trilby*. His appearance at that time was afterwards described by his great friend Tom Armstrong, in *Reminiscences of du Maurier*. "It is curious," wrote Armstrong, "that my recollection of our first meeting should be so vivid, but I suppose his personality from the beginning attracted me. . . . I can revive the picture of him in my mind's eye sitting astride one of the Utrecht velvet chairs, with his elbows on the back, pale almost to sallowness, square-shouldered and very lean, with no hair on his face except a slight moustache . . . he certainly was very attractive and sympathetic, and the other young fellows with whom I was living felt much as I did. We admired his coats with square shoulders and long skirts after the fashion of the day, and we admired his voice and his singing, his power of drawing portraits and caricatures from memory, his strength and skill with his fists, and above all we were attracted by his very sympathetic manner. I think this certainty of finding sympathy was one of his greatest and most abiding charms. His personality was a very engaging one, and evoked confidence in those who knew him very little. Music was a powerful influence in du Maurier's life. He used to say that literature, painting and sculpture evoked no emotion which could be compared with that felt by a sensitive person on hearing a well-trained voice or a violin

. . . in those days he spent much more time at our hired piano than he did before an easel."

The Little Billee existence might have continued much longer, or at least long enough for Kicky to become a great painter, but this was not to be. For suddenly, in the summer of 1858, the tragedy of his life occurred. He lost the sight of his left eye. And for a time it was feared he might lose the sight of both. The agony and misery of the months that followed he described many years later in *The Martian.*

He moved from Antwerp, where he had been sharing a studio with a fellow student, Felix Moschelles, to the little town of Malines. For a while he felt he would never recover from the blow; he even had dark thoughts of suicide. His mother, who came out to be with him, could not comfort him; for though he made light of the tragedy in public, and laughed and joked about it when his friends came to Malines to see him, showing them his dark glasses and saying he was an *aveugle,* she knew, and they suspected, what his inner suffering must be.

Money was scarce. They had nothing to live upon but the annuity his mother had inherited from Mary Anne Clarke, the original hush money from the Duke of York. His brother Gyggy was a constant source of worry, always in debt as his father had been, and his sister Isobel, now a pretty girl of nineteen, must also be supported, for although she played the piano beautifully she could hardly earn her living by doing so, nor was she likely to find herself a rich husband. It seemed to Kicky at that time that he, who had hoped to be the main prop of the family, had become, in a few short months, its greatest liability. It would be better if they were rid of him altogether.

And then Isobel wrote from London, where she was staying with a school friend, Emma Wightwick, to say that Mrs. Wightwick had heard of an oculist at Grafrath, near Düsseldorf, who had cured hundreds of people near to blindness, and who was said in fact to be the finest oculist in Europe. What was more, there was a school for painting in Düsseldorf itself. Why did not Kicky and her mother leave Malines, and try their luck in Germany? This suggestion saved her brother from suicide, and in the spring of 1859 young George du Maurier and his mother moved to Düsseldorf, the charm and gaiety of which went to the young artist's head immediately, and life seemed once more possible.

The oculist could not restore the sight of his left eye, but he did promise that, with care, the right one would remain sound to the end of his days; and so Kicky's natural optimism returned and he began to draw again—he even drew a flattering likeness of the oculist himself—and he and his mother plunged into the lighthearted society of Düsseldorf, where life was bohemian and manners easy, and money did not matter too much because it went so far.

His sister Isobel came out to join them, flirting happily with all the impecunious German counts and princekins, and Kicky did the same with a Miss Lewis, who was the beauty of that particular season. Artist friends drifted down from Paris and Antwerp to join in the fun, and in the work too, which was rather haphazard and not very steady. There were plenty of sketches lying about in the studio which du Maurier shared with a young Swiss friend, all showing promise but few of them finished; and it was not until his closest friend, Tom Armstrong, came to stay in the spring of 1860, and told him frankly that he was doing no good and was allowing himself to drift, that Kicky took stock of himself. Tom was perfectly right. He *was* doing no good. He was living on his mother, he was selling no pictures, and he was getting himself entangled with girls he could not possibly afford to marry.

Tom Armstrong showed him *Punch's Almanack*, which he had brought over from London, and pointed out the drawings of Keene and Leech, insisting that if Kicky chose to do so he could draw as well as either. If a fellow wanted to earn his living by his pencil, London was the place to start, Tom Armstrong urged. He was returning himself in May, he could get Kicky introductions to *Punch* and to other weekly illustrated papers. Several of their friends had moved from Paris to London, and artistic London was a world away from the dreariness of Pentonville and chemical laboratories. There was every reason why the move should be made now, before it was too late and Kicky had allowed himself to settle to the life of a second-rater in a German provincial town. How about it?

Young du Maurier looked about him. The season in Düsseldorf was beginning once again. The same little narrow circles meeting at the same parties. The same concerts, the same idle chatter, the same frothy flirtations meaning nothing. Amusing last year, coming as it did after the anxiety with his eye, but amusing no longer. He was fit again, he was well, and he wanted to draw, he wanted to be independent, and he wanted to be able to keep his mother, instead of his mother keeping him. He was twenty-six. If he did not pull himself together he would become another Gyggy, reduced to the ranks after bad behaviour.

Once again, as in Malines, it was Wightwick influence that finally decided him. Not Mrs. Wightwick this time, but the daughter, Emma. She and her mother had come out to Düsseldorf to see the du Mauriers, and especially Isobel, who had stayed with them in London. Kicky remembered Emma as a long-legged, handsome schoolgirl, with a plait swinging from her shoulders. She was now grown up and very lovely, with a pair of eyes that made Miss Lewis's seem like boot buttons. When she looked at him, gravely, yet with understanding, it did something to his heart that no woman had done before. He decided to go to London. . . .

So in May 1860, borrowing ten pounds from his mother's annuity, young George du Maurier set forth from Düsseldorf to London, travelling with Tom Armstrong and the Wightwicks. The personality that Tom Armstrong found so sympathetic reveals itself clearly enough in the letters that he wrote to his mother, with its moods at times sanguine, at times despondent, but more often than not eager for life and for experience, and for what he could contribute towards both. In those days he used to feel within himself two persons: the one serious, energetic, full of honest ambition and good purpose; the other a wastrel, reckless and careless, easily driven to the devil. It seemed to him, in such a mood, that only the love and influence of Emma Wightwick could save him from disaster. Possibly, like all young men, he was too introspective. He had yet to learn the philosophy of the middle years. He wrote very fully to his mother, keeping little or nothing from her. He shared with her both his gaiety and his disillusions. Some robust quality of understanding in her, inherited surely from Mary Anne, made it easy for him to be frank with her on matters delicate. She even twitted him, during his long engagement, on his excessive purity, telling him it was bad for his health, and quite unnecessary. Sure of her faith in him, he could not help showing her, from time to time, a little-boy conceit. He was anxious, so desperately anxious, to do well. Therefore he must pretend sometimes that he had already arrived, that editors were running after him, that critics were openmouthed, that London society—and especially the women of that society—were kneeling at his feet. This quality of cocksureness, this tendency to show off, to talk big, betrayed itself to the mother who bore him as inner doubt and fear of failure, as a sort of bolster to his youthful pride so swiftly wounded by a careless word. Because of it he endeared himself to her all the more, and knowing his faults, unable to help herself, she loved him the better for them.

Emma Wightwick, who was to become his wife, saw no fault in him at all, except that, when he was not with her, he was inclined to become tipsy at evening parties. Also he smoked over-many cigarettes. And sometimes he worked too hard, and stayed up too late, and was apt to talk nonsense to his friends. Besides, rather foolishly, admiring too many pretty faces, which he would sketch from memory on the backs of old envelopes. She felt that Paris had induced bad ways in him which she must correct, and his tendency to think of himself as a Frenchman, and a bohemian, was something it would be better for him to forget. He must learn to become an Englishman, and a respectable one at that. Which indeed he did, without too much agony of the spirit. But that France and its memories still possessed some part of him, he showed in his novels some thirty years later. . . .

There is a description of him by a contemporary, the daughter of Frith the artist, who, writing her memoirs in 1908, remembered young George du Maurier in the 1860s, when he had not been married very long, and was still making his way in the London world. Here is what she says of him:

"When I first knew du Maurier he was living in rooms over a shop quite close to the British Museum, and in great terror of losing his sight.

"He was never a robust man, but had immense vitality, and was one of those charming natures which gives out hope, life, and amusement to all who come in contact with them, and I should

sum him up in one word—joyous. Naturally he had his dark days
and times, but these he never showed in public. In the days I
knew him he was not at all well off, and he had an increasing
family, but he had married one of those wives of that period, the
women who lived for their homes and their husbands, and there
was not a load that Mrs du Maurier did not take from his shoulders when she could, not a thing she would not do to help him,
and see that no small worries stood between him and his work.

"She was one of the loveliest creatures of her time, and from
her statuesque beauty her husband drew his inspiration, and has
immortalised her over and over again in the pictures in *Punch*.
She had quantities of lovely dark hair, and in those days often
twisted a yellow riband among her locks with a most ravishing
effect. It was always a delight to me to watch du Maurier draw,
while Mrs du Maurier sat and sewed, and the children played
about the floor unchecked.

"Du Maurier became a rich man, and had a big house, but I
question if any days were happier, although all were happy, than
those first days when he sang at his work in the front room over
the corner shop. . . .

"His talk was most delightful, but above all the delight caused
me by his singing is a thing I shall never forget.

"He would sit down to the piano, and in a moment the room
would be full of divine melody, not loud, not declamatory, but
music in the fullest sense of the word; a nightingale singing in an
orchard full of apple blossom was not as sweet, and I have heard
a sudden hush come over a large assembly should he sing, albeit
he liked a small audience. I have only to close my eyes, and I
can hear him once more—a perfect silence would fall upon us all.

"*Der Lieben Langen Tag* wailed out across the night, and I
was gazing at the moon across the sea, listening to the mingled
ripple of the waves on the shore and the lovely voice in the
drawing-room, my eyes filling with tears, I do not quite know
why, and my heart beating as sentimentally as that of any lovesick maiden in her 'teens. Never did any moon shine before or
since as that did, or any sea and voice mingle as did those. Then
the tone would change; dainty little ripples ran along the keys of
the piano; we were in France. Despite the very obvious moonlight on the sea the sun shone, soldiers clanked along the boule-

vard, girls came out and beckoned and smiled, the leaves rustled on the trees, and all was spring, and gaiety and pleasure. One never had to ask him to continue; one little song after another would make the evening memorable; he knew his audience, knew that we could never have enough, and he played upon us all with his voice, another Orpheus with his lute, until we travelled miles into the country of make-believe, and wandered with him along the myriad roads of fancy. How I wish I could reproduce that *voix d'or!* At any rate, I possess it always, and can never forget the evenings when we were sung to by du Maurier.

"I always think that those who knew and loved such a genius as his can never lose him; he may die, he himself may pass into the shadows, but how much he leaves behind. . . ."

The Matinee Idol

[1973]

My father Gerald was born on the twenty-sixth of March 1873,
so if he were alive today he would be a hundred years old. The
words make no sense to me, and by no possible feat of the imagination can I conjure up a vision of some lean and slippered
pantaloon sitting in a wheelchair propped up by pillows, deaf,
perhaps, mouth half open, fumbling for telegrams of congrat-
ulation.

When he died on April 11, 1934, at the comparatively early
age of sixty-one, after an operation for cancer—and I have it on
good authority that with the surgical skill and medical treatment
of today they could have saved him—he knew, despite plans for
convalescence and smiles of reassurance to my mother, sitting by
his bedside (he died on the thirty-first anniversary of their wedding day), that his time had come. Ripe old age was not for him.
The weeks and months ahead held no promise. He had neither
the energy nor the inclination to read plays which he would be
bored to direct and equally bored to perform; and as for hanging
about a film studio all day waiting to speak half a dozen lines
that would later be cut, this might serve to pay off what he owed
for income tax, but would only increase the sense of apathy
within. To what end? An expression he often used in those last
years, half joking, half serious, and then would follow it up with
his favourite quotation: "Now more than ever seems it rich to
die, to cease upon the midnight with no pain."

Well, he had his wish. He had no pain. My aunt, who was
with him at the time, told me he had a curious, puzzled look in
his eyes, as if asking a question. I can believe it. He had the

same look when I smiled at him from the doorway and waved good-bye before his operation.

This is no way to start an article about a matinee idol. The end before the beginning. The trouble is that, as his daughter, I never saw the beginning, only grew up through childhood and adolescence when the tide of his popularity was running at full flood. He was thirty-three in 1906, a year before I was born, when he made his first big success as Raffles, the cricketer turned cracksman, a play packed full of action from start to finish, a novelty in those days, which delighted his Edwardian audiences as much as a similar theme about a Georgie Best turning out to be one of the Great Train Robbers would enthrall a pack of shouting teen-age fans in 1973. In 1906, however, his applauders were not children—except on half holidays: they were respectable fathers of families, middle-aged matrons, wide-eyed spinsters, stolid businessmen, sisters and aunts up from the country, anyone and everyone who had money enough in his pocket to pay for a seat in gallery, pit or stall, and desired above all things not to be made to think but to be entertained. It was exciting, and rather shocking, to have the hero of a play a burglar—and not an obvious burglar, the spinster ladies told themselves, who wore a cloth cap and a muffler, but a gentleman strolling about with his hands in his pockets. It gave them a *frisson*. And the men in the audience nodded in agreement. Nonsense, of course, but jolly good fun, and how easy du Maurier made the whole thing look, from lighting a cigarette to handling a gun. No wonder the women were mad about him.

Easy, perhaps, but in 1906 this sort of acting was new, and a critic of the day was even more impressed than the audience. "To play such a scene as this, slowly but surely working to a tremendous emotional climax, with few words and the difficulty of an assumed calmness which needs much subtlety, is the achievement of a tragedian of uncommon quality."

I wonder if Gerald read this notice and whether, for a moment, he thought, "Tragedian? Me? Could I ever? Dare I ever?" then, with a smile, threw the thought away with the newspaper, and continued to give his public what it wanted. Arsène Lupin, a French crook and a duke, Jimmy Valentine, the safe opener, one impossible con man after another, and the greatest crook of them all, Hubert Ware in George Bancroft's *The Ware Case,* who murdered his brother-in-law by drowning him in a lake, and lied his way out of the witness box with the help of a down-at-heel accomplice. Immoral, if you come to think of it. No message to the masses. It did not send the audiences home pondering about world problems (it was first produced in 1915, and the men who shouted their applause were all in khaki), but it allowed them to forget that they were going back to the trenches: the murder of a brother-in-law in a lake made sense and war did not.

Lists of plays that were popular successes between the years 1906 and 1918, all produced at Wyndham's Theatre, where Gerald had gone into management in 1910 with a non-acting partner, Frank Curzon, would be of little interest to the reader of 1973. He will never see them. None, except those of J. M. Barrie, is likely to be revived. Suffice it to say they were of their era, and Gerald, who had a genius for knowing when the moment was ripe for something old or something new, a revival once popular and acclaimed a second time or a novelty catching the passing mood, never failed to "bring them in," as the saying went. "House Full" boards went up outside the theatre, the queues lengthened, the taxis rolled.

This, it could be argued by the young of today, sounds somewhat tame. Bourgeois, middle class. Nothing like a Pop Festival in Hyde Park or the Isle of Wight, where boys and girls will sleep out in the open and wait twenty-four hours in the rain to hear the beloved reach for his mike or twang his guitar. Football players are mobbed as they leave the ground, film stars (and they grow fewer every day) besieged outside their hotels, disc jockeys accosted in the streets; anyone who happens to hit the headlines in the morning appears on television that same evening and is seen by millions. Instant fame is the order of the day. Herein lies the difference between our time and forty, fifty, sixty years ago. There was no hysteria then. Applause, yes, and plenty of it, and boos and catcalls too, when a play had offended, reviews the following morning written by critics of repute who did not hesitate to damn author and cast alike if they deserved it, yet at the same time spared the newspaper reader the cheap gibe or flourish of wit.

Dignity, perhaps, was the operative word. Dignity, and ease of manner. Recognition of talent, technique and training, and understanding on the part of critic and playgoer alike that the men and women on the other side of the footlights had worked long and hard during the weeks of rehearsal to bring pleasure to those who sat and watched. If they had failed, too bad; the play would be withdrawn, the cast dismissed, the management lose money, and a start must begin all over again to find a play that would please the audience better.

A point in favour of the old actor-manager of the past was that those he endeavoured to entertain connected him with one particular theatre. The playgoers from 1910 to 1925 did not have to search the newspapers to discover where Gerald du Maurier was performing: it could only be at Wyndham's Theatre. (And after 1925, when the partnership with Frank Curzon ended and Gilbert Miller took his place, the St. James's Theatre became the new home.) The cast changed, of course, from play to play, but there was continuity in the theatre staff, the commissionaire in front of the theatre, the stage doorkeeper, the cleaners, the dressers, the stage manager, the manager in the box office. Thinking back, after all too many years, I can feel the swing doors with the bars across them under my hands; surely I had to reach up to them? And Bob, the stage doorkeeper, smiling down from his stool. The stairs to the dressing room, stage entrance on the left, stairs to the other dressing rooms on the right. The musty, indefinable theatre smell of shifting scenery, with stage hands moving about and Poole, Gerald's dresser, who had rather a red face and mumbled as he spoke, hovering at the entrance to the dressing room.

The colour of the room, in retrospect, seems to be green. There were playbills all over the wall on the left. A large mirror on the right, and a flat sort of divan beneath it on which my sisters and I used to sit. It was good for dangling our legs. A curtain, seldom pulled, divided the inner sanctum where Gerald changed and made up. A different smell came from it, not musty —grease paint (I'm told they don't use it today), eau de cologne and something else, cool, clean, that must have been Gerald himself.

To us children there was nothing singular or surprising that in a moment he would come bursting in from the door that led

directly to backstage, calling for Poole, and that we would hear
the distant sound of applause which meant that the audience
was still clapping after the final curtain, before "God Save the
King." This was his life. Other children's fathers, perhaps, went
to an office; ours went to the theatre. Then, perhaps, friends or
acquaintances who had been to the matinee would come round
to see him, which meant standing up and shaking hands on our
part, and listening, yawning, while the chatter passed over our
heads. The people who came always seemed excited, thrilled, entering the star's dressing room was an event. It was a relief when
the exclamations and the congratulations were over and we were
just ourselves, with Gerald sitting down and taking off his make-
up at the dressing table. Pity, though, I sometimes thought. He
looked nicer with it on, bolder, somehow, and his eyes very
bright. Still, it was all part of the game of make-believe that was
his, and ours as well. Life was pretending to be someone else.
Otherwise it was rather dull.

I suppose I must have been about six, or possibly seven, when
I first realised that Gerald—Daddy, as we called him—was recognised, known, by strangers outside the theatre. We were entering
a restaurant—it was probably the Piccadilly Hotel, because he
had not yet started his custom of going to the Savoy, and for
some reason or other he was taking us out to lunch; perhaps it
was my elder sister Angela's birthday. There were several people
standing about and I was lagging behind. Then a tall woman—all
adults seem unbearably tall to a small child—nudged her companion with a knowing look and said, "There's Gerald du
Maurier." She sounded excited, and there was a gleam in her
eye. The escort turned and stared, and a knowing look came into
his eye too. Both of them smirked. Somehow, I don't know why,
I found this offensive. I looked up sharply at my father, but he
was humming softly under his breath, as he often did, and took
not the slightest notice of either the tall woman or her escort, but
I knew that he had heard the exclamation, and he knew that I
had heard it too. Waiters suddenly approached, bowing, pulling
back chairs from our table. Heads turned. The same gleam, the
same nudge. We sat down and the business of the lunch proceeded, and the whole scene sank into a child's unconscious
mind, but the penny had dropped.

From then on I knew that strangers, people we should never know, never speak to, were in some curious way gratified when he passed by. The applause, the clapping of hands, the little knot of men and women, mostly women, waiting outside the stage door when we left the theatre to go home after a matinee, was all part of the same thing. Because Gerald—Daddy—had pleased them by pretending to be someone else; like Raffles leaping out of the grandfather clock in the last act, he also pleased them by going into a restaurant and having lunch. And the strange thing was that it made *them* feel important, not him. He didn't care. And somehow, to a child of six or seven, this was tremendously important. If Gerald had smirked back, or thrown them a glance over his shoulder—those two in the restaurant—or in any way shown himself aware . . . *my* idol would have crashed.

This cool disregard on the part of the well-known towards the pointer, the starer, was not, I think, peculiar to Gerald, but was characteristic of his fellow stars as well, half a century and more ago. They were not concerned about their image. I suspect that it is different today. With rare exceptions a public figure who does not wave, grin, exchange jokes with his admirers and continually show himself conscious of his fans would be accused of having a swollen head. The fact that Gerald ignored nudges and whispers in the street or in restaurants did not mean that he despised the crowds who came to applaud him in the theatre, or indeed the many fans who wrote to him or waited outside the stage door, autograph book in hand. Letters were answered promptly, though I have no recollection of who did the secretarial work before my aunt Sybil—Billy, my mother's sister—took it on around 1919. Hands were shaken, autographs written, and all with a good grace, after the matinee, in that dark passage between Wyndham's and what was then the New Theatre; then to the car drawn up at the front of the house, with Dan—or was it Martin?—throwing open the door, and so back home for an early dinner at a quarter to seven, then twenty minutes' shut-eye before the evening performance. Eight performances a week, bed never before midnight or later, but first supper—eggs and bacon or sausages—cooked by my mother, who had waited up for him in her dressing gown and now listened to the gossip of his day.

Stage, film and T.V. stars nowadays have marriages that come apart with the first row. An absence for a few weeks on tour or on location is asking for trouble. Somebody's eye wanders, is caught, and the curious modern custom of telling all to the innocent partner so as to appease personal guilt is followed through to its inevitable conclusion, and the innocent partner, pride outraged, sues for a divorce. Everyone marries again. Perhaps it will be second or third time lucky.

Gerald, who had learnt the facts of life as a young actor from Mrs. Patrick Campbell and others, fell in love with my mother, Muriel Beaumont, when they were acting together in Barrie's *The Admirable Crichton* at the Duke of York's Theatre in 1902. She was very pretty, rather naïve, had a will of her own and adored him. Adoration was mutual, and continued unchanging until his death thirty-one years after their marriage in 1903. How fully my mother was aware of his wandering eye I shall never know. Perhaps she closed her own, realising, with the wisdom of her particular generation, that he would always place her first. Not a marriage of convenience, but a marriage of love and understanding. Twice I saw her really roused, with a high colour and stamping foot. The first occasion was when she opened her bill from Fortnum & Mason and saw, in the middle of a list of items she had ordered, a large case of tea that had been sent round, on Gerald's instructions, to the apartment of his current leading lady. Let him order goods on the side if he must, she told him, but not put them down to his wife.

The second occasion was more serious. Driving into London from Hampstead in her own small car, she noticed, with astonishment, Gerald's Sunbeam parked outside a terrace house on the fringe of St. John's Wood. The house was inhabited by a young actress who had a small part in his current production. My mother—Mo, as she was always called—drove on to town, whether to shop or to visit friends I don't know, but on the return journey, a few hours later, she saw that the Sunbeam was still there. Crisis threatened. Dinner before the theatre that evening was an ordeal. I know, because I was there. What passed between my father and my mother in the way of accusation, denial, acknowledgement, contrition, I shall never know, except for the quick whisper in my ear from Gerald on his way to the theatre, "Mummy's so angry with me, I don't know what to do."

How old was I? Nineteen, twenty? I don't remember; but I felt then as if he were my brother, or indeed my son. The father-daughter relationship had entered a deeper phase.

Ten years or so previously the relationship had been more personal, more emotional. If Gerald's most popular successes to date —and I am now speaking of 1917—had been chiefly those of what we should now call the cops and robbers variety, the thrill of the chase, it took J. M. Barrie to draw the finest acting out of the matinee idol of the day. In *Dear Brutus*, surely Barrie's best play, the least sentimental, the most perceptive, Gerald took the part of a jaded, spoilt, successful painter, at odds with his wife and with the world. The title—taken from Cassius in *Julius Caesar*, "The fault, dear Brutus, is not in our stars, But in ourselves, that we are underlings"—gives the theme of the play: a group of people, the painter amongst them, as they wander in an enchanted wood, are shown, by their host magician, what they would have done with their lives had they been given a second chance. Gerald, as Will Dearth, is still an artist, but unsuccessful, with no possessions except a daughter in her teens, whom he loves, and who loves him. The transformation of the jaded, successful man in the first act to the happy-go-lucky father in the second saw Gerald at his peak. He was himself, yes, but also every man who carries in his soul a seed of discontent, of wishing that his world was other than it had turned out to be. There was nostalgia, too—memories of his own artist father, who had known success but had remained his generous, unspoilt self.

The third act brought realisation. The second chance was nothing but a dream. He was Will Dearth, who had conquered the artistic world, but he had no daughter. "When I was in the wood with Margaret," Gerald said, "she . . . she . . . Margaret . . ." and then he lifted his head and looked about him, at the walls of the house enclosing him, no wood, no child, and it was as though he shrank into himself, and the expression in his eyes, bewildered, lost, anguished, was something that his real daughter, a child of ten, has never forgotten, can never forget. Filial identification? Possibly. But the hushed audience identified also, and this is surely the whole meaning of communication between the actor on the stage and those who sit and watch him; they have a bond in common, they see themselves.

The natural school of acting that Gerald founded had much to answer for in later years. Mumbled speaking, sloppy gestures, actors with small talent believing that, without years of training and hard thought, they could walk an easy road to success. It was not so. Either they achieved a temporary popularity, or they fell by the way. Only those with real genius knew how to develop the technique and build upon it, and I do not think it is fancy on my part, or filial pride, when I think of the two greatest actors of our day, Laurence Olivier and John Gielgud, who, in their youth, must have seen *Dear Brutus* and watched Gerald in his prime.

It can be argued, of course, that when Gerald appeared on the stage for the first time in 1894, at the age of twenty-one, without any training, he did so through favouritism. Sir John Hare happened to be a friend of his father and was pleased to give the lad the humble part of Fritz the waiter, with little to do and still less to say. His only experience until then had been in amateur theatricals during school holidays from Harrow, and at Harrow his sole claim to distinction had been his ability to imitate Sir Henry Irving up and down the corridors, to the amusement of masters and boys alike. Possibly an added inducement to Sir John Hare was the fact that two years previously the boy's father, George du Maurier, had published his novel *Trilby*, which had proved to be the literary event of the season in both England and America. The *Punch* artist, a celebrity anyway, was now world famous. Nothing succeeds like success, and it is doubtful if the critic who wrote of Fritz the waiter, "Mr du Maurier in a very few words showed that he had probably found his vocation" would have noticed the young man but for the familiar name in the programme.

A familiar name on its own, however, does not carry its bearer far unless the talent is there, and the will to work, and Gerald possessed not only talent but determination too, qualities that were developed in the following years under the brilliant tuition of Beerbohm Tree and Mrs. Patrick Campbell. From Fritz the waiter to Will Dearth may not have been a hard road or an uphill climb, but it took three-and-twenty years to achieve, which is a fair step, if you come to think of it. Charm and ease of manner may win popularity in a night, but artistic genius within a man must be nurtured by perception, experience and integrity, if it is to survive for more than a decade.

"Why was Daddy knighted?" I asked my mother when, after his death in 1934, I was making notes for his biography. She looked up from her embroidery with a thoughtful expression in her eyes. "I don't think we ever knew," she replied, which seemed to me then, and now, a delightful attitude to honours, and one that was undoubtedly Gerald's own. I assumed that the knighthood was laid upon him in 1922 not because of the wild popularity of Bulldog Drummond, a very different role from that of Will Dearth, nor for the somewhat quixotic gesture which he made in his mid-forties in 1918 by throwing up *Dear Brutus* and joining the Irish Guards as a cadet (a tribute, I suspect, to his beloved brother Guy, who had been killed in action in 1915), but plainly and simply "for services rendered to his profession." He was president not only of the Actors' Orphanage but of a number of other charitable organisations, never sparing himself when he could make money for those less fortunate than himself. Wasn't it Will Dearth in the enchanted wood who had said to his daughter Margaret, "We lucky ones, let's always be kind to those who are down on their luck, and when we're kind, let's be a little kinder"? No one ever asked Gerald for a loan and was refused, and needless to say the money, if any attempt was made to return it, was not accepted. He was never a rich man, as riches are known today in the world of film and pop star, but what he earned was generously spent, needy relatives taken care of, friends paid for on holiday. Make other people happy while you have the means to do so, and to hell with the future and the Inland Revenue. . . .

If the matinee idol of the war years was now Sir Gerald with added responsibilities, he carried the burden lightly; and although in the 1920s he was the undoubted head of his profession, and had turned fifty, he was still youthful in appearance and young in heart. No one who remembers *The Last of Mrs Cheyney*—Freddie Lonsdale's witty comedy at the St. James's Theatre —in which he co-starred with Gladys Cooper, will forget the brilliance of these two, their consummate ease and grace, their timing, the sense of fun that pervaded the whole production. Now there were two sets of fans waiting at the stage door after a performance. His and hers. And if nobody screamed or fainted when Gladys finally emerged, I do recollect the murmur that arose from her excited adorers, gradually swelling in volume as she passed between them, and hands would be stretched out to touch her coat as though the very texture had magic properties. Gladys smiled, and waved, and made a dash for her car, and if by chance I scrambled in her wake, being an adorer in my own fashion, I used to wonder how swiftly a waiting crowd might be moved to anger, the murmur of approval turn to a roar of hate, the hands outstretched to touch reach down for stones. Anyone who has heard boos and groans and whistles at a first night after a flop will understand me.

The great day for the fans, of course, was the annual Theatrical Garden Party, in aid of the Actors' Orphanage, originally held in the Botanical Gardens in Regent's Park, but in postwar years in the Chelsea Hospital Gardens. This would be the nearest thing, fifty years ago, to the pop festivals of our own time. The whole theatrical profession would be there, stars, supporting players, understudies. The sight was something between a circus and a fun fair. Walk up . . . walk up . . . Come bowl for a pig with Owen Nares. Dig for buried treasure with Phyllis Dare. Buy Gladys Cooper Face Cream from her own hands. The biggest draw, as might be expected, was a vast marquee at the end of the grounds covering a built-up stage, with a curtain and rows of seats for a paying audience, where Gerald, with a picked cast of actors and actresses, gave a knockabout performance known as *The Grand Giggle*. If memory serves me right, the skit or farce would last about thirty minutes, the action proceeding at a cracking pace to whoops of laughter. Then the audience would troop out to allow their successors in the queue outside to take their place. An exhausting afternoon for the players, but a field day for the fans. Even the performers' families basked in reflected glory. My mother, with a bevy of helpers, would preside over a hoopla stall with all the grace of a queen consort, with my sisters and myself as a doubtful added attraction, the whispered "Ooh! aren't they dears?" bringing blushes to our cheeks. It was much more fun to roam the other stalls incognito than to pose as prize exhibits.

Well, it's all over now. Grand Giggles and hoopla stalls belong

to a bygone age. Some of those who drew the crowds in the
twenties now live in the Denville Home for retired actors and
actresses, of which Gerald was also president. The art of acting
is ephemeral, especially in the theatre. We can see the film stars
of yesterday in yesterday's films, hear the voices of poets and
singers on a record, keep the plays of dead dramatists upon our
bookshelves, but the actor who holds his audience captive for
one brief moment upon a lighted stage vanishes forever when
the curtain falls. The actors and actresses of two generations ago
live on in the memories of those who had the good fortune to
watch them and applaud, and if this is poor consolation for the
absence of voice and smile and gesture, at least something of
their presence lingers still, to bring courage and inspiration to
their successors.

When a young player today glances instinctively over his
shoulder, alters position, changes tone and speaks with greater
clarity—none of which has been laid down for him in the script
or urged upon him by the director—is it fanciful to believe that
something of the talent possessed by others has brushed off on
his shoulders, and that as he treads the boards of a well-worn
stage the very dust of a predecessor rises to become part of him?
Sentimental, perhaps, but your born actor has sentiment bred in
the bone, and superstition too. He feels, he is aware, and no matter how many theatres fall on the scrap heap—the St. James's is
no more, the old Criterion is threatened, Wyndham's may one
day give place to an office block—the few square acres of London where he works, from Covent Garden to Piccadilly and beyond, are haunted by a happy breed of men who one and all
were strolling players in their time. Applause was theirs for a
night and a day in their world of make-believe, but the emotion
they engendered in themselves and in those about them was for
posterity.

When I think of Gerald—and scarcely a day passes without
some reminder, from the photographs and mementoes round the
house down to his signet ring, which I wear upon my finger—it is
not as a father that I see him most clearly, bowling to us children
at cricket on the lawn at Hampstead and assuming a different
personality with each delivery of the ball; nor as the producer,
directing rehearsals of a play with intense concentration from a

corner of the stage or from the stalls; nor yet as the actor, putting every ounce of energy and thought into a first-night performance and then standing, with the cast beside him, to take his bow and receive the shouting acclaim at the final curtain. No, he has pottered downstairs to the drawing room one fine morning in search of cigarettes, while Mo is upstairs having a bath, and he is wearing silk pyjamas from Beale & Edmonds of Bond Street, topped by a very old cardigan full of holes that once belonged to his mother. He switches on the gramophone, and the hit song of the day, a sensuous waltz, floats upon the air. He holds out his arms to a non-existent partner and, closing his eyes, circles the room with the exaggerated rhythm of a musical-comedy hero, languid, romantic, murmuring with mock passion:

> *"I wonder why you keep me waiting,*
> *Charmaine, my Charmaine . . ."*

Unseen by friends or fans, and unobserved, so he imagines, by any member of his family, Gerald obeys the instinct of a lifetime, and is acting to himself.

Sylvia's Boys

All childhood memories are visual. A face, a figure, somebody smiling or frowning, and the image stays forever. A moment in time, held captive. Sometimes the drone of adult conversation sounding as a foreign language suddenly becomes clear. A sentence becomes imprinted on the memory box. No explanation. Silence again.

I do not remember my aunt Sylvia, the second daughter of my grandfather George du Maurier, and the little I do know was told to me, through the years, by my father Gerald, the youngest of the family. He adored all three sisters, and his brother, but somehow I formed the impression that Sylvia, who married Arthur Llewelyn-Davies and bore him five sons, was the sister he loved the best. As I have said, I do not remember her, for she died when I was barely three years old; yet my mother used to tell me that she would ask for me to be taken down to see her, when she was lying in bed already suffering from the cancer that would kill her, so that she could hold me in her arms. This was no mark of favouritism. My sister Angela would go too. But Sylvia adored babies. So I have often wondered why my memory box does not hold the impression of that dying woman, beautiful, witty, tender and loving, whispering words of comfort, or possibly even jokes, to a shy and stubborn baby.

I am three, I am four, I am five, and why is it that Cousin Jack, Aunt Sylvia's second son, already a midshipman surely in naval uniform, takes to calling at Cumberland Terrace, where we live, to bring me sweets, and once a balloon?

"Someone to see you," says the parlourmaid. "Just go into the dining room."

I wander in and he is there, sitting in the chair at the far end of the room.

"Hullo, Daphne," and he stands up and smiles at me. At four, at five years old, I am smitten on the spot. Cousin Jack is the only one in the world for me. But now, in retrospect, why did he come? Was it because he knew that his mother Sylvia loved little children, and when I sat on her bed as a baby he remembered this? I do not know.

The image of Cousin Jack persists. He has come to see all of us in the country, where we are spending the summer. He climbs an enormous tree in the garden with supreme confidence. Yet to enter the dining room and say, "Hullo, Cousin Jack," over-whelms me with shyness. My heart beats. I nearly faint with embarrassment.

Another image. We are at Ramsgate. Our grandmother takes a house there every summer. We go to stay, and the cousins too. I overhear my mother say, "I don't know why the Davies boys have to have the best front rooms, and our children are put at the back."

At five, six, I know the answer. The Davies boys are *boys*. Hurrah for them! They are all playing in a front room, and we join them. Some sort of hide-and-seek, and Cousin Michael knocks into me inadvertently. I begin to cry. Cousin Michael rushes from the room. Cousin Nico, nearer to my age, though some four years older, comforts me.

"Look. Look at this picture in *Punch* of a plum pudding. It's Michael."

This is funny. I stop crying and laugh.

"Come and see Michael, he's ashamed," says Nico. We go into the adjoining room. Michael is sitting in a chair with a rug over his face. "Kiss him," says Nico, "go on." Instinctively I know that, although I would like to kiss Cousin Michael, he would not want me to do so.

Overheard conversation. It is between their nanny, Mary, and ours.

"Michael has bad nightmares. He dreams of ghosts coming through the window." Yes . . . Yes . . . I stare at the window of our night nursery in London, and I understand. But what about Peter Pan? Peter Pan came through the window to the night nursery of the Darling children, and he was not a ghost. *Peter Pan.* The play that we act in our own nursery endlessly. The play that we go to see every Christmas. Uncle Jim, who wrote

the play for the cousins, and looks after them now that Uncle
Arthur and Aunt Sylvia are dead, comes to see us act it in our
nursery. But I don't remember when he came.

The memory box switches to Cousin George, the eldest of our
cousins; he is tall and dark, smiling down at us from another
seaside house at Bournemouth that our grandmother rented. Almost a man. Not a boy.

"Let's all play hide-and-seek in the garden," somebody says—
Nico? It will be doubly exciting if Cousin George will play too.

"Doris will play as well," says Nico, always game for anything.

Cousin George looks embarrassed. "I don't think I'll play," he
says. "You children go instead."

Am I seven years old? I can't remember. But the thought came
to me then, "Perhaps Cousin George would feel shy if he caught
Doris." Doris is our nursemaid.

And almost instantly it's the war. Uncle Guy, Daddy's brother,
is killed. And a few weeks later we are told, back in Cumberland
Terrace, that Cousin George has been killed like Uncle Guy. We
wear black bands on our arms for both of them. And the following Sunday we are at the zoo. Uncle Jim is there, with Nico, and
we stare at the lion's cage. But surely if Cousin George has been
killed we should not go to the zoo? I don't understand. I am confused. Why aren't Uncle Jim and Nico crying? Nico is laughing
at the lions. Daddy cried when Uncle Guy was killed. Angela,
Jeanne and I have no brother. Why? I shall pretend to be a boy,
then. Like the lady who acts Peter Pan at the Duke of York's.

Three years pass. They are rehearsing *Dear Brutus* at Wyndham's Theatre. Uncle Jim and J. M. Barrie merge into one person, and I am no longer a child. I understand what is happening.
Daddy—Gerald—has to be the father of a girl called Margaret,
and they are alone together in a magic wood. I begin to identify.
The daughter might be me. Then Uncle Jim calls me up onto the
stage.

"Daphne? Shall we show Faith Celli how to walk?"

Up and down, up and down, he takes my hand and we walk
together. Everyone rehearsing watches. But I can't identify any
more. I feel silly, awkward. Daddy tells me to go back again and
watch the rehearsal from the stalls. I know then I would hate to
be an actress. I couldn't even be Peter Pan.

Meanwhile the cousins have grown up. Jack, the onetime idol, is married, out of my thoughts. Peter, a more distant figure, also a grown man. Michael, whom I wanted to kiss and never did, is at Oxford. Nico is at Eton, and sometimes we go to the great day there, the Fourth of June, and although he is still the same laughing, joking Nico there is a grandeur about him, he is in Pop, he belongs to the élite.

I am fourteen, no longer a child, at any rate in my own eyes, and one day, saying the customary "Good morning" to our parents in the bedroom, I hear the dreadful news. The night before Uncle Jim had gone round to Wyndham's Theatre and said to our father Gerald, "Michael's dead. . . . Drowned." And he broke down, there, in the dressing room. I can't put it out of my mind. Uncle Jim loved Michael best of all the boys. There is a funeral. Michael is buried in Aunt Sylvia's grave, next to Grandpapa and Granny, in the Hampstead churchyard. Michael, I never knew you as we all know Nico, where have you gone? Why did it happen?

One morning, some days after the funeral, when we go for our daily walk into the town to buy biscuits or whatever is needed in our schoolroom, I slip away from the governess and buy some violets with my pocket money. Then I go to the churchyard and put them on the grave. "These are for you, Michael." Perhaps he heard. But would he be there? I don't know. Then I go quickly away to find the others. "Where *have* you been?" No answer. I shan't tell anyone. Let them scold. Aunt Sylvia, George, Michael, perhaps they are all laughing at me together.

The years pass. Ten, twenty, thirty years, the remaining boys are married, myself as well, and I am now a writer, Peter and Nico publishers. Uncle Jim is dead. Peter wants to bring out a book about our grandfather, George du Maurier, and asks me to write the Introduction. Peter, the shadowy boyhood figure, becomes a close friend. We meet at the Café Royal, and talk and talk. Always about family; ours. Grandfather George is Kicky to us, as he was to himself and to his friends. We never discuss the world of today. Always the past. Do all of us carry a seed of melancholy within, except perhaps Nico? Peter thought yes, I could not be sure. Then, within a few years, Peter himself was dead. Jack was dead. Nico, dear Nico, remains.

My Name in Lights

I believe that success and the enjoyment of it are a very personal and a very private thing, like saying one's prayers or making love. The outward trappings are embarrassing, and spoil achievement. There come moments in the life of every artist, whether he be a writer, actor, painter, composer, when he stands back, detached, and looks at what he has done a split second, perhaps, after he has done it. That is the supreme moment. It cannot be repeated. The last sentence of a chapter, the final brush stroke, a bar in music, a look in the eye and the inflection of an actor's voice, these are the things that well up from within and turn the craftsman into an artist, so that, alone in his study, in his studio, on the stage (and the stage behind the footlights can be the loneliest place on earth), he has this blessed spark of intuition. "This is good. This is what I meant."

The feeling has gone in the next breath, and the craftsman takes over again. Back to routine, and the job for which he is trained. The pages that must link the story together, dull but necessary; the background behind the sitter's head; the scenes in the actor's part which come of necessity as anticlimax: all these are measures of discipline the artist puts upon himself and understands, and he works at them day after day, week after week. The moment of triumph is a thing apart. It is the secret nourishment. The *raison d'être*.

The moment, rare and precious, must never be confused with those occasions which come, alas, only too often, when the writer —full of complaisance and conceit—becomes blunted to his own style, and believes he has only to dash off a few thousand words and the result is literature. The moment of the inner glow, and the purr of pleasure, are two very opposite things. The inner glow can bring despair in its train, or a high temperature, or such fever of intensity that nothing but a ten-mile walk or an icy swim will break the spell and release the writer to the world of day-by-day. The purr of pleasure is an indication that the writer has never left the world at all. He has been watching himself at work, hearing his own voice; and the fret with which he waits for public opinion—the criticism of friend, publishers, reader— points to the doubt within. He must be praised, he must be flat- tered, he must be boosted by some means other than his own life spark: otherwise there is no momentum, all is sound and fury, signifying nothing.

The supreme moment can come to anyone, from Shakespeare penning a sonnet to a clown turning a double somersault. The flash is no respecter of persons, but each and all share one thing in common at the moment of impact, and that is integrity. A kind of purity within. Like a prayer, like the giving of love to a beloved, the feeling says, "This is what I have to offer." Anatole France put it best when he wrote his story of the Juggler of Notre Dame, who, demanding no audience, his being filled with the inner glow, did his circus turn before the statue of the Blessed Virgin, a tribute and a triumph all in one.

After the private homage the public homage is anticlimax, and worse than anticlimax, second rate. Values go awry. We have learnt in our generation to misdoubt, even to dread, mass hyste- ria. The mob which sobs and screams at a boy with a guitar is the same mob which hanged Mussolini and his mistress upside down. Tip the scales, and the hands that acclaim the artist be- come the hands that tear him to pieces. The wreath of laurel is the crown of thorns. The actor and the writer are especially vul- nerable today, when world-wide publicity through press and tel- evision makes them into that treacherous thing, a "personality."

In other days rogues, vagabonds and scribblers clung together, if they clung at all, and, gently mocked at as a race apart, were left mercifully alone. In the 1950s they are expected to pro- nounce on the H-bomb, enter Parliament, open hospitals, shut bazaars, and—surely the most surprising activity of the lot— crown carnival queens! In moments of cynicism I like to ponder on what would have happened over a hundred years ago if two sisters from Haworth had been inveigled into Leeds for an after-noon at an art gallery, and found themselves thrust upon a stage before a gaping audience while ringing tones announced, "Char-lotte and Emily Brontë, This Is Your Life. . . ."

Certainly no moment of triumph for them. Only disgust and horror. Living as we do in an age of noise and bluster, success is now measured accordingly. We must all be seen, and heard, and on the air. What toothpaste do we use? Do our husbands snore? What about A.I.D. and foot and mouth? To answer these ques-tions counts as sucking up. To refuse to answer is high-hat. No remedy for the artist today.

My own dislike of the trappings of success dates from watch-ing my father, the theatre idol of his time, push his way through a crowd after a first night. Adoring, and fiercely proud, I felt in-stinctively as a small child that the clamour was false, the praise unreal. What the mob really wants is for the artist to fail, so that the whispering campaign can begin. "Poor chap, he's had his day. The thing's misfired . . . a flop. Tear down the bills." De-stroy the idol.

When my father went to Harrow at fourteen the first thing that happened to him was to be made to stand up, in class, while the rest of the boys stared at him for having a famous *Punch* art-ist for a parent. This was in 1887. When I went to finishing school in Paris in 1925 the girls goggled round me because I was Gerald du Maurier's daughter. There is a lad at school in 1958 who gets chaffed and ragged because he is Daphne du Maurier's son. A circus family has no illusions about success. They tumble from the cradle, and are used to taking knocks. It is the amateur and the dilettante who hide their heads in shame when the jeers begin; or, swift to offence, hit back in anger.

If fan letters do not surprise me, or begging letters either, it is because I read my father's and my grandfather's as well. The people who write these letters are sincere, but they are lonely. They are writing to an idol, to a myth—never to an individual. Sometimes, answering them, I have wondered what would hap-pen if I followed up my acknowledgement with a ring on the bell, a knock on the door, and a request, "You said you wished you knew me. Here I am. May I share your home?" What bewil-dered stares! What stammering denials!

If those of us who have been successful with what wares we peddle are truly honest, we will admit a certain snob value to praise. The college girl who empties her heart from Texas is tossed aside more quickly than the poet from Corfu. The old lady who knew an aunt in Cambridge is answered, reluctantly, on Friday, but that fellow author we so much admire, and find to our delight and gratification admires us too, he is answered the very afternoon that his letter came.

Vanity, vanity, all is vanity, said the preacher, except during that moment when the writer felt the flash and wrote . . . what did he write? The flash has gone. It's as swift as that, as ephemeral, as fierce, but, like the song that ended, the memory lingers on.

Quite otherwise the trappings. I remember coming out of the underground in Piccadilly. I was alone, it was raining, and I had no date for the evening and very little money on me, not enough for a taxi. I looked up and saw my name in lights, and the title of the current film, *Rebecca*. There were lines of people standing in a queue, waiting to go in. I did not join them. Moment of success? Perhaps.

Romantic Love

There is no such thing as romantic love. This is a statement of fact, and I defy all those who hold a contrary opinion. Romantic love is an illusion, a name given to cover up an illicit relationship between two people, one of whom is married, or betrothed, to somebody else. The great love stories of the world that have been handed down to us through the centuries, whether in verse or prose or sung upon a lute, have had for theme forbidden passion, for nothing else would stimulate the reader, or in earlier days hold the attention of the listener, as he or she sat before the hearth and waited upon the teller of old tales. Battles, yes, the gorier the better, slaughter, blood, Hector dragged round the walls of Troy; but Helen was the prime cause, who left her husband Menelaus of her own free will and fled with her lover Paris, son of the Trojan King Priam. If ever illicit love brought disaster in its train this did, some twelve hundred years B.C., causing the deaths of thousands, Greeks and Trojans. Her lover Paris slain in battle, the beautiful Helen returned to her husband Menelaus, and at his death retired to the island of Rhodes, where she was almost immediately strangled by order of her onetime friend Polyxo.

Romantic love? If so, a bloody business, with unhappiness for all.

Theseus, King of Athens, was one of the most celebrated heroes of antiquity, but he was no romantic lover, unless making love to two sisters at the same time can be called romantic. He eloped with Ariadne, elder daughter of the King of Crete, to Naxos, and then deserted her and married her younger sister Phaedra. She, in due course, succumbed to a hopeless passion for Hippolytus, the son of Theseus by a former marriage; and because he did not return the love of his stepmother she accused

him of rape, when he fled to the seashore and was drowned in
his own chariot by a great wave which Neptune, in answer to
Theseus' prayer, caused to rise up from the sea. On hearing of
his death Phaedra hanged herself. A charming relationship.

Theseus, her husband, not content with one abduction in his
life, invaded the underworld and tried to carry off the Queen of
Hades but, foiled in the attempt by the god Pluto, King of
Hades, he returned to Athens to find a usurper in charge, and
then, lacking a family and a kingdom, he retired to Scyros,
where he fell to his death from a precipice.

These were the tales that stimulated our ancestors in bygone
centuries, and if the loves of mortals palled they could always
fall back upon the amours of their gods. Zeus, or Jupiter as the
Romans called him, reigned in heaven—Olympus—with his consort Hera, Juno, but his appetite was prodigious, and nothing
pleased him more than to adopt a disguise when making love to
earthly beings. He impregnated Leda, wife of the King of
Sparta, in the guise of a swan, and she brought forth two eggs,
from which, as they cracked, emerged four children, Castor and
Clytemnestra, Pollux and Helen.

Castor and Pollux are twin stars in the sky, you can see them
any night when the sky is clear, and as for Helen, we already
know what happened to her. Clytemnestra, if she lacked her
sister Helen's beauty, had inherited her swan father's appetite,
for while her husband Agamemnon was away at the Trojan wars
she lived in sin with her cousin Aegysthus, and then when her
husband returned murdered him, only to be slaughtered in her
turn by their son Orestes.

These stories, savage, brutal, utterly amoral, are the founda-
tion of our literary culture. They spread from Greece to Rome
and so throughout Europe, and although the gods died their
deeds lived after them. New stories arose, based upon the old,
but the main themes were the same: illicit passion, betrayal, and
a grim death for the lovers. The coming of Christianity may have
changed the course of history, although the birth of a heavenly
son to a virgin has a curious similarity to the Greek myth preceding it, but despite the Jewish tradition of devout and strict family life, which had a supreme influence on Christian morals,

when it came to singing songs and telling tales the main theme was still illicit love.

Arthur and Guinever . . . Guinever who betrayed her husband King Arthur with the greatest knight of all the world, Sir Lancelot, as the old romances of the Round Table described him; Tristan, son, not nephew, of King Mark of Cornwall, who, sent to Ireland to fetch his father's bride, fell in love with her himself, and she with him, so bringing jealousy and despair to the father's heart. Is it possible that the Tristan story is really an adaptation from the Theseus, Phaedra and Hippolytus tale, handed down from singer to minstrel, from Greece to Gaul, from Gaul to Brittany and Cornwall? During the telling of it the theme has softened. Tristan has become nephew, not son, thus drawing a veil over the incest barrier. King Mark has become an aged, crusty old man, the two lovers Tristan and Isolde both young and innocent, sleeping, when they fled his wrath to the woods, with a drawn sword between them.

Not so originally. Béroul, the first Frenchman to take up the tale and make a poem from it, described the love affair with all the robust humour inherited from some earlier source. King Mark sprinkles the bedroom floor with flour so that Tristan, creeping to Isolde's bed, will leave his traces there. Tristan, disguising himself as a pilgrim, waits by a ford which the Queen and her retinue cannot pass, and offers himself as carrier. Then, with the Queen upon his shoulders, he stumbles in the mud, and they fall together to make play with one another in the shallows, and later the Queen can tell her husband the King, without speaking an untruth, that she has "lain" with no man except a pilgrim.

This is true bawdy, and certainly not romance. Here was the stuff that made our ancestors slap their thighs and roll in their seats, but it did not serve at a later date. The women demanded romance, as they continue to do today in their novels and magazines, and, if they can get it, on their television screens as well. Lovely Guinever, noble Sir Lancelot! Gallant Tristan, unhappy sweet Isolde! They couldn't help falling in love. It just happened to them.

Another famous pair of lovers were Paolo and Francesca. Francesca, married to a lame husband, Giovanni Sciancato

(John the Lame), falls in love with his younger brother Paolo, but not, let me remind the reader, until both the innocent young people are sitting together reading the story of Lancelot and Guinever. (Which proves that reading about illicit love can corrupt the reader.) Then, as the poet Dante has it, *"Noi leggiavamo un giorno per diletto, di Lancialotto, come amor lo strinse!"* or, in matter-of-fact prose, "One day we read of Lancelot, and how love constrained him. We were alone, and without all suspicion. Our eyes met, and when we read how the fond smile was kissed by such a lover, he, who shall never be divided from me, kissed my mouth all trembling." The deed was done. Fate ran its course. John the Lame discovered what was brewing, and murdered both his wife and younger brother.

Of course Dante, being a good Christian, a Catholic to boot, and not a Greek or Roman poet, had the two lovers condemned forever to circle on the winds in hell. You can read of them in the Inferno. And yes, Helen of Troy is there too, and Tristan, and other illicit lovers, including—but possibly she deserved it—Cleopatra, though Antony is not named. Dido is amongst the damned, simply because she killed herself for love after her husband's death—he was her uncle, incidentally—and this has always seemed to me a curious choice on Dante's part, because poor Dido had committed no ill deed. Whether it was the suicide, or the marriage to the uncle, that caused Dante to shake his head I have never discovered. As for Paolo and Francesca, and the other band of doomed sinners, surely the Greeks would have turned them into stars? We lost much when Olympus fell.

Shakespeare, living three centuries after Dante, had a lighter touch with lovers. True, the jealous husband plays his customary role, and though Desdemona, unlike Isolde and Guinever, is innocent of adultery, her spouse Othello smothers her with a pillow. But then Shakespeare never claimed his play was a romance. *Othello* is a tragedy, and so is *Antony and Cleopatra,* in which Egypt's Queen (an inhabitant of Dante's Inferno) puts a poisonous snake to her bosom after her lover Antony has died of his wounds at her side. We may suppose, though we cannot say for certain, that there was much writhing and contortion, groans as well, upon the Elizabethan stage when the leading characters died. The spectators, pressing forward, would watch breathless as the boy actor, playing Cleopatra, put the asp to his breast and murmured, "Peace, peace! Dost thou not see my baby at my breast, That sucks the nurse asleep?" They were spared, probably from scenic difficulties, the drowning of mad Ophelia in *Hamlet,* but were told how "her garments, heavy with their drink, Pull'd the poor wretch from her melodious lay To muddy death."

Shakespeare's most famous pair of lovers were undoubtedly Romeo and Juliet. Here at last, you will say, we have romance. Nothing illicit in this play, the tragic ending has us all in tears. Well . . . it must not be forgotten that in the first act Romeo declares himself burning with love for one Rosaline, whom we are never permitted to see, alas; but for a young man supposedly suffering from a broken heart Romeo recovers very swiftly at first sight of Juliet. Juliet, at twelve years old, is equally stricken, but one wonders how much this mutual attraction between the two young people is whipped to a point of frenzied passion by the knowledge that any alliance would be forbidden by their shocked and horrified parents. Once more we have illicit love, and this makes the spice of the story, or did so at any rate for its Elizabethan audiences.

Had the course of true love run smooth, had Romeo and Juliet stood hand in hand a bridal pair in the final scene with Capulets and Montagues smiling, the whole point would have gone. Happy endings were implicit in Shakespeare's comedies, but these plays were mostly given before selected audiences, written for specific occasions, guests at court and so on, when, having dined well, the assembled company preferred to be soothed and entertained rather than horrified or stirred. Hence in *Twelfth Night* the jaded palate of the sophisticated visitor or courtier could be tickled by the spectacle of a lovesick duke becoming unconsciously attracted to a girl disguised as a page, with the widow for whom he has sighed in vain so long herself seeking the favours of the same supposed youth. Shakespeare, tongue in cheek, knew only too well what went on behind the scenes of Queen Elizabeth's court. The same sort of deception delighted those who watched *As You Like It.* Girls dressed as boys; Portia did it too in *The Merchant of Venice.* A fairy besotted by a fool with an ass's head was the final touch of irony spun in *A Mid-*

summer Night's Dream. Shakespeare was well aware that to make a comedy savoury you had to play it witty, coarse and quick, or you would have your audience on the yawn.

Therefore today, when we upbraid the modern playwright for pornography, let us remember that the tradition is long-standing, handed on by masters of the game, Aristophanes surely being the supreme example. They did it, however, with more finesse. To show lovers naked in the act would have dulled the appetite.

The great dramatists were never romantic, any more than the great novelists. Tolstoy did not portray a happy wife in *Anna Karenina*. She deceived her husband for a pretty worthless lover, and when he went to the wars preferred to throw herself under a train rather than live without him. Flaubert's Madame Bovary, bored with provincial life and her doctor husband, lacked courage at first to console herself with a lover, but when she succumbed to Rodolphe Boulanger and Léon Dupuis corruption set in, lies, deceit, debts, all sense of honour left her, and in the end, deserted by her lovers, her still-loving husband absent, she died a slow and painful death from self-administered arsenic. A fine romance.

Hardy's Tess of the D'Urbervilles was dogged by fate from the start. Raped by a man she did not love, then married to one she did, who spurned her on the wedding night when he learnt the secret from her own lips, she passed a wretched existence desired by the first, desiring the second, and in the end, having stabbed to death, while he slept, the man who had first possessed her, she ran away after her true husband Angel Clare, seeking forgiveness, which at last he gave, even the murder, but it was too late for happiness. The officials of the law came to arrest her, and, as Hardy himself put it, the immortals had finished their sport with Tess. Here is the essence of Greek tragedy, but in nineteenth-century England.

Wuthering Heights has been acclaimed as a supreme romantic novel, but what is romantic about its hero Heathcliffe, who marries a woman he despises in order to ill-treat her and to spite her brother, who mistreats in equal measure the delicate son he has by her, and tries to turn this son's wife into a kitchen slut? And all this because Cathy, his foster sister and the only being in the world he has ever had feeling for, marries another and then dies in childbirth? There is more savagery, more brutality, in the pages of *Wuthering Heights* than in any novel of the nineteenth century, and, for good measure, more beauty too, more poetry, and, what is more unusual, a complete lack of sexual emotion. Heathcliffe's feeling for Cathy, Cathy's for Heathcliffe, despite their force and passion, have a non-sexual quality; the emotion is elemental like the wind on Wuthering Heights.

Emily Brontë, striding over the Yorkshire moors with her dog, did not conjure from her imagination any cosy tale of happy lovers to console women readers sitting snugly within doors. A romance, according to my dictionary, is a tale "with scenes and incidents remote from everyday life," and a romancer a "fantastic liar." Well, fair enough. If a romantic tale is what editors of magazines demand for their reading public they may get it, but not quite in the form for which they hoped: instead, jealousy, treachery, deceit, passion, ending all too often in a violent death. It is not, alas, the gods who make men and women mad, but the chemistry in the blood. "Men have died . . . and worms have eaten them, but not for love. . . ."

This I Believe

In my end is my beginning. The ill-fated Mary Stuart, Queen of France and of Scotland, chose this cryptic saying as her motto. It was embroidered, in French, upon her chair of state—*En ma fin est mon commencement*—a puzzle to those who looked upon it, but the truth was that the quotation came from a fourteenth-century lyric written by a priest, Giles de Machant, and the song doubtless took her fancy when she was young and gay and lived in France with her youthful husband the Dauphin, later François II, before she had any presentiment of his early death or of her own future tempestuous life and unhappy middle years.

We, knowing her history, remembering the blindfolded figure stumbling towards the block, may venture to transpose the words and read into them greater significance—In my beginning is my end. Mary Stuart carried within her from birth the potential seeds of disruption, doom and tragedy; such were the qualities and traits inherited from her forebears that, no matter what road she had followed, and even if she had reigned neither in Scotland nor in France, she would have caused disunity and stress.

In our beginning is our end. The colour of our eyes, our skin, the shape of our hands, the depth of our emotions, the bump of humour or lack of it, the small talents we may put to good account, even the ill-health that suddenly in later life descends without apparent reason—these are the things that make us what we are. There is no cell in our bodies that has not been transmitted to us by our ancestors, and the very blood group to which we belong may predispose us to the disease that finally kills. We are all of us chemical particles, inherited not only from our parents but from a million ancestors; and because of this we beget in turn, passing on to our descendants at best a doubtful, sometimes a disturbing, legacy.

I find these facts, of which I knew little in my youth, exciting, even exhilarating. They stand for order, for a plan. They make for sense in what too often in the past seemed a senseless world. If the particles that we now are came originally from an explosion in or near the sun, and the sun itself from yet another explosion in a kindred universe, then there is no limit either to the past or to the future, life of some sort is continuous, it has no beginning and no end. Our world may burn, disintegrate: there will be others. New explosions will form new particles, which will unite. Life will go on. Creation is at work, has always been at work, will always be at work.

The image of a super-Brain, sitting before a blueprint of a million universes and commanding, "Let there be light," does not convince me, nor that such a super-Brain should point a finger at the particle I am and demand subservience to its authority. The super-Brain, if it exists, has made too many errors of judgement through the ages to deem itself omnipotent, and so win our allegiance. The automaton that gives life has, like our own inventors, second and third thoughts when working out a problem. What cannot adapt is scrapped. The first insects, the first reptiles, were too large, too cumbersome. They became redundant. Giant bats with wings and claws that pawed the sky were mistakes and—to use a modern term—were quickly scrubbed, along with the lumbering mammals glimpsed by our first ancestors. Plants, fishes, birds, apes are tried, found wanting, vanish. Races die out. Civilisations crumble. Not because an Almighty Ruler deals out punishment to offending sinners, but because certain particles of matter have failed to adapt to the changing circumstances of a particular period.

I have never understood why this belief—for belief it is—cannot be reconciled with a firm faith in all the finer feelings and qualities that have evolved in man since he first stood erect. Self-preservation, the instinct to reproduce his species, was part of his genetic inheritance. He had to destroy to live and, by forming into tribes, into groups, achieve greater stability. Awareness of others, the feeling for his young shared by all birds and beasts, enabled him to keep his unit strong.

The bird that trails its wing to avert danger to its chick and so deceives the pursuer, the lioness that guards its cub, the woman who snatches her child from the road on the approach of a car, these things are done from an agelong impulse to preserve the species, to adapt, to meet the future; and the chemical change that fires the impulse, the discharge of adrenalin into the bloodstream that directs the action, these are all part of our inheritance, transmuted from those first particles that gave us life. I do not see what all this has to do with God unless God is another name for Life—not omnipotent, not unchanging, but forever growing, forever developing, forever discarding old worlds and creating new ones.

If we are particles made to a repetitive pattern, our actions and our thoughts frequently predictable, no more able to change our pattern than a plant, cross-fertilised to bloom purple, will turn yellow, nevertheless we can come to terms with our inheritance, recognise the good within us, and the ill. As an individual living here and now I am only too well aware that I possess feelings, emotions, a mind and body bequeathed to me by people long since dead who have made me what I am. Generations of French craftsmen of the tight-knit glass-blowing fraternity, provincial, clannish, have handed on to me a strong family sense, a wary suspicion of all who are not "us." Drawing their life and sustenance from the deep forests of Vibraye and Montmirail, they have made me to their pattern, and thus inevitably, it seemed, I sought wooded shelter, the protection of great trees, for what ultimately came to be my home. Respect for tradition vies in me with a contempt for authority imposed from above, a legacy of French temperament passed on from that nation of individualists.

In my beginning is my end; and having passed through many phases and attempts to be other than I am, I have reached my fifty-eighth year with the realisation that basically I have never changed. The child who rebelled against parental standards rebels against them still in middle age. The sceptic of seven who queried the existence of God in the sky, of fairies in the woods, of Father Christmas descending every London chimney in a single magic night, remains a sceptic at fifty-seven, believing all things possible only when they can be proved by scientific fact.

The child who avoided the company of adults, and of her own contemporaries with the exception of the immediate members of her family, preferring solitude in the countryside and an interchange of conversation with her own self, does so still. A hatred of injustice fills me now as it did then. Kindness seems to me the one quality worth praising, but today I give it a longer word and call it compassion.

I have known only one person in my life whom I would truly call good, and that was my maternal grandmother, a little woman of great simplicity and charm, who, when she entered a room, made it warm with her bright presence. English to the core, a native of the Cambridgeshire fens, "honest cathedral stock," as my father used to say in playful mockery of his mother-in-law, no adversity of circumstance defeated her. She was always smiling, always serene, the light and centre of her modest home. Kneeling beside her in St. Jude's Church, Golders Green—I would have been about nine and she in her late fifties— I remember watching her bowed head, her closed eyes, and the fervent movement of her lips as she murmured the words of the Confession at Morning Service, and the sight of such humility filled me with outrage against the vicar, against God, that both should deem it necessary for someone as gentle and as unselfish as my little grandmother to admit to uncommitted sin.

"We have followed too much the devices and desires of our own hearts. We have offended against thy holy laws. We have left undone those things which we ought to have done; and we have done those things which we ought not to have done; and there is no health in us. But thou, O Lord, have mercy upon us, miserable offenders. . . ." The miserable offender was the final straw. If God demanded such self-abasement from one who brought only happiness to those about her, then I wanted no part of Him. I questioned, at that moment, all authority from heaven. I had no compulsion to obey God's holy laws. I was not a miserable offender any more than was my grandmother but, unlike her, I would not ask for mercy. As for sin, the word was meaningless. It is so still. The only sin then, as now, is cruelty, and today I know that cruelty is bred from ignorance out of fear.

Prayer is different, too habit-forming ever to be shed. I pray nightly upon my knees today as I did then, ending with the

childish words, "Let everything be all right," as if, by so express-
ing myself, I may come to terms with fate. Yet I know in my
heart that the only worthwhile prayer is a prayer for courage,
courage to bear the ills that may come upon me, and the ills that
I may bring upon myself. I know now that the good we do returns to us in full measure, and the evil that we do rebounds also
—the lies, the deceits, the evasions which we have inflicted on
other people.

Dante's Inferno is not so far from the truth. Hell is what we
make it. The damned endure torment not from the underworld
but from within. Hell is not other people, as Sartre would have
it, but ourselves. We inflict our own punishment. Meanwhile
centuries of civilisation have not yet devised a cure for crime.
Society imprisons the criminal instead of directing his interest towards a panacea for the committed crime. It would be more hu-
mane, and might be more successful, to train those who assault
the old and feeble to care for the sick and aged, to make the rap-
ists of young women work as midwives, put the poisoners into
laboratories to discover some means of saving life rather than de-
stroying it.

There are certain fundamental laws which have helped to
shape us as human beings from the earliest days, and without
which we should perish. The strongest of these is the law of the
family unit, the binding together of a man and a woman to produce children. In the process of time this may become unnecessary, the test-tube baby turn out to be a more practical, less
wasteful method of begetting and rearing the young. In our present state of development we cannot do without the unit. Emotionally, we should be starved. We seek, even in the sexual act, a
long-lost comfort. A basic peace, reunion with ourselves. The
fact that marriages so often fail is our misfortune. Incest being
denied us, we must make do with second best. The perfect husband or wife is an illusion, a hero or a heroine born of fantasy,
something we seldom recognise until, as Hamlet phrased it, the
heyday in the blood is tame.

Society, as we know it, must disintegrate once the family dis-
solves. Nothing but the family bond will hold men and women
together. Already women, emerging from centuries of submis-
sion, fret against their more passive role, demanding equality in

all things as their right, but in achieving this they lose their first purpose in life, which is to preserve, to maintain the family. Women have not yet learnt how to serve their families and their own ambitions without conflict, and until they do so husband and children suffer, as well as they themselves. This is the greatest problem of our time. Our own and succeeding generations must learn to adjust to the ever changing status of women in our modern civilisation, for without a home, without a centre, we become disoriented, lost orphans without shelter, faith and confidence collapsing about us like a house of cards. Chaos reigns.

The second great problem of our time is how to live without religion. I believe that the dawn of the religious instinct in man came about through his first encounter with death. Death which slew his father and his mother, so that his groping mind sought consolation in a greater Father, a greater Mother, whether in the sky or in the bowels of the earth. He saw disease or misadventure strike down the beings upon whom he had hitherto depended. He saw them wither and grow old. This could not be. Therefore he created in his imagination the immortal ones. They would never let him down. The eternal Father would command him, praise him, punish him, the eternal Mother nourish him. Whatever he could not understand was of their doing. The laws of his own parents became confused with the sterner laws of his gods, and the necessity for sacrifice arose. The earthly parents, those frail creatures who grew old and died, losing all strength and beauty by so doing, were then transformed into immortals too. They lived on, but in another sphere, in the Islands of the Blest, or beyond the stars. Death, the last enemy, was thus defeated.

Belief in gods and demons became ingrained. The gods were good, the demons evil. Man was the tool of both, torn in conflict by opposing wills. The necessity to worship, to do homage to something greater than ourselves, is bred in the bone. It is part of our heritage, irrevocably intertwined with the basic need for family, for security. Deprived of our gods, of God, we are children without parents, hungry, lonely, fearful of the dark. Mankind, in this present century, balks against dogma, against what our forefathers called Divine Authority. Yet if those we revere on earth deceive us, to whom then shall we turn?

There is a faculty amongst the myriad threads of our inheritance that, unlike the chemicals in our bodies and in our brains, has not as yet been pinpointed by science, or even fully examined. I like to call this faculty the sixth sense. It is a sort of seeing, a sort of hearing, something between perception and intuition, an indefinable grasp of things unknown. Psychologists have called this sense the Unconscious Mind, the Superego, the Psyche, the Self. Scientists, to date, are not prepared to acknowledge such a sense, or, when they do, explain it as a memory storehouse, connected to the brain. This may well be, but, whether it proves so or not, it is also a storehouse of potential power. The phenomena of precognition, of telepathy, of dreaming true, all come from this storehouse, and the therapeutic value of hypnosis, still in its infancy, depends upon it too. The sixth sense, latent in young children, animals and primitive peoples, more highly developed in the East than in the West, has long lain dormant in most civilised societies.

I believe that neglect of this sixth sense has contributed to our problems throughout the ages. It can act as guide, as mentor, warning us of danger, signalling caution, yet also urging us to new discoveries. This untapped source of power, this strange and sometimes mystical intuitive sense, may come to be, generations hence, mankind's salvation. If we can communicate, one with another, by thought alone, if a message from the storehouse can act as a panacea to pain, so curing the body's suffering, if recognition of a fault, a crime, can be understood before it is committed, if dreaming in time can recapture from the past certain events known to our forebears but unperceived by us, then surely a series of possibilities, multitudinous, astonishing, may lie ahead for our children's children.

Naturally there is danger in the use of the sixth sense. There is danger in the misuse of electricity, of atomic power: dabblers in magic, in the occult, in so-called spiritualism (telepathy in another guise) and the quack hypnotists, all can use the sixth sense to their own advantage. The combat between the good within us and the evil will always be with us. It is again part of our inheritance. The serpent under the tree, the demons from Pandora's box, these figments of our doubts and fears will continue to threaten us until they are perceived and understood. Each one of us is Perseus, who, cutting off Medusa's head, saw her reflection in the mirror and recognised himself. The sixth sense can help us to this recognition and, by fusing the conscious with the unconscious, broaden our vision so that all things become possible. When Jesus said, "The kingdom of God is within you," I believe he meant just this. As prophet and seer, with the sixth sense more highly developed possibly than in anyone before his time or since, he knew the potentialities of the inner power and drew upon it, believing, as one of Jewish faith, that the source was Yahweh.

The gospels, their message blurred though beautiful, show us a messianic figure of compelling personality at once loved and often misunderstood by his immediate followers, speaking in riddles. Was the historical Jesus, the healer of the sick, the worker of miracles, the opposer of buying and selling in the Temple, more deeply involved in a struggle to help the oppressed peoples of Israel than we have hitherto been told? Can the shouts of the populace calling "Hosanna . . . Hosanna . . ." in that fateful Passover week be interpreted as "Free us . . . Free us . . ."? Did that cry of agony from the cross, in Aramaic *"Eli, Eli, lama sabachthani,"* mean "My power, my power, why have you gone from me"?

This, to the devout Christian, will seem blasphemy, a denial of all later teaching, reducing the Son of God to the Son of Man. Yet the cry of Jesus, however it was phrased, was the eternal question put by man in the face of death since the beginning of time. No answer from the heavens. No answer from within. The historical Jesus nailed to his cross, the mythical Prometheus chained to his rock, both dared to refashion men on earth by breathing fire upon them, to turn them from figures of clay and matter into living gods. Their failure was their glory. For only by daring can man evolve, shake himself free, triumph over the hereditary shackles that bind him to his own species. Only by daring can the spirit, hitherto a prisoner in matter, break away from the body's ties, travel at will across time and space, discarding the body's aids that have served in ages past, the eyes, the ears, the heart, the lungs, and venture into the unknown, untrammelled, free.

Nothing is impossible, no vision too distorted that cannot become reality generations hence. A hundred years ago men would have laughed to scorn the idea that, sitting at home in their armchairs, they might watch and hear events taking place thousands of miles away, that they themselves could travel in a few hours across the sky from one end of the globe to the other, that drugs would combat madness and disease, that atomic power would bring light or destruction to whole continents, that their great-great-grandchildren might land upon the moon. Man is forever seeking, forever probing, and although as individual particles we must conform to a pattern, to a design, the great process of adaptation still continues, changing us imperceptibly, so that we cannot foresee what we shall ultimately become.

In my beginning is my end. The I who writes this essay lives and dies. Something of myself goes into the children born of my body, and to their children, and those children's children. Life, whatever shape or form it takes, goes on, develops, adapts.

Humbert Wolfe, a poet of my youth now dead and seldom, so I am told, read by the young of today, wrote a long poem, first published in 1930, called *The Uncelestial City*. Three verses caught my attention in those days, over thirty years ago, not particularly for their language but for the attitude expressed, and they sum up for me now, as they did then, all that I have been trying to say in the foregoing pages.

> Continue! knowing as the pine-trees know
>   that somewhere in the urgent sap there is
> an everlasting answer to the snow,
>   and a retort to the last precipice,
>
> that, merely by climbing, the shadow is made less,
>   that we have some engagement with a star
> only to be honoured by death's bitterness,
>   and where the inaccessible godheads are,
>
> that to plunge upwards is the way of the spark,
>   and that, burning up and out, even as we die
> we challenge and dominate the shameless dark
>   with our gold death—and that is my reply.

Death and Widowhood

[1966]

Death, to the novelist, is a familiar theme. Often it is the high spot of a particular tale, turning romance to tragedy. A character, his demise planned for a certain chapter while the story was still in notebook form, vanishes from the manuscript, and the author, like a successful murderer whose victim has disappeared, decides that the killing was well done. I have done this several times in my novels. I can even confess I enjoyed the killing. It gave a certain zest to the writing, and if I felt an inward pang for the loss of the character I had created, the pang was soon forgotten and the memory faded. The fictitious person was, after all, only a puppet of my imagination, and I could create others to take his place. The writer, like a spider, spins a web; the creatures caught in the web have no substance, no reality.

It is only when death touches the writer in real life that he, or she, realises the full impact of its meaning. The deathbed scene, described so often in the past, with fingers tapping it out upon a typewriter or pen scratching it on paper, becomes suddenly true. The shock is profound. Sometimes this encounter with reality can so awaken the writer from the imaginary world that he never recovers. I believe that this is what happened to Emily Brontë. The fantasy world of Gondal that had been hers, peopled with heaven knows how many persons, coupled with the harsher, wilder land of Heathcliffe, Cathy and *Wuthering Heights,* faded on a certain Sunday morning when her brother Branwell, his dragging illness accepted with resignation for so long, of a sudden died. A cold, caught at his funeral and then neglected, hastened her own decline and death barely three months afterwards. It does not account for her stubborn refusal to see a doctor, her silence with her two sisters, her complete withdrawal within herself, which can only be explained by shock, or trauma as we would call it today, occasioned by direct experience of death. The death of a brother, for which she blamed her sisters and herself. They had neglected him. Therefore, she argued, she must be neglected likewise. It was an unconscious form of suicide, not uncommon to the suddenly bereaved.

I am a writer too. Neither a poet nor a great romantic novelist like Emily Brontë, but a spinner of webs, a weaver of imaginary tales; and when my husband died in March of this past year it was as though the sheltered cloudland that had enveloped me for years, peopled with images drawn from my imagination, suddenly dissolved, and I was face to face with a harsh and terrible reality. The husband I had loved and taken for granted for thirty-three years of married life, father of my three children, lay dead. If by writing about it now I expose myself and my feelings, it is not from a sense of self-advertisement, but because by doing so I may be able to help those readers who, like myself, have suffered the same sense of shock.

Like Emily Brontë, one of my first reactions, after the first bewildered fits of weeping, was to blame myself. I could have done more during the last illness, I should have observed, with sharp awareness, the ominous signs. I should have known, the last week, the last days, that his eyes followed me with greater intensity, and instead of moving about the house on trivial business, as I did, never left his side. How heartless, in retrospect, my last good night, when he murmured to me, "I can't sleep," and I kissed him and said, "You will, darling, you will," and went from the room. Perhaps, if I had sat with him all night, the morning would have been otherwise. As it was, when morning came, and the nurses who had shared his vigil expressed some anxiety about his pallor and asked me to telephone the doctor, I went through to him expecting possibly an increase of weakness, but inevitably the usual smile. Instead . . . he turned his face to me, and died.

My readers will have heard of the kiss of life. We tried it, the nurses and myself, in turn until the doctor came. But I knew, as I breathed into his body, that it was useless and he was dead.

His eyes were open but the spark had gone. What had been living was no more. This, then, was the finality of death. Described by myself in books time without number. Experienced at last.

The aftermath of shock must alter the chemistry in the blood, for it forced me to action instead of to collapse. I had to telephone my children. Make arrangements. See that necessary things were done. These responses were automatic, numb. Part of my brain functioned, part of it seemed closed. The part of it that was automatic and dissociated from emotion ordered an immediate autopsy so that the doctor's first assessment of death by sudden coronary thrombosis could be verified. The part of it that was numb began to fuse with the emotions, every instinct urging me to perform those actions he would have wished carried out, the wording to *The Times* making clear that by his own request the cremation should be private, there would be no memorial service, instead his friends might send donations to the Security Fund for Airborne Forces—those Airborne Forces he had commanded in 1942, 1943 and 1944, his beloved "paras," his glider pilots.

It was not until the cremation was over, which only my children and a few close friends attended, and I had scattered my husband's ashes at the end of the garden where we often walked together, and my children had returned to their own homes, that I knew, with full force, the finality of death. I was alone. The newly discovered tenderness of my daughters, the sudden maturity of my son, himself to become a father within a few months, had not prevailed upon me to go back with one of them, to recover, as they put it, from the strain. "No," I told them. "I want to face the future here, in my own home, by myself." To go elsewhere, even with them, would postpone the moment of truth. What had to be endured must be endured now, and at once, alone.

In marriage one partner—unless both are killed simultaneously —must go before the other. Usually the man goes first. Generations of wives have known this. Now I knew it too, and must adapt. I must force myself to look upon the familiar things, the coat hanging on the chair, the hat in the hall, the motoring gloves, the stick, the pile of yachting magazines beside his bed, and remind myself that this was not the separation of war that we had known twenty years earlier, but separation for all time.

To ease the pain I took over some of his things for myself. I wore his shirts, sat at his writing desk, used his pens to acknowledge the hundreds of letters of condolence; and, by the very process of identification with the objects he had touched, felt the closer to him. The evenings were the hardest to bear. The ritual of the hot drink, the lumps of sugar for the two dogs, the saying of prayers—his boyhood habit carried on throughout our married life—the good night kiss. I continued the ritual, because this too lessened pain, and was, in its very poignancy, a consolation.

I wept often because I could not prevent the tears, and possibly, in some way beyond my understanding, tears helped the healing process, but the physical act of weeping was distressing to me beyond measure. As a child I seldom cried.

I thought long and often about the possibility of life after death. Baptised and confirmed in the Christian faith, I acknowledge no denomination, yet have an instinctive yearning for survival, as indeed the human race has always done, since man first sought to come to terms with death. I liked to think of my husband reunited with the parents who had gone before him, and with his comrades of two world wars. I liked to think that all pain, all suffering, had been wiped out, that he knew, as none of us can know here on earth, indescribable joy, the "peace which passes all understanding"—a line he used to quote.

Yet I had seen his empty shell. I had seen the light flicker and go out. Where had it gone? Was it blown to emptiness after all, like the light of a candle, and does each one of us, in the end, vanish into darkness? If this is so, and our dreams of survival after death are only dreams, then we must accept this too. Not with fear and dismay, but with courage. To have lived at all is a measure of immortality; for a baby to be born, to become a man, a woman, to beget others like himself, is an act of faith in itself, even an act of defiance. It is as though every human being born into this world burns, for a brief moment, like a star, and because of it a pinpoint of light shines in the darkness, and so there is glory, so there is life. If there is nothing more than this, we have achieved our immortality.

Meanwhile, for the bereaved, who will never know the answer here on earth, the practical living of day-by-day continues. We must rise in the morning, eat, go about our business, watch the seasons pass, our life no longer shared. To plan for one, instead of two, brings a sense of apathy. Instinct says, "Why bother? What can the future hold?" The sense of urgency is lacking. A younger woman, with a family to rear, would be spurred by necessity to action. The older woman has no such driving force. Her children are adult, they can fend for themselves. The older woman must seek her reason for living either in outward forms—good works, committees, the demanding tasks of a career—or look inward, deep within herself, for a new philosophy.

"At least," said a kind, well-wishing friend, "you have your writing," as though, with a magic wand, I could conjure at will a host of dancing puppets to grimace and do my bidding, their very antics proving an antidote to pain. Yes, I have my writing, but the stories that I fashioned once were fairy tales, and they cannot satisfy me now. Death, surely, will make me more aware of other people's suffering, of other people's ills, of the countless women there must be who, widowed like myself, have no form of consolation from without or from within. Some lack children, sisters, friends; others are financially bereft; a vast number lived in their husband's shadow, and with the shadow gone feel themselves not fully individuals, unwanted and ignored. What life can these women make for themselves, how will they adapt?

The widow, like the orphan, has been an object of pity from earliest times. She received charity. She lived, very often, with her married son or daughter, and earned, sometimes rightly, the hostility of her daughters- or sons-in-law. Her place was the chimney corner, and in more modern times the little flat upstairs or the bungalow next door.

The Hindu woman, in old days, committed suttee. She laid herself on the funeral pyre of her husband and was burnt with him. This was one way out of her dilemma. My own grandmother, widowed at the same age as myself, at fifty-eight, entered upon old age with grace and dignity. She donned her weeds and her widow's cap, and I can see her now, a kindly, grave, if rather formidable figure, endeavouring to teach me, a child, how to knit, in the First World War.

I look down today at my own weeds, dark slacks, a white pullover, and I wonder if the change in garb is basic, a symbol of woman's emancipation, or simply a newer fashion, while fundamentally the widow's sense of loss remains unchanged. No matter how brave a face she puts upon her status, the widow is still a lonely figure, belonging nowhere, resembling in some indefinable manner the coloured races in a world dominated by whites. The attitude of the non-widowed is kindly, hearty, a little overcheerful in the attempt to show the bereaved that nothing is different, just as the liberal white will shake his black brother by the hand, smiling broadly, to emphasise equality. Neither is deceived. Both are embarrassed. The widow, aware of her inadequacy, retires into her shell, while the other, dreading the floodgates of emotion, beats a hasty retreat. Carried to extremes, the division results in apartheid, the widowed and the non-widowed withdraw to their separate worlds, and there is no communion between the two.

The old adage, Time heals all wounds, is only true if there is no suppuration within. To be bitter, to lament unceasingly, "Why did this have to happen to him?" makes the wound fester; the mind, renewing the stab, causes the wound to bleed afresh. It is hard, very hard, not to be bitter in the early days, not to blame doctors, hospitals, drugs, that failed to cure. Harder still for the woman whose husband died not by illness but by accident, who was cut short in full vigour, in the prime of life, killed perhaps in a car crash returning home from work. The first instinct is to seek revenge upon the occupants of the other car, themselves unhurt, whose selfish excess of speed caused the disaster. Yet this is no answer to grief. All anger, all reproach, turns inward upon itself. The infection spreads, pervading the mind and body.

I would say to those who mourn—and I can only speak from my own experience—look upon each day that comes as a challenge, as a test of courage. The pain will come in waves, some days worse than others, for no apparent reason. Accept the pain. Do not suppress it. Never attempt to hide grief from yourself. Little by little, just as the deaf, the blind, the handicapped develop with time an extra sense to balance disability, so the bereaved, the widowed, will find new strength, new vision, born of the very pain and loneliness which seem, at first, impossible to master. I address myself more especially to the middle-aged who, like myself, look back to over thirty years or more of married life and find it hardest to adapt. The young must, of their very nature, heal sooner than ourselves.

We know, and must face it honestly, that life for us can never be the same again. Marriage was not just another love affair, an episode, but the greater half of our existence. We can never give to another what we gave to the partner who has gone. All that is over, finished. And the years that lie ahead, ten, twenty, perhaps even thirty, must be travelled alone. This is a challenge, just as marriage, in the first place, was a challenge.

I remember on our wedding day, in July 1932, the good priest who married us drawing a comparison between the little boat in which we were to set forth on our honeymoon and marriage itself. "You will embark," he said, "on a fair sea, and at times there will be fair weather, but not always. You will meet storms and overcome them. You will take it in turns to steer your boat through fair weather and foul. Never lose courage. Safe harbour awaits you both in the end."

Today I remember this advice with gratitude. Even if I must, of necessity, steer my boat alone, I shall not, so I trust, lose my bearings but, because of all I have learnt through the past three-and-thirty years, with my fellow helmsman at my side, come eventually to my journey's end.

One final word to my contemporaries. Take time to plan your future. Do not let your relatives or friends, anxious for your welfare, push you into some hasty move that later you may regret. If it is financially possible for you, stay in your own home, with the familiar things about you. We need many months to become reconciled to the loss that has overtaken us; and if at first the silence of the empty house may seem unbearable, do not forget it is still the home you shared, which two persons made their own.

As the months pass and the seasons change, something of tranquillity descends, and although the well-remembered footstep will not sound again, nor the voice call from the room beyond, there seems to be about one in the air an atmosphere of love, a living presence. I say this in no haunting sense, ghosts and phantoms are far from my mind. It is as though one shared, in some indefinable manner, the freedom and the peace, even at times the joy, of another world where there is no more pain. It is not a question of faith or of belief. It is not necessary to be a follower of any religious doctrine to become aware of what I mean. It is not the prerogative of the devout. The feeling is simply there, pervading all thought, all action. When Christ the healer said, "Blessed are they that mourn, for they shall be comforted," he must have meant just this.

Later, if you go away, if you travel, even if you decide to make your home elsewhere, the spirit of tenderness, of love, will not desert you. You will find that it has become part of you, rising from within yourself; and because of it you are no longer fearful of loneliness, of the dark, because death, the last enemy, has been overcome.

Moving House

[1969]

Moving house, after twenty-six years, is rather like facing a major operation. Especially if the home one leaves behind has been greatly loved. As a young woman I moved often, being married to a soldier, and we were never more than eighteen months in the same place. This did not greatly worry me, because my husband organised everything, even to writing out the labels for the removal men and deciding where the various pieces of furniture should go. He would always try to make the new home as much like the old one as possible, for, although very go-ahead and progressive as a soldier, he was a stickler for routine in personal life. So, while desks were placed in new living rooms in identical corners beside new fireplaces, and while he arranged the familiar objects in the right order, I would wander around in a daze, trying to picture the sort of people who had lived in the house before. Also I felt sorry for the house we had left; I was sure it would be melancholy without us. This feeling passed, and soon I would "grow" into the new house, taking something of its atmosphere into myself and giving something in return. Anyway, we were both young, and life was an adventure.

When the war came and my husband was serving overseas, I took a bold step and moved house on my own, with a nanny and three young children. I rented the old manor house Menabilly that I had written about in *Rebecca*, which had no electricity and no hot-water system, and was full of dry rot. My husband, in far-off Tunis, told his brother officers, "I am afraid Daphne has gone mad."

The madness paid off. When he came on leave for Christmas,

expecting to find us squatting in camp beds with the rain pouring through the roof, he found the telephone installed, electric light in all the rooms, a hot bath waiting, and the furniture brought from store and put in just the right places he would have chosen himself. There were sprays of holly behind every picture.

"Well, I must confess, I didn't know you had it in you," he told me.

He grew to love it as much as I did, and forever after, during his lifetime, Christmas was always the high spot of the year.

In 1964 we knew that our lease was coming to an end and that we should have to look for another home. The thought of moving from this particular bit of Cornwall was unbearable to both of us, and, like a miracle, unspoken prayer was answered. The lease of the onetime dower house to Menabilly, Kilmarth, fell vacant, and it was only half a mile or so away, with a splendid view over the sea beloved so well. We walked round the empty rooms, as desolate as Menabilly had been before we lived there, and he said to me, "I like this place. I can see ourselves here." He signed the lease a few weeks before he died.

This was all of four years ago, and in the intervening period, between writing books, I have been planning what I hope will be my final home. I finally moved into Kilmarth in June of this year, 1969, and count myself very fortunate that I had so much time to make the change. Day by day, week by week, month by month, I would visit the empty house, walk round the rooms, plan the decorations, watch the necessary alterations, decide where the furniture would ultimately go. The architect, the builder, the builder's craftsmen, could not have been more helpful or more kind. We felt ourselves a team, creating a renewed Kilmarth which I felt very certain its predecessors had loved.

The Roger Kylmerth who lived here in 1327 may have been different in character from the one I have written about in my novel *The House on the Strand*, but the foundations of his home are beneath me now. The Bakers, merchants in the seventeenth century, touched these walls. Younger sons of Rashleigh parents bided here before inheriting Menabilly, rebuilding upwards from the foundations, while later tenants, so I am told, kept packs of collie dogs and even peacocks! I like to think of the latter strutting the walk where I now exercise my own West Highland terriers.

Kilmarth, today, has a slated eighteenth-century front, with twentieth-century additions on either side. The front garden is enclosed by walls and railings, giving a formal touch, and, although it was suggested I should take down the Victorian porch, I am glad I kept it; it has a delightful, old-fashioned air. The drawing room, or long room as I call it, is on the right of the hall, and to the left are my small dining room and library. When the doors of all three are opened you can see from one end of the house to the other, thus giving a sense of space. The french windows of the long room have been opened wide all summer long, facing due south, and I can see myself sitting here through the winter too.

The original dining room of my predecessors, three steps up from the hall, has been turned into a kitchen. Light paper on the walls, a warm brick-coloured floor and modern wall units with an electric cooker, this is one of the nicest rooms in the house. Once it was dark and narrow, but a wide window now gives light where the chimney breast used to be. The cramped rooms beyond, used in old days for staff or nursery, are now a separate suite for visiting grandchildren. The little ones can romp, the teen-agers play their pop records, and their grandmother in the front of the house be none the wiser! What is more, they have their own staircase and their own entry, and the wing has all the appearance of a miniature house on its own.

The basement, useful for storage now, held the onetime kitchen, pantries, laundry, stillroom of former tenants, no longer practicable today. Here are the cellar walls of antiquity, and I have turned one recess into a tiny chapel. To exorcise unquiet spirits? Perhaps. Who knows, it may have been a place for prayer in centuries past. The yard without, which surely once led from the mediaeval farmhouse building, has been relaid with the cobbled stones that, now lying about the grounds, may have graced it long ago.

Let us make our way above once more to the front of the house. The staircase leads to my own quarters, and to the guest rooms for family and friends. Here I admit to doing myself in style. Furnishings and fabrics are not new, they have been with

me for much of my married life, but I have never before had a
suite of dressing room, bathroom and bedroom; and the view
from the bedroom, which overlooks the sea, is the best I have
ever known. Ships anchor in the bay before proceeding to Par
Harbour, and the ilex trees have a magic quality, outlined
against the sky. It is a very pleasant room by day or night. The
guest room along the landing I call the pink room. It contains
my father's four-poster bed, and the closet adjoining is now a
bathroom. A narrow corridor leads to two double guest rooms
and one single room, with their own bathroom and W.C. So
when Christmas comes again I can, at a pinch, put up children,
grandchildren, in fact the entire family, although there might be
a certain amount of juggling with camp beds.

I hope, in time, to get the overgrown garden back into some
sort of order. Last spring I planted dahlias, but none of them
came up. The roses had the blight. Most of the undergrowth and
brambles have been cleared, and new grass sown where the net-
tles grew. The apple trees are long past their prime, but the
windfalls have gone into apple tart on Sundays. My husband's
old boat stands in her final resting place, and she shall have a
coat of paint next spring. And so I look about me, planning the
months ahead: one day, perhaps, reclaim the tennis court in the
orchard, where Victorian ladies played patball with one another,
though for tennis I feel it has probably had its day. A football
pitch might be the answer for growing grandsons. Two meadows
lie beyond, let for grazing to the neighbouring farmer, and I
shall have to watch any battles between Chelsea and Spurs in
case the flying ball should fall amongst, and startle, his pedigree
herd of cattle.

I shall miss the acres of woodland that surround Menabilly.
Here the only "plantations" worthy of the name are those bordering the road leading to the village of Polkerris, and a winding
shrubbery at the back of the house. Never mind. Wildlife
abounds here as much as there. Badgers scratch the earth beneath tumbled leaves, jackdaws roost in the taller trees, owls
hoot by night, and the long summer through swallows and mar-
tins built under the eaves. As for butterflies, the place abounds
with them. Tortoise-shell, swallowtail, admirals, flitting amongst

the overgrown buddleia, and so, I regret to say, do wasps as well.

The pleasantest spot at evening is an old summerhouse, built by one of my predecessors, where one can sit sheltered from cold winds and watch the sun go down across the bay. Steps lead down from the wall to the field below. Perhaps a peacock strutted here, his tail spread wide. And the collies surely rampaged in search of erring sheep. For my own part, rejoicing in a long hot summer, I have crossed the field most afternoons after tea and descended to the cliffs and the beach beyond. The sea, milky white from the sediment of china clay, has a strange attraction, to me at any rate, though I have heard grumbles at its stickiness from summer visitors. At high spring tides the water laps the cliffs and there is a strong undertow, dangerous, I would think, to the non-swimmer. Now, with the visitors departed, the only intruders upon the beach are oyster catchers and gulls.

Indeed, I tell myself, as I climb the steep hill back again to Kilmarth (Thrombosis Hill, I have called it, and time will prove if it lives up to its name), I am most blest and truly fortunate. The house I looked upon with misgiving before I moved, wondering whether I should ever settle down in new surroundings, no longer gives me the somewhat dubious impression of a pleasant holiday residence lent to me for a season by obliging friends, but is transforming itself, day by day, week by week, with the familiar furniture and objects all about me, into the friendly warmth and comfort of a place well loved, where I am made welcome. In short, we are at one, and I am at home.

A Winter's Afternoon,
Kilmarth

It is the idle half hour succeeding lunch, when, having written a number of unnecessary letters all morning, I can sip black coffee and smoke the first cigarette of the day. The back pages of yesterday's newspapers are still unread, and it is my whim to contrast the current weather report with the advertisements for winter holidays in Cornwall.

"The ridge of low pressure now approaching our western seaboard will deepen, and the showers at present falling on the Scilly Isles and Cornwall will become heavy at times, turning to hail and thunder on higher ground. Winds will increase to gale force, veering southwesterly to west, and later in the day temperatures may fall to 28 degrees. Outlook for the next two days cold and unsettled, with gales locally."

I glance out of the window. My informant on the radio was right. The pine trees beyond the garden wall, planted by some Victorian predecessor in the belief that whatever suited the Scottish climate would defy the elements equally well in Cornwall—and how wise he was—are beginning to sway, while massive clouds, driven by some demon force, bank the far horizon, reminding me of a rather too elaborate production of *Macbeth*.

I turn to the advertisements in the newspapers. "Double Your Sunshine and Come to Lovely Looe." Looe is a few miles along the coast, and that foremost cloud, vast as a witch's trailing cloak, will be upon it in exactly four minutes. There are, however, further blandishments westward across the bay. "Visit Mevagissey, the Fishing Village with the Continental Touch." Mevagissey is already blotted out with rain, but doubtless some winter visitor, lured by summer memories of the Côte d'Azur, is now scurrying from the quayside in search of a casino with an affable croupier in charge bidding him "*Faites vos jeux.*" There may be one or two slot machines still in action, but I doubt it.

The hotels along the coast offer more tempting vistas still. "A gleaming jewel on a sun-drenched bay. Balconies to every bedroom . . ." But enough. Being myself no visitor to these shores, but an inhabitant, on and off, for over forty years, and having recently moved from a sheltered house in woodlands to my present home on "higher ground" threatened by that same hail and thunder announced over the radio, I am anxious to prove my mettle. There is, perhaps, an "Award Scheme for Courage Displayed by the Over-Sixties" brewing in the minds of princes, and I could qualify. Besides, the dog needs exercise.

Dressed like Tolstoy in his declining years, fur cap with ear flaps, padded jerkin and rubber boots to the knee, I venture forth. Moray, my West Highland terrier, taking one look at the sky, backs swiftly into the porch, but brutally I urge him on, and we cross the garden to the fields beyond. Where I lived before, at Menabilly, there was a shaded path known as the Palm Walk, and on rainy or windy days, flanked by tall trees, I could amble along it peacefully, snipping at the drooping heads of blue hydrangeas still in bloom. Here, at Kilmarth, I know no such lassitude. The sloping field I am bound to traverse, if I walk at all, is under plough, and the herd of South Devon cattle who tramp daily across the as yet unsown soil, having first satiated themselves with roots a little further down, have turned the field into another Passchendaele. "This," I tell myself, "is what Tommy endured as a subaltern in the First World War," and, inspired by the thought, I sink into craters made by the South Devons, wondering if Mr. Mitchell the farmer could have crossbred his prize herd with yaks from Tibet. The cattle, less courageous than myself, did not linger long on the "higher ground" but have already sought shelter in the farmyard out of sight, having advanced milking time by at least two hours.

Shaking my feet clear of Passchendaele, and avoiding the electric fence that guards the roots, I climb over the stile that leads to the grazing land above the cliffs, thinking how closely I must resemble a veteran at the Battle of Ypres. Moray, flicking his ears, runs like a greyhound to a favourite molehill, which he is wont to anoint as a matter of routine. This ritual, if nothing else, will make his day. Mr. Mitchell's flock of sheep, taking him for a marauder and mistaking the action, begin to scatter. Heavy with lamb, some of them strangely decorated about the head with brambles, they have the bizarre crowned appearance of beasts bound for some sacrificial slaughter. Remembering the doomed flock plunging over the cliffs to destruction in the film of *Far from the Madding Crowd*, I hold my breath; but after a brief and hesitating pause they labour up the hill in a northwesterly direction, making for home, and I breathe again. It is Moray and I who turn seaward to brave the full force of the gale.

It is a stupendous sight that meets my eyes. Thirteen ships are anchored in the bay, rolling their guts out in a cauldron sea. I can make out a couple of Dutchmen, a Dane, a German, and I think a Norwegian flag amongst them, but the shelter of Par Harbour will not be theirs this night, for it is already high water, and the docks are full. What if their cables drag, a mile distant, off this lee shore? The only hope up-steam and out of it, rounding the Gribben head to the Fowey estuary.

I put up my arm in salutation, not to the courage of the seamen on board but in a vain attempt to keep the hail out of my eyes. Below me the sea thunders on Bûly beach, so called because of the white stones—*bûly*—that lie upon it. Rounded, flat, scattered here and there upon the sand, these stones make excellent targets on a summer's day for the anointing Moray while I swim. Now, as the incoming rollers break upon them and lash the cliffs, only to withdraw with an ominous sucking sound, the white stones have a ghastly resemblance to drowning ewes, and for a moment I fear that my vision of the scene from *Far from the Madding Crowd* has in part come true. The stones do not loll, though, in the surf but remain submerged, and I am spared winning an award for gallantry and plunging to the rescue of mangled carcasses; indeed I could not have done so, for the descent to the beach itself is swept by a sea at least six feet high. This is disappointing. There is a cave on Bûly beach into which the hail would not have penetrated, and, although it is damp and eerie and smells of old bones, had it been half tide I could have stood there like Prospero, watching the storm, the faithful Moray Ariel at my side.

Which reminds me, where *is* Moray? I look about me, shouting in vain against the wind. Seized with sudden panic, I climb up the stony track, away from the beach, to the cliffs above. I can just see his white rump disappearing along the muddied path in the direction of the only shelter known to his dog instinct, a hedge of thorn about a hundred yards distant that overhangs a drop known locally as Little Hell. The place is aptly named. God only knows what drowning seafarer in centuries past caught a glimpse of it from an upturned boat and cursed it as he sank. Or, perchance, an irate farmer, predecessor of Mr. Mitchell from Trill Farm, driven to frenzy by a scolding wife, hurled himself and her to merciful oblivion. Either, or all three, dubbed the spot thus. The ravine is cut out of the cliff face, and the potential suicide is only spared from the goal he seeks by a strand of barbed wire, and what appears to be the single bar of an old bedstead—doubtless forming part of the frenzied farmer's connubial couch—with three straggling thornbushes beyond. He cannot see the depths below, so steep is the incline, and a torn sack masks the final sickening drop, but at high tide, as it is today, an evil hiss surges some two hundred feet beneath him, fair warning of the fate awaiting trespass.

Moray has sense, all the same. The thornbushes, bent backwards over the muddied path, make an effective arbour in a space about three feet square; it is, in fact, our only haven in a world gone temporarily mad. He awaits me, hunched and disapproving.

We crouch side by side above Little Hell, enduring some of that same discomfort which political prisoners experienced in the torture chamber of the Tower of London known as Little Ease, but at least the hail is no longer in my face and the rain is driving slantways above my head, missing my humped knees by a few inches. It is some comfort to think of all the things I would rather *not* be doing. Ringing the front doorbell of people I don't know well, but whose invitation to drinks has been reluctantly accepted, and as the door opens being met by the conversational roar of those guests already arrived . . . Standing in the model gown department of a smart London store, endeavouring to squeeze myself into an outfit designed for someone half my age, and, as I grapple with a zip fastener that will not meet, becoming aware of the bored and pitying eye of the saleswoman in charge . . . Circling any airport in a fog, or, worse still, waiting for the fog to lift and sitting in the airport lounge hemmed in by bores, all of them bent on exchanging their life history . . .

Meditation, after twenty minutes or so, is cut short by the realisation that a stream from the field above, which disappeared mysteriously under the muddied path on which I crouch, is pouring its tumbling waters into a miniature Niagara behind my back, before descending to Little Hell. It is time to move. Struggling to my feet and glancing upward, I perceive that, miraculously, the hail has ceased, the black pall of the sky has parted into jagged shades of blue, and the sun itself is breaking through, gold, all-powerful, like the face of God. The scene is utterly transformed. The rollers in the bay are milky white, boisterous, lovely, even wilder than before, and graced now with the sun's touch, all malevolence gone. The vessels plunging at their cables dance as if to a fairground's tune, and one of them, the Dutchman, lets forth a siren blast of triumph and begins to move slowly, majestically, towards Par Harbour.

The port is jammed with shipping. Every berth seems full. Derricks appear to intertwine, crisscrossed at every angle, and now that the wind has shifted a few points west it brings the welcome sound of industry, power plants at work, engines whining, men hammering, chimneys pouring out great plumes of smoke, white and curling like the sea. Pollution? Nonsense, the sight is glorious! Later the remaining ships at anchor will dock in turn, load up with china clay, and plough back across the Channel to their home-port destination. The white waste from the clay, regretted by some, scatters a filmy dust upon the working sheds, and the bay itself has all the froth and dazzle of a milk churn spilt into a turbulent pool. Tourists may seek the golden sands of holiday brochures if they like, but to swim in such a sea is ecstasy—I have tried it, and I know!

Suddenly, out of nowhere, the birds appear. Oyster catchers, with their panic call and rapid wingbeat; curlews, more mysterious, aloof, the whistling cry surely portending sorrow, and then like leaves uptossed in all directions, but swerving, dipping, to their leader's flight; a flock of starlings, soaring for the sheer joy of motion, their ultimate destination the ploughed fields of Passchendaele above. Which, cowardlike, I cannot face. Not for a second time this afternoon those craters and muddied depths. Nor the climb itself, so easy to descend, but seen from Little Hell the peak of Everest itself. So, for Moray and myself, the easier gradient of the cliff path that will finally lead us in roundabout fashion to a little wood of about four and a half acres, which forms part of Kilmarth domain.

My lease made mention of certain "sporting rights," and for this splendid bonus I pay a shilling a year. I am not sure what I had in mind when the lease was signed. Possibly sons-in-law wearing tweeds, armed with Purdey guns and calling "Over" as pheasants swerved above their heads, the same pheasants gracing the dinner table at a later date. Or, on a less ambitious note, the more doubtful pleasure of lunching on pigeon pie. (I read once that pigeon eaten on three consecutive days brought certain death.) Be that as it may, the pheasant's call and the pigeon's flutter are alike absent this afternoon; the only thing to stir except the trees themselves is a ragged crow, who launches himself from a dead branch at my approach and croaks his way to Passchendaele.

It is not everyone, however, who is sole tenant of sporting rights, and, as Moray plunges into the wood and I pitch after him, I must admit I walk the narrow path with a certain swagger. Possession is short-lived. As I trip over a rhododendron root and round a corner, I come upon an elderly man leaning against a tree, a gun at the ready. Moray barks, and he turns and stares. Is this the moment to stand, as they say, my ground? One of my predecessors at Kilmarth, a formidable lady by all accounts, who held sway some fifty years ago and was said to commune with the spirit world, had for escort when she walked a flock of peacocks, a pack of collie dogs and a donkey wearing a beribboned hat; she would have handled the situation with aplomb. Not so her present-day successor.

I advance timidly, forming appropriate words of welcome. "Any luck?"

He shakes his head. I shrug in sympathy. "Too bad, it must be the weather. Well, don't shoot yourself instead of the absent birds."

I wave a cheerful hand as I pass, and the slow smile that

spreads across his features suggests that the impression I have made is poor. Ah, well . . . He must have walked and shot that wood, man and boy, for nearly fifty years himself. I am the intruder, not he, and as I shuffle along beneath the dripping trees I no longer swagger. Moray, of course, is disgusted with me. The ankles of all strange men are suspect, and the elderly sportsman promised easy game. He follows me, muttering, and I "shush" him under my breath, relieved when the wood is left behind and I climb through the fence to the plot of garden surrounding the house itself. Here, at least, I am mistress of all I survey, and I can relieve my sporting inclinations by fetching a long pruning implement, during the ten minutes of fine weather that remains, and beheading the grotesque tops of a clump of bamboos which, shaking in the wind and masking the sea view from one of the windows, have the horrible appearance of African witch doctors engaged in some tribal rite. I attack them with ferocity, and then, arms aching, honour satisfied, make my way indoors before the hail strikes. The thought of tea is doubly welcome after these efforts, legs stretched out before flaming logs.

I fling off my Tolstoy outfit, replace the pruning implement, and open the door of my living room.

I am driven back by clouds of evil-smelling smoke. The pile of logs, balanced with such loving care before I set out for the walk, the paper beneath them gently touched with a lighted match, instead of welcoming me with the roaring blaze I had expected has turned jet black. Not even a tongue of flame arises from them. I kneel beside the grate, bellows in hand, but not so much as a spark glints from the stinking ashes. I sit back on my heels in despair, remembering all the remaining logs awaiting transport from the old boiler room in the basement. These were to see me through the winter, and I have no others. Hewn from a giant fir laid low in the autumn by a crosscut saw, they were my pride and joy as much as the sporting rights.

I hurry to the nether regions to bring up kindling wood, but this has been cut from the same fir, and when laid upon the corpses of the blackened logs it emits one protesting spark, sighs, and is extinguished. Too late to double back to the wood and search for twigs of stouter brand. I should lose yet more face before the sportsman with the gun, and anyway the heavens have burst again; what momentary glory shone from the sky has gone forever.

> Pear logs and apple logs
> They will scent your room.
> Cherry logs across the dogs
> Smell like flowers in bloom.

Somewhere, in a desk, I have the whole poem about logs, sent to me by an obliging friend and expert, recommending those that give warmth and scent, and warning against those that do not. Feverishly I search for it amongst a heap of papers, and run my eye down the printed page.

> Fir logs it is a crime
> For anyone to sell.

I never thought to read the poem before having the fir tree felled. . . .

> Holly logs will burn like wax,
> You should burn them green.

I can bear no more of it, and go to the kitchen to make tea, but as I drink it in front of the non-existent fire, wearing dark glasses to protect my eyes from the festoons of smoke hanging like Christmas decorations about the panelled room, I think of the many stunted hollies in the shrubbery behind the house, and plan destruction.

Tea passes without further incident, and supper on a tray watching television—a play showing teen-agers making love on one channel and a very old film about the American navy in Korea on the other, offering doubtful entertainment to my jaded palate—takes me up to bedtime.

The increasing sound of the gale without and lashing rain against the windows gives warning that there is one remaining hazard to face before I climb the stairs. Moray must be put out, not at the front door where he would be blown over the wall and never seen again, but down to those same nether regions where the logs are harboured, and through the hatch door of the boiler room opening on the "patio," where he can do his worst in comparative shelter.

The winding stair to the basement does not deter me, nor the memory of those characters dead for centuries who may have walked the basement in days gone by. Fourteenth-century yeomen, sixteenth-century merchants, eighteenth- and nineteenth-century parsons and squires, are shades that I can brave with equanimity. The idea of the Edwardian lady,' however, who communed with the spirit world flanked by her peacocks, is more disturbing. It was in the basement kitchen, no longer used as such, that she used to give her orders for the day to the trembling cook, and I have it on good authority that a parrot, chained to its perch, let fly a torrent of abuse at her approach. I stand shivering at the hatch door, while Moray sniffs the cobbles in disdain, and then, to test both our nerves, I switch out the light. This surely should bring an award for stamina.

Nothing happens. No clatter of a cane upon stone flags. No screech from protesting peacocks. No cry of "Pieces of eight . . . pieces of eight . . ." from the parrot. A door bangs in the distance, but this is probably the draught. My formidable predecessor of more affluent days may be a silent witness to my challenge, but thank heaven she does not materialise. May she rest in peace.

The door is bolted, Moray scampers ahead of me up the winding stair, and we proceed to our own quarters and the bedroom that was, I am glad to say, built on in later years, after the peacock lady's day. It faces seaward, and thus receives the full force of the sou'westerly, or indeed of any gale, but the effect of this is stimulating, like being on the enclosed bridge of a ship, without the rocking. I look out of the window and see the riding lights of those vessels that have not yet sought refuge in Par Harbour, and the thought of the seamen possibly battened down below, at the mercy of every lurching sea, makes me turn to my own bed with a sense of well-being, even of complacency. Moray retires to his lair and, leaning back on my pillows with a sigh of satisfaction, I open the unfinished newspaper I was reading after lunch. "You too can enjoy the thrills of camping in Cornwall."

Brushing the advertisement impatiently aside, I turn to matters of greater moment. The thrust and parry of political parties, the feuds and international problems of our time.

Something splashes upon my pillow. An ominous drip. It is followed in a moment by a second, and then a third. A tear from an unseen presence? I look up to the ceiling and perceive, all complacency gone, that a row of beads, like a very large rosary swinging from a nun's breast, is forming a chain immediately above my head and fast turning into bubbles. Drip . . . Drip . . . The water torture, practised in the Far East and said to be more swiftly effective than our own mediaeval rack. Hypnotised, I watch the row of beads expand and fall, its place immediately taken by another, meanwhile my pillow taking on the sodden appearance of the sack cast away at Little Hell.

This is the end. . . . I will *not* be forced out of the double bed I have slept in for thirty-five years and seek asylum elsewhere. No heating switched on in the spare rooms, beds not aired, lamps lacking bulbs.

"You too can enjoy the thrills of camping in Cornwall."

I leap out onto the floor and, risking hernia, proceed to drag my double bed into the centre of the room. The floorboards groan. Moray, disturbed from sound sleep, sits up and stares at me, a look of intense astonishment on his face. "What on *earth* . . . ?"

I fetch towels for the cascade to splash upon, and then, marooned on a flat surface, headboard gone, pillowless, install myself on the desert island that has become my bed. Moray continues to look astonished, even aggrieved.

Tommy's photograph, beret at the familiar jaunty angle, smiles at me from the dry wall opposite. I am reminded, only too well, that it was always my berth, in our old sailing days, never his, which suffered the inevitable leaks from the deck above. My discomfort produced delighted chuckles, and although the following day the leaks would be stopped, with each successive craft we owned the one wet patch would invariably form itself, in an otherwise perfect boat, over my head.

The smile is infectious, and whether a happy echo from an unforgettable past, or a signal from the Isles of the Blest, it has the required result. Sense of humour returns. I make a long arm and switch off the light, reckoning up the follies of one more useless day, yet knowing in my heart that, but for the absence of the departed skipper, I would not change it for the world.

Sunday

[1976]

"Six days shalt thou labour, and do all that thou hast to do; but the seventh day is the sabbath of the Lord thy God. On it thou shalt do no manner of work. . . ."

Yes, but even in the time of Moses animals had to be cared for and fed, the lost sheep sought and brought back to the fold, fires kindled in winter, water brought from the well. Farmers do the same today. Railwaymen drive trains for those who must travel. Seamen man ships. Pilots guide aeroplanes. These people labour, though many others take their ease. The Jewish Sabbath—still sacrosanct, I understand—became the model, through the centuries, of the Christian Sunday, when almost everybody, men, women, children, went to church to do homage to their Maker.

The numbers have decreased in the mid-twentieth century, and the faithful are mostly middle-aged. Why so? Churchmen, laymen, scholars, attenders and non-attenders argue the reasons, the more frequent excuse being that there is more to do for a family on Sunday nowadays than ever there was in the past. Outings, picnics, family gatherings, television, or simply rising late and reading the Sunday papers. The habit has been lost. Church bells are no longer a summons. Religious conscience is stilled. Belief in the Maker is dormant, if it exists at all.

As a writer, a widow, approaching seventy years of age, how do I look upon Sunday? Possibly the answer to this goes back into childhood.

At five or six Sunday meant putting on clean underclothes, which were prickly and uncomfortable. Woollen combinations and stockings that itched. A different dress from weekdays. And because it was my actor father Gerald's day of rest, we children

were bidden downstairs to shake hands with his friends before
they departed for golf. This was shy-making, a penance. Then, at
a slightly older age, came Going to Church. Matins was dull. But
my aunt, who was also my godmother, was a fervent Anglican,
and when I accompanied her to high mass I thoroughly enjoyed
it; there was plenty to watch, like going to the theatre. One thing
worried me, however, whether at matins or at mass, and this was
the humble, even obsequious attitude of all the adults to their
Maker. "We are miserable sinners . . . there is no health in us."
Why must they cringe and crawl? Surely this was not what God
wanted? So later, when my father Gerald, who never went to
church, suggested that I should go for a walk with him on
Hampstead Heath instead, I readily agreed. His religion
consisted of being kind and generous to people "down on their
luck," and of kissing the photographs of all his dead family, father, mother, brother and sisters, before he went to bed. I saw
the point of this. It made sense, perhaps, to God too.

Nowadays, with one sister a High Anglican like my godmother
and the other a Roman Catholic, I still do not attend either
matins or mass. But, because I have a deep respect for Christianity, I read a Catholic missal every Sunday morning after
breakfast. A slight show-off, in a way, because I like to test my
Latin. And this particular missal was published by Monseigneur
Gaspard Lefebvre, who of late has been in trouble with the
Pope.

And after reading the Mass for the Day, what then? I do my
weekly accounts and pay all outstanding bills, which at least
puts me right with any debts. Then, as my housekeeper has the
day to herself, I cook my lunch, so testing my culinary talent.
Sometimes a great success. Sometimes a slight failure. But no
matter whichever way it goes. And, observing the old Sabbath
rule, I never "work" on Sundays. By working I mean writing,
which has been my profession for forty-five years. But I do clear
up my mail and answer outstanding letters. Then a walk, or in
summer a swim, and afterwards long hours with the Sunday
papers. Starting, naturally enough, with the *Sunday Telegraph*.

It is a day which, unless members of my family happen to be
staying with me, I invariably keep to myself. I give no invitations
and accept none. A day for privacy, except for neighbouring cat-

tle and sheep, with which I am on excellent terms, speaking to them in their own language. (I baa better than I moo, nevertheless they appear to understand the drift of my conversation; even Romany of Trill, the bull, acknowledges my presence with a courteous inclination of his horns.) As to the birds, they flock to the bird table in winter for their food, ignoring my welcoming twitter. I can hear them chattering amongst themselves: "Silly old fool, eat up and don't take any notice of her, she's quite harmless," upon which I tactfully withdraw, and observe them from the cover of a window.

It may be thought, by churchgoing readers, that during the course of this peaceful Sunday I continue to neglect my Maker. On the contrary, conversing with beast and bird is my way of giving thanks. And if anything deepens belief in a Creator, it is by watching wildlife in the countryside, a constant miracle, and noting the changes in their routine through the four seasons; something that applies equally to the colour and growth of trees, plants and shrubs, even weeds. They all obey natural law, which is surely God's law.

One of the greatest miracles of all is the migration of swallows. The first week in May I stand in my small front garden and wait and watch. They never fail to arrive, though not always on a Sunday. I wave "Hurrah, and welcome!" and they make for my roof, or the old nest that was their home the preceding year inside my garage. Here they rear their young, generally two broods, and by September they begin to prepare for the autumn flight. They fly overhead in a restless manner. "Safe journey, and a good winter!" I call. The following day they have gone. They are obeying natural law.

There are several questions I would like to ask the Creator, though—and this is one fault I find in my missal, that nobody asks a question—and one of the questions is, "In prehistoric days, before You thought of man, were You evolving too, and occasionally making mistakes? If not, why create species like the brontosaurus, like the mammoth, like other gigantic beasts, and let the species die, unless at the period of their creation and development You had a thing about size, and thought big was best? Then gradually realised You had made an error of judgement. Yes or no?"

A simple question, but a direct answer would be helpful. If an error is admitted, then there must have been others through the ages. Faulty genes, chromosomes, in man, which cannot be blamed on man himself. And what about the million million stars? Have some of them life? Must they be swallowed up eventually, and our world too, by something called a black hole? Someone will say that it is not for us to question the mind of the Creator. I disagree. Curiosity is a fundamental instinct within all of us. So these are some of the things I ponder about upon a Sunday afternoon, sitting, perhaps, at what I call the Look-Out, staring down across the fields to the sea. Then I come indoors and make myself a cup of tea, the hall sadly empty since the death of my faithful dog companion in the summer heat wave, my constant shadow for twelve years. I will replace him in the spring with a couple of pups, and life, along with natural law, will continue.

Telephone calls to my family follow. Everybody well and happy? Good. I can settle with an easy mind to television for the rest of the evening, switching channels at whim; the faster the police chase in New York or San Francisco the more relaxed I am, sloping into my chair, only to sit up with a jerk and realise I have missed the denouement. Time for bed, for filling hot-water bottles, for saying my prayers. Sunday is over.

"Give peace in our time, O Lord. And may those who by Thy counsel lead the peoples of this earth give a right judgement."

POEMS

The Writer

Not for me the arrow in the air,
  Nor the mountain snows,
  Nor the dumb ocean,
  Nor the wind on the heath,
  Nor the warm breath
  Of the bare bright sun upon my hair.

Not for me the mist of the white stars,
  Nor the singing falls
  Nor the deep river,
  Nor the flung foam
  Upon the hard beach,
  Nor the other mountains that I cannot reach.

Mine is the silence
And the quiet gloom
Of a clock ticking
In an empty room,
The scratch of a pen,
Ink-pot and paper,
And the patter of the rain.
Nothing but this as long as I am able,
Firelight—and a chair, and a table.

Not for me the whisper in the ear,
  Nor the touch of a hand,
  And that hand on my heart,
  Nor the quick pattering of feet
  Upon the stair, nor laughter in the street,
  Nor the swift glance, intangible and dear.

Not for me the hunger in the night,
   And the strength of the lover
   Tired of his loving,
   Seeking after passion the broken rest,
   Bearing his body's weight upon my breast.

Mine is the silence
Of the still day,
When the shouting on the hills
Sounds far away,
The song of the thrush,
In the quiet woods,
And the scent of trees.

Always the child who loved too late,
The poet—the fool—the watchman at the gate.
I am the actress mother who must make
A pretended cradle of her arms, lifeless and bare,
Who has never borne a child.

I am the deaf musician, calm and mild,
Singing a battle symphony, who has never heard the guns,
Nor the thunder in the air.

I am the painter whose blind gaze defiled
Would conjure an ocean, who has never seen the sea break
On the wild shores of Finistère . . .

Not for me the shadow of a smile,
   Nor the life that has gone,
   Nor the love that has fled,
   But the thread of the spider who spins on the wall,
   Who is lost, who is dead, who is nothing at all.

Another World

[1947]

Last night the other world came much too near,
    And with it fear.
I heard their voices whisper me from sleep,
    And could not keep
My mind upon the dream, for still they came,
    Calling my name,
The loathly keepers of the netherland
    I understand.
My frozen brain rejects the pulsing beat;
    My willing feet,
Cloven like theirs, too swiftly recognise
    Without surprise.
The horn that echoes from the further hill,
    Discordant, shrill,
Has such a leaping urgency of song,
    Too loud, too long,
That prayer is stifled like a single note
    In the parched throat.
How fierce the flame! How beautiful and bright
    The inner light
Of that great world which lives within our own,
    Remote, alone.
Let me not see too soon, let me not know,
    And so forgo
All that I cling to here, the safety side
    Where I would bide.
Old Evil, loose my chains and let me rest
    Where I am best,

Here in the muted shade of my own dust.
    But if I must
Go wandering in Time and seek the source
    Of my life force,
Lend me your sable wings, that as I fall
    Beyond recall,
The sober stars may tumble in my wake,
    For Jesus' sake.

A Prayer?

[1967]

Gentle Jesus, meek and mild,
Look upon a little child.

His the agony, the loss,
His the burden of your cross.
Mocked and scourged, with garments torn,
He must wear your crown of thorn.
Look upon his vale of tears
Flooded for two thousand years.
Hatred, bitterness and strife
Promise him eternal life.
In the tomb where you were lain,
Jewish boy and Arab slain
Kick the earth and bite the dust,
Victims of the law of lust.
Water once was changed to wine
In your name in Palestine,
Wine to blood flows merrily
On the shores of Galilee.
Falsely listened he who heard
Heaven's kingdom in your word.
This your message, blessed Lord,
Peace I bring not, but a sword.

Gentle Jesus, meek and mild,
Look upon a little child.